SAILORS AND TRADERS

SAILORS AND

A Maritime History of

TRADERS

the Pacific Peoples

Alastair Couper

University of Hawai'i Press
HONOLULU

© 2009 University of Hawai'i Press
All rights reserved
Printed in the United States of America
14 13 12 11 10 09   6 5 4 3 2 1

LIBRARY OF CONGRESS CATALOGING-IN-PUBLICATION DATA
Couper, A. D.
  Sailors and traders : a maritime history of the Pacific peoples / Alastair Couper.
    p. cm.
  Includes bibliographical references and index.
  ISBN 978-0-8248-3239-1 (hard cover : alk. paper)
  1. Pacific Islanders—History. 2. Sea Peoples—Pacific Area—History. 3. Sailors—Pacific Area—History. 4. Shipping—Pacific Area—History. I. Title.
  GN662.C68 2009
  995—dc22
                    2008038710

University of Hawai'i Press books are printed on acid-free paper and meet the guidelines for permanence and durability of the Council on Library Resources.

Designed by University of Hawai'i Press production staff

Printed by The Maple-Vail Book Manufacturing Group

For Callum, Rona, Katrina, and Roddy

CONTENTS

ACKNOWLEDGMENTS ix

NAUTICAL GLOSSARY AND ABBREVIATIONS xi

Introduction: A Seafaring Perspective 1
1 Sailors, Myths, and Traditions 6
2 The First Pacific Seafarers 22
3 Settlements, Territories, and Trade 43
4 The Arrival of Foreign Ships 60
5 Pacific Commercial Shipowners 75
6 Under Foreign Sail 100
7 Dangers, Mutinies, and the Law 118
8 Companies, Colonies, and Crewing 136
9 Island Protests and Enterprises 150
10 Contemporary Local and Regional Shipping 165
11 The Global Pacific Seafarer 186
Epilogue: Some Contemporary Resonances 207

NOTES 209

BIBLIOGRAPHY 237

INDEX 253

ACKNOWLEDGMENTS

I WAS FORTUNATE in being a research scholar at the Australian National University, Research School of Pacific and Asian Studies, in the halcyon days of the 1960s. It was highly stimulating intellectually and socially to be alongside so many of the greats in Pacific Studies, including Harold Brookfield, Jim Davidson, Jack Golson, Harry Maude, Oskar Spate, and Gerry Ward. Their influences will be evident in this volume.

More recent acknowledgments are due to my academic friends and colleagues—Dr. Hance Smith of Cardiff University; Professor Sarah Palmer of the Greenwich Maritime Institute, University of Greenwich, London; and Professor Glyn Williams of Queen Mary, University of London—who read and commented on early drafts, as did Dr. Ronald Hope, former director of the Marine Society. I have drawn also on some of the work by former colleagues at the Seafarers International Research Centre (SIRC) at Cardiff University on the medical aspects of the health of seafarers. I thank also Dr. Paul D'Arcy of the Australian National University for his kind and valuable comments on the draft manuscript, and I appreciate the helpful reviews by an anonymous appraiser from the University of Hawai'i Press, as well as the professional attention of copy editor Rosemary Wetherold, who greatly improved the work.

I wish to thank Phillipa Grimstone of the Pepys Library, Magdalene College, Cambridge, for arranging the reproduction of the sixteenth-century painting from the Schouten voyage, and Elaine Greig of the Writers' Museum, Edinburgh, for all her help in providing photographs and notes. These and my own series of photographs were reproduced by Alun Rogers of Cardiff University, who also drafted the maps of the Pacific. I am very grateful to him for this and for much valuable advice, and also to Tim Robinson for photographic assistance. I particularly wish to thank Louise Deeley of SIRC, who helped in so many invaluable ways from start to finish in the production of the book.

There are many friends in the maritime community of the Pacific ashore and as shipmates to whom I have been indebted over the years. I can acknowledge here only the more recent. During 2001, I was welcomed as a visiting colleague by Professor G. Robin Smith and Dr. Joeli Veitayaki to the University of the South Pacific. I thank Captain Carol Dunlop for discussion at her home in Suva, and Captain Tomasi Cama Kete of Fiji for our meetings and the arrangements he made with seafaring colleagues. Also important was the cooperation of Captain John Hogan, Maritime Programme manager, Secretariat of the Pacific Community; Toloa Kaitece and Norate Anteriea of the Seafarers' Union of Kiribati; Julia Wakolo, Seafarers Union of Fiji; and Dave Morgan of the New Zealand Seafarers Union. Likewise, I am grateful for interviews and correspondence with R. Weiss of the South Pacific Marine Services and Hamburg Süd Line and with John MacLennan, chief executive of the Pacific Forum Line.

Finally, my thanks to David Cockroft of the International Transport Workers' Federation, who assisted in my travel to Kiribati, and Professor Helen Sampson for use of facilities at SIRC. Not least, I am, as always, grateful to my wife, Norma, who carried out work in the islands, sailed the Pacific, and helped in so many ways in the production of this book.

NAUTICAL GLOSSARY AND ABBREVIATIONS

altitude	The angle between a celestial body and the sea horizon below it.
azimuth	The magnetic compass bearing of a celestial body, when compared with the true azimuth (bearing) derived from the annual *Nautical Almanac*, gives the error of the magnetic compass for the course being steered.
BIMCO	Baltic and International Maritime Council.
boatsteerer/harpooner	The crewman who first harpoons a whale and then takes over steering the boat while the mate does the killing with a lance.
fathom	6 feet (1.829 meters).
furling	Taking in sails and securing them to the yards by line gaskets.
ISF	International Shipping Federation.
ITF	International Transport Workers' Federation.
master	The captain of a merchant ship; in the eighteenth century a noncommissioned officer in the British Royal Navy.
missed stays	Failure to go from one tack to another, when the head hangs and falls back on the previous tack. Dangerous when there is little sea room or when tacking away from a lee shore.

nautical mile	6,080 feet (1.853 km). Unless otherwise stated, all sea distances in this book are in nautical miles.
navigator	Taken as synonymous with the "captain" of an indigenous vessel, e.g., *tia borau* (Kiribati), *rimedo* (Marshalls), *pelu* (elsewhere in Micronesia), and *tou tai* and variations (Polynesia).
ratings	Usually there are three departments on a cargo vessel: deck, engine, and catering. Each has three levels of crewing: officers, petty officers, and ratings. On-deck ratings comprise mainly ordinary seamen (OS) and able-bodied seamen (AB); in the engine room they are mainly motormen (MM), firemen, and greasers; and in catering, various assistants. Some of these designations have changed with technology and minimal crewing, but AB and MM have been retained.
reefing	Shortening sail by gathering it up and tying it with line reef points.
scudding	Running before a gale when the speed of the vessel equals the speed of the following sea. Creates the danger of losing steering and of a heavy sea coming on board astern (pooping).
SPC	Secretariat of the Pacific Community. Has consultative and advisory roles in maritime affairs.
stability	Ability of a vessel to return to an upright position when it heels over. Determined by a righting lever, which is a function of the relationship between the center of gravity and the center of buoyancy. The distributions of cargo, passengers, and free water surfaces can be crucial.

supercargo	The superintendent of the cargo and the trade room. Knows products and customs of the trading areas (Fijian: *vunivola ni waqa*).
tonnage	Before the late eighteenth century the tonnage of merchant ships was usually expressed as the weight of the cargo and stores carried (tons burden). For warships the weight of the ship was added to the total contents (tons displacement), as it still is. The tonnage of modern bulk-carrying ships is expressed by the weight of the cargo, fuel, and stores carried (tons deadweight). The tonnage of the general cargo and passenger ships is, at its basic, expressed as the gross tonnage (GT)—the volume of the total enclosed space of the ship in cubic meters, multiplied by a constant.

Introduction

A SEAFARING PERSPECTIVE

WRITING IN THE *American Historical Review* of June 2006, Kären Wigen reminds readers that the sea is "swinging into view" and is "being given a history, even as the history of the world is being retold from the perspective of the sea."[1] When we consider the millennia of exploration and settlement of the islands of the Pacific, and the continuum of maritime activities in the region, it would not be much of an exaggeration to define the history of the Pacific as "a history of seafaring." It is the role of indigenous seafarers and related traders in Pacific history that is the main theme of this book.

Centuries before the Pacific was revealed to Europeans, flotillas of vessels carried thousands of men, women, and children, together with plants and animals, to virtually every island in a vast ocean that covers about one-third of the surface of the globe. They settled in homelands with considerable diversity, ranging from the high islands of Papua New Guinea to small volcanic peaks that rise from the deep seabed, and a myriad of coral atolls and reef islands.

In recent times the islands of the Pacific have been grouped into twenty-two political entities. Ten are independent states, six are variously associated with former colonial administrations, and six are politically parts of distant countries (France, three; United States, two; and New Zealand, one). Their aggregate population is about nine million, of which over five million are in the mainland and islands of Papua New Guinea. These figures do not include the indigenous peoples in Hawai'i and New Zealand.

When the Europeans gradually "discovered" these lands widely distributed in an ocean on the other side of the world, they saw the inhabitants as isolated and insular. It was a view not shared by island people. Their oral traditions in stories, songs, and creation myths told of great voyages. They were anything but insular, as the navigator Tupaia from Ra'iatea demonstrated to Cook in 1769. His map showed seventy-four islands he could name, and he related many others he had knowledge of. Tupaia's map extends over an area of the Pacific equivalent to a region of Europe encompassing Ireland and Spain in the west, Denmark in the north, Italy to the south, and beyond to the Caspian Sea and Russia to the east.[2]

The scope of this book lies in the continuity of seafaring from the ancient ancestors of Tupaia to the modern Pacific sailor.[3] The purposes of this introduction are to provide a perspective of the various cross sections in time and to emphasize that there are several common features in the shipboard work and lifestyles of mariners that constitute a form of "ship culture."

Chapter 1 makes comparisons between the traditions of Pacific sailors and others. The similarities are important because they help explain the ease of crew mobility between ships regardless of national and ethnic diversity. This is not to say that seafarers the world over have more in common with each other than with people in the societies from which they were drawn; nor would it be entirely true that maritime traditions on board do not vary between national and ethnic groups. What is observable is that there are traditions, terminology, and even modes of dress that are common to sailors at various periods and cut across national and ethnic differences. These distinctive common components of the seafaring way of life arise from the dangers of the sea, living and working in an enclosed and inescapable ship space, separation from families, continuous travel, the ease of adjustment to multiethnic settings on board and in "sailor town" enclaves when ashore, and exposure to exotic diseases.

Sailors similarly share experiences of alienation from society on shore. They acquire outlooks on life that differ from those of their land-based contemporaries. It was said of sixteenth-century Spanish mariners that "sailor's eyes would carry engraved on their retinas images of a diverse and exotic world, which made events and landscapes of daily life on land seem insufferably monotonous."[4] This is still true of Pacific sailors returning to remote island villages after international voyages.

The more chronological sequences in the book start with the second chapter, which goes back into the mists of time to identify characteristics of the first Pacific seafarers. This endeavor is attempted through what Eric Sager calls "intuitive perception, the facility that allows us, with varying degrees of success, to recreate in the mind experiences from the past that are otherwise unrecoverable."[5] I have approached aspects of prehistoric seamanship in this way from the point of view of a professional mariner with experience in island trading and Pacific island crews. Other material includes the observations of researchers sailing with indigenous navigators, including those on replica vessels; archaeological and DNA data;

and the decoding of ancient myths and metaphors by Pacific scholars. It has likewise been assumed that contemporary indigenous trading systems embody some spatial and ceremonial components from the distant past. Descriptions of such components are derived from publications, port surveys, and personal experience.

The period of the first arrival of the Europeans is considered in terms of the relationships between foreign sailors and the maritime communities of the islands. Regarding this, only the records of the Europeans are available. The journal of George Robertson of HMS *Dolphin* in 1767 reveals the attitudes of sailors. The journals of Cook and others from 1768 are primary documents in many respects, including descriptions of the use of sea power by chiefs in interisland conflicts. The points of view of island people are more difficult to ascertain, but there is some help in the accounts of James Morrison, bosun's mate of the *Bounty* who lived eighteen months in Tahiti from 1789, and of young William Mariner, brought up as a Tongan from 1806 to 1810.

There were more widespread and intrusive arrivals by commercial trading and whaling ships. Particularly useful are the accounts of voyages by the English supercargo John Turnbull (1800–1804) and the American sailor Stephen Reynolds (1810–1813). Their records afford brief views of the changes in Tahiti and Hawai'i, the recruitment of islanders, and trading with the coastal and island peoples of the Pacific region of the American Northwest. Such commercial contacts were accompanied by a remarkably rapid adoption by island rulers, chiefs, and the Maori communities of European designs of vessels and adjustments to commercial trade. For a short time they successfully competed as shipowners in seaborne trade with the Europeans and Americans.

The Pacific seafarers who sailed vessels owned by island chiefs went on to crew the enormous fleets of foreign merchant ships and whalers in the late eighteenth and early nineteenth centuries. This return to the sea in a different capacity by Pacific islanders lasted for only a few decades. Captains were encouraged by authorities in New South Wales to recruit "native crews" from New Zealand and Polynesia. Many of these crewmen, like their European and America shipmates, suffered abuses. They responded by desertion and mutiny. Records of such events are from court cases and also from accounts by Europeans who recorded at first hand the experiences of a few Pacific sailors.

By the late nineteenth century, bigger foreign merchant companies with steamships were dominant. This accelerated the pace of colonization. Among other effects were the actions by Australasian and American maritime trade unions in defense of their members against the use by shipowners of cheap labor on their national flag vessels. This saw most Pacific seafarers confined to employment on small interisland traders within specific colonial territories. Continuous attempts by Pacific people to usurp foreign dominance over trade and shipping took the form of obtaining more local craft, protest movements and boycotts, as well as the temporary rise of a few island-based maritime trade unions and related strike actions in port towns.

As is shown in several chapters, the Pacific islanders clearly were never simply observers of the colonization of their lands or the total domination of their seas. Indigenous noncommercial maritime trade also continued, and ceremonial events were carried along, entwined with commercial ventures on island- and foreign-owned vessels.

In the early twentieth century when the values of island resources fell, some of the foreign commercial companies withdrew. The island mariners and shipowners now included mixed-race descendants of sailors and settlers. The role of this sector is examined for its importance in local trades. The second half of the century was a period of political independence for most islands, the founding of national shipping lines, and the regional Pacific Forum Line. These were accompanied by considerable technological change, and the book focuses on the impacts of such developments on the skills, training, and welfare of seafarers, as well as new attitudes toward women at sea. In order to deal with this multiplicity of issues a case study of the interisland shipping of Fiji is presented. Similarly, the complexity of the modern international employment of Pacific Island seafarers is examined through an analysis of one hundred crew lists of foreign ships on which Pacific sailors served. This likewise leads to an in-depth case study of Kiribati, chosen because it is the major Pacific source of seafarers engaged on foreign ships. This study includes life at sea, impacts of homecoming, gender issues, family stresses, and problems of disease.

This book differs from most others in the history of the Pacific by its emphasis on sailors and related traders. Apart from novels, there has not been much of a focus in the past on merchant seafarers in Pacific literature. In academic publications there have always been references to the importance of the sea—not least in the concepts of Epeli Hau'ofa.[6] When it comes to sailors, however, they have usually been relegated to mere ciphers, as "ships crews" in commerce, and generalized as operational adjuncts in traditional exchange voyages. In practice the safety and success of these ventures were literally in the hands of sailors. This tendency to ignore the reality of the life of a sailor is partly due to the lack of written accounts by sailors, a sparseness of observers at sea, and land-oriented officials who never thought it necessary to keep crew records. Even in Britain it was only in the mid-nineteenth century that official statistics began to be kept on ages, places of origin, and deaths at sea of merchant seamen.

There are exceptions to the total anonymity of Pacific sailors. References are made in major studies of historical events, whaling, and trade, in which Pacific sailors feature. These are referred to in several chapters and are listed in the bibliography. Only three volumes focus specifically on indigenous sailors. Paul D'Arcy has carefully analyzed the information for many interisland contacts in Polynesia and Micronesia between 1770 and 1870.[7] He shows these as agents of social and technical change, independent of European activities. David Chappell, in the absence of statistics, has dedicatedly drawn together statements and anecdotes on the employment of Pacific seafarers on foreign ships during the eighteenth and nineteenth centuries.[8] Richard Feinberg has brought together very detailed accounts of the sea life of people in a group of small island communities in the Polynesian outliers during the modern period.[9] *Sailors and Traders* provides perspective for these and other studies by extending over a wider compass of space and time in order to record more of the remarkable heritage of the modern Pacific sailor.

CHAPTER ONE

Sailors, Myths, and Traditions

THE PACIFIC SAILOR who is waiting for a jumbo jet at Nadi International Airport in Fiji has been in transit for almost three days. He has travelled by local boat from his home island of Nanouti in Kiribati to Tarawa, the principal island of Kiribati, and from there by small plane to Fiji. He is bound for Townsville, Australia, via another flight from Sydney to rejoin a large bulk carrier as an AB (able-bodied seaman). The ship will probably be heading next for the United States. It is owned by a German company in Hamburg and flies the Liberian flag. This ship once again will be his home and workplace for the next twelve months.

A similar procedure is repeated in various ways throughout Oceania. Some eight thousand or so young men, and a very few young women, move from their home islands to world ports to join foreign-going ships. They are recruited as sailors by agencies of the global labor market and will be sailing worldwide on vessels carrying cargoes of raw materials, oil, chemicals, and consumer goods in containers. Rarely, if ever, will they sight their home islands during these trips.

The sailor from Kiribati was born on a small, flat coral atoll close to the equator (0°40' S). The atoll is remote and only twenty-four miles long and ten miles wide. There are nine villages, with a total population of about 3,200. These are subject to drought conditions, when water and island foods are scarce, and survival has depended on sea resources. When growing up, the future sailor was never beyond the sound of the wind and sea, and at an early age he learned to swim, dive, sail, and fish. Few strangers would have come to his village. Only when an interisland vessel came through the boat pass and anchored in the lagoon to unload flour and other goods by workboat would there be any significant changes in the repetitive rhythm of daily life. The boat would load copra off the beach, which is the only cash product on Nanouti and can be depleted during droughts.

As a youngster, the I-Kiribati sailor would have known male relatives who returned on leave from foreign-going ships. They would tell sailors' yarns and bring money, radios, perfumes, toys, and other attractive items. These were soon distributed within the extended family through the social obligations of *bubuti* (sharing on request). Some of the younger unmarried sailors would spend only the minimum time on leave at home. They preferred to return to the company of mariners from other islands who congregated in South Tarawa, with its cinema, cafés, bars, and girls and its distance from the rule of the old men and the eyes of the clergy on their home islands.

The Nanouti sailor is following in the footsteps of the itinerant sailors of the past. He is twenty-nine, has qualified at the Marine Training Centre in Tarawa, and has already served three years at sea. He is now a well-paid (by island standards) AB. His young wife and baby daughter have been left on Nanouti, where he has also left part of his personality. From now on, he will adapt to the ways of shipboard life, with its terminology known only to fellow seafarers, its discipline, and its food and customs. He has likewise been transformed in appearance. While on leave on his home island, he lived the relaxed life of a bare-bodied, barefoot villager in a wraparound lavalava. He is now wearing a T-shirt, blue jeans, a baseball cap, sunglasses, and an outsize pair of trainers. He carries a case and a bag, which contain shirts, pullover, socks, underwear, a woollen cap, a boilersuit, boots, shoes, hard hat, oilskins, and a knife, all previously supplied by the company.

Onboard discipline is exercised by a German captain and, on deck, three Polish officers. The engine room has similar numbers and nationalities in charge. The cook is from the Philippines; consequently, for the next twelve months he will not eat the "true food" of Kiribati—fish, coconut, and taro, supplemented by bread, rice, tinned meat, and on occasion pig and fowl. Instead the daily diet will be German and Polish dishes cooked by a Filipino. But he is happy that at least six other ratings will be from the islands of Kiribati. He could of course have found himself in a much more ethnically diverse seagoing community. In any event he will be different in many respects from what he was on his home island.

Like other oceanic sailors, some of the Kiribati crew may recall being told half-remembered stories of founding ancestors. There is that of Batiauea, a female spirit who in the course of a voyage met Baretoka, a male spirit. Batiauea's canoe was stretched into a curved shape and called Taraea, or Tarawa, where the two spirits dwelt and raised a family. There are numerous such metaphorical legends in the Pacific that recall ancient voyagers to whom islanders are related genetically and through threads of sea-oriented culture. To these are added many other inherited and acquired beliefs of Pacific and fellow seafarers worldwide. This diversity is illustrated below by comparisons between the traditions (if not the myths that are specific to the Pacific) and beliefs held by Pacific islanders and other sailors in the past and present.

Na Keiki o Ke Kai (The Children of the Sea)

The relationships between Pacific people and the vast sea around them are more than geographical; they go to the very heart of people's birth and being. The ancient creation myths and cultural metaphors lie deeply embedded in collective memories. They have been transmitted orally over generations, often by hereditary storytellers. More recently they have been decoded and interpreted by Pacific Island scholars and are valued as voices from a remote past. At a basic level of interpretation several of the myths can be reduced to accounts of ancient voyages of discovery and the founding of communities on uninhabited islands. For the prehistoric peoples out of Asia who reached the westward beaches of Oceania and eventually embarked on the first explorations by sea toward the distant eastern horizons, their discoveries of new lands and, for some, their return from these with stories of abundance, were epoch making.

These seafaring migrants from Southeast Asia possibly carried the widespread belief in Tangaloa, or Tangaroa (Lord of the Ocean), to the Pacific. This hearkens back to the Sulawesi word for "ocean," *togaloang*. In the Pacific, legends of related sea gods have similarities in widely separated islands. They range from the activities of the demigod Motikitiki in the eastern Solomons[1] to the Maui myths found over the whole of Polynesia. I. Futa Helu of Tonga recounts how the demigod Maui pulled the Polynesian islands from the bottom of the sea.[2] Helu sees this as referring to the chance landfalls made by the earliest Pacific voyagers. In the Tongan story, Maui starts as a navigator and ends his days in Tonga as a farmer. The transition from sea to land epitomizes the long evolution of Tonga from a predominantly marine culture and economy to one based primarily on cultivation plus some fishing.

Pat Hohepa, professor of Maori studies at the University of Auckland, refers to the version whereby Maui brought a giant fish to the surface.[3] This, along with Maui's canoe, became the North and South Islands of Aotearoa (New Zealand). The new land was simultaneously a vessel and a fish, "a progeny of Tangaroa the Sea Lord." Some twenty generations after the creation of Aotearoa, the navigator Kupe was sent away from

Hawaiki, the legendary homeland of the Maori (possibly Rarotonga, Cook Islands, or Ra'iatea, Society Islands), to search for a southern continent—centuries later, another great navigator, James Cook, was given the same task. Kupe decided to seek the fish of Maui (Te Ika a Maui). He found it petrified as Aotearoa and spent two generations exploring both islands before returning to Hawaiki with the news.

Another twenty generations passed, so the folktale goes, before people in a double canoe left Hawaiki to follow "the path" (sailing directions) of Kupe. They did so, Hohepa interprets, to take their families away from the hunger and wars over resources in Hawaiki, which had suffered droughts, perhaps from a severe El Niño. Five generations afterward, successive fleets of canoes made voyages of over 1,600 miles from Hawaiki to Aotearoa. These people eventually dispersed over Aotearoa, as recounted in Maori folklore and genealogy, to occupy tribal territories, some of which carried the names of great canoes.

The remembrances of voyages of founding seafarers have been preserved in other forms elsewhere in the Pacific. Joel Bonnemaison discusses the links between canoes, territories, ancestors, and people in southern Vanuatu.[4] Each territory is identified with a canoe, as is the social organization. The descendants of those who occupied the front of the canoe had special status (lords). The helmsman was the captain and, when ashore, a chief. This concept and the memories of the community are carried onward to new territories on migration, thereby combining the essential "rootedness" to an original homeland with the mobility of voyaging.

Another component of voyage-related myths lies in the celestial dome covering the Pacific. The stars, sun, planets, moon, and even comets appear in the stories of the gods of Oceania. The oral transmission of Tahitian myths, for example, shows detailed astronomical observations.[5] Ta'urua (Venus) prepares a canoe and sails west to dwell with his wife, Rua-o-mere (Capricornus). In Kiribati the myth of the courtship of Nei Auti (Pleiades) and Rimwimata (Antares) sees them engage in an endless race with each other across the sky. Their risings mark the seasons for good and bad voyaging (see chapter 2). The many long and convoluted accounts reciting apparent movements of godlike celestial bodies may have aide-mémoire functions in the oral traditions of Pacific Island navigators. Arthur Grimble, writing in 1931, confirms, "If you want to find an expert on stars you must ask for a *tiaborau* or navigator."[6] There are many such myths and interpretations. There are also traditions and images of ships and the sea that have been carried by sailors and shared and assimilated among nationalities. Despite technological changes some of these have persisted, with adaptations, into modern times as common heritages of global seafaring.

Images of the Ship

The vastness of ocean spaces and weather could be overcome only with a ship that could be relied on. The ship was consequently endowed with mythical properties and symbols. At an individual level in the Pacific there is even the symbolizing, through body tattooing, of the unity of the person, vessel, sea, and sky, as described by Laurence Carucci. These were depicted on the bodies of some Kayapo people in the Marshall Islands at the beginning of the twentieth century (before tattooing was denounced by the Congregationalist mission). The central motif of the tattoos was the body embarked on a voyage: "The upper pectoral triangle represented the body of the canoe, the lower pectoral triangle the ocean swells. The belt like band of wavy lines extending across the stomach are clouds, the mast runs from neck to navel. . . . The body fully fashioned, is the vessel islanders use to face the voyage of life."[7]

In the oral traditions of several maritime societies the canoe symbolizes male and female relationships: "A man is equated with the hull and a woman with the outrigger. Thus when visiting neighbours in Enewetak Island in the Marshalls, a common query directed to a man about his wife takes the form—'*ewi kobaak eo?,*' where is the outrigger?"[8] The outrigger has the vital function of stabilizing the canoe against capsizing in strong winds; the metaphor clearly relates to the function of women during the rougher passages of matrimony. The attributing of human characteristics to all or parts of a vessel, as in the outrigger allusion, is common. A ship for seafarers is of female gender. Joseph Conrad advises sailors that they must always treat a ship with "an understanding and consideration of the mysteries of her feminine nature[;]then she will stand by you faithfully."[9] Pablo Pérez-Mallaína, writing of sixteenth-century Spanish seafarers, describes how they formed such an identification with their ship that they got into fights to defend her honor. The ship becomes in these respects almost a surrogate wife or family.[10] A British rating is recorded by J. M. M. Hill with the comment that for seamen "the sea and ship provide a family background without doing anything drastic like marrying someone."[11]

The ship as a symbolic family is encountered in the southern Moluccas of Indonesia (one of the possible places of origin of ancient voyagers into the Pacific). The stern board of the ship, with its animal motifs, including a cock, a bird, and a water snake, is the symbolic helmsman: "The union of the 'boat' and the 'helmsman,' woman and man, sets the family on course."[12] Traditionally, a pair of gold earrings is bound to the joint between the keel beam and stern beam. Nobody knows the precise significance of this, but anthropologists in the region consider it to represent semen. With similar Freudian connotations, the mythical "golden rivet," said by European sailors to be the last one driven into the hull of a ship before she takes to the sea, is a feature from modern maritime folklore out of the age of the iron ship.

In the Caroline Islands the indigenous female imagery of the ship is that of a "mother"—she "holds the food, holds the crew," and "the navigator is the father because he distributes the food to his sons, the crew."[13] There can be even more reverence for the ship. The strange European-type ship was perceived by some people as a god in an early contact, as distinct from its seafarers, who were viewed as goblins. The famous account of the Maori Horeta Te Taniwha, who as a child met Cook, is cited in most histories of New Zealand: "When our old men saw the ship they said it was an *atua*, a god, and the people on board were *tupua*, strange beings."[14]

Images of the Sea—Death and Rituals

The sea, like the ship, is often referred to by sailors in anthropomorphic terms. It needs to be approached with respect; it can be bountiful and can give nurture to people who know how to treat it. The sea can be peaceful, also wild, and always treacherous; it can snatch an unwary sailor. In the cold northern latitudes it is referred to as the "gray widow-maker," and its waters are "mothers' tears." High risks in the course of their day-to-day life, with little access to legal protection or medical care, once again marks off sea people from land people. A farmer can lose a crop in bad weather; a sailor can lose everything, including his life.

Over the ages there has been an expectation of sailors and their families that they may not return from the sea. The weather of the Pacific is considered relatively benign in this respect, but even if ancient migratory voyages avoided sailing in the hurricane season, they would still be vulnerable to losses. A vessel heavily laden with women, children, and livestock could be overwhelmed in the sailing season by waves of squally conditions such as the *bogi walu* in Fijian waters or the *aho valo* in Tonga. These are very complex winds, which blow violently for eight days and eight nights. Or their vessels could be dashed to pieces on hidden reefs or, in long calms, be carried far away from a sighted island by ocean currents. Such concerns are evident in this ancient Tuvalu song:

Our father speaks
Exhorting the current to have mercy
And flow towards the island.[15]

We have no idea of the death rate on ancient migratory voyages from storms, adverse currents, and stranding as well as disease, thirst, and starvation. Even allowing for a more favorable climatic period, deaths were probably no less than those for other people of the sea. For the mariners in the days of Pacific whaling, the evidence of death is compelling. Nathaniel Philbrick writes of the community of Nantucket with a population of seven thousand: "Death was a fact of life with which all Nantucketers were thoroughly familiar. In 1810 there were forty-seven fatherless children in Nantucket, while almost a quarter of the women over the age of twenty-three (the average age of marriage) had been widowed by the sea."[16] The British Royal Commission of 1885 recorded six times as many deaths of merchant seamen as of underground miners.[17] Today seafaring is still the most dangerous of occupations.

It might be expected that people of the sea, exposed to sudden death, would have predilections to superstitions and propitiation rituals. They do, but with more skepticism than that of, say, large island inland communities. The latter would, certainly in the past, have fears of night travel, sorcery, and magic in their forested and mountainous habitats. Those at sea would always know very well the real nature of the immense physical dangers they faced and how to combat these with seamanship. Even in the deeply religious society of sixteenth-century Spain, Pérez-Mallaína describes how seafarers in a storm would turn to religion only as a last resort: "Even in the midst of a storm, if the mariners continued to curse, passengers could know that things were not too bad, but if the curses turned to prayers, then the situation was really desperate."[18]

Attitudes toward death on board as with related rituals were, and still are, often simple, utilitarian, and sardonic. It is considered unlucky to keep a dead body on board. Unless there is adequate refrigeration or proximity to land, a dead sailor is sewn up in canvas by the bosun, and with grim humor it is said he puts the last stitch through the nose. In the past, weights such as cannonballs or fire bars were added. A simple service is conducted, and the body is slid overboard from a hatch cover. European and American sailors would say that their shipmate was now bound for Davy Jones' locker—the refuge of a malignant sea spirit who stalks mariners. On the other hand, the dead sailor might be metamorphosed into an albatross and fly toward the South Pole. At the pole he would find a revolving open hatch. On entering, he would return to his natural form and arrive at the sailors' paradise of Fiddler's Green, which lies "seven miles to the loo'ard of hell." Here he would find good-looking women and free smokes and drinks.[19]

The albatross as the soul of a dead sailor is a totem; Coleridge's "Ancient Mariner" recalls in his horror,

And I had done a hellish thing,
And it would work 'em woe:
For all averred, I had killed the bird
That made the breeze to blow.

For the Pacific mariner, one of the totemic birds of the traditional society was the frigate bird. Like the albatross, it has an immense wingspan and glides over the ocean. It became known to sailors generally as the man-o'-war because of its piratical and fearless behavior. It closes on other seabirds at great speed and forces them to regurgitate their meal, which it then catches with great skill in midair. The frigate bird was admired, as well as feared, by Pacific island sailors. The belief was that it could communicate between spirits and humans "and carried the souls of the departed to the kingdom of the dead."[20]

While these beliefs at sea are precautionary, most seafarers are practical enough to know that in reality their safety depends only on a well-found ship and a good crew. Each of the crew has to know his job and be reliable, and each one looks out for the other. The most significant protection in the past and present relates to the integrity of the crew and the vessel; any flaw in either could mean disaster. Conrad says, "A ship is a creature which we have brought into the world, as it were on purpose to keep us up to the mark. In her handling a ship will not put up with a mere pretender."[21]

Despite technical advances, what seafarers still admire are the skills of mariners with a "feel" for the sea and the behavior of the ship. This trait is derived from years of experience. In the Pacific the feel of the underlying swell (as distinct from local waves) and the refraction effects of distant islands were used by experienced navigators to determine the direction of the islands (see chapter 2). A similar technique was utilized by the sailors of South Sulawesi, Indonesia, which they termed *omak tua* (everlasting swell), and by the fishermen of the Shetland Islands. The Shetlanders, when fishing in the North Atlantic in fog, would feel the *moder dai* (mother wave), which would guide them home. Similarly, experienced seafarers could interpret the shuddering and vibration of their vessel in a seaway, and the tenderness or stiffness as she rolled to a beam sea. A captain of a modern ship is also likely to waken from a deep sleep on feeling a sudden alteration of course, as will a chief engineer with the change in tone of an engine. No doubt the ancient Pacific mariners would likewise have responded to the creaks and groans coming from the flexible movements of lashings and timbers of a vessel as she labored in bad weather. These are human senses for which technology has brought no real substitutes.

Protecting the Ship

In the matter of ship integrity, the building and launching require great practical experience, but to make sure, it was, and is, hedged around with rituals. In the Pacific the choice of the right trees for construction of a vessel was accompanied by the sacrifice of pigs at the trees' base.[22] The building was then in the hands of craftsmen from hereditary clans. In Fiji they served the god Rokola (the son of Degei, the most important god of Fiji),[23] and the methods of construction corresponded to the guidance of sacred chants and were accompanied by ceremonies. The building of a massive war canoe was of such significance that "human blood was a necessary adjunct to the construction, launching and first sailing" and "heavy hulls were sometimes launched over the bodies of slain enemies."[24] A. M. Hocart, writing of ships built in the Lau Islands for Tonga, noted that "of old as many as five men would be killed on those occasions, baked and eaten, or a woman would be brought raw."[25] James Morrison, the bosun's mate of the *Bounty* who spent eighteen months in Tahiti in 1789 and 1790, described how a man would be secretly selected and his skull smashed with a club at night and put on board as a sacrifice. In the western Solomons, "when sacrifices were required for the launching of new canoes or the inauguration of new canoe houses—around which headhunting and fishing ritual revolved—an unsuspecting captive would be clubbed and used."[26]

It was customary in Fiji for the owner of a vessel to provide feasts for the builders when the keel was laid and when the vessel was delivered. In West Africa in modern times the building of quite a simple fishing canoe is accompanied by feasts and rituals, and the builders carry the canoe to the owner, who has prepared gin, eggs, and fowl.[27] In advanced shipbuilding countries of today, a woman usually performs the launching ceremony. She smashes a bottle of champagne on the bow and calls upon God to bless the ship and all who sail in her.[28] The woman receives a launching present, and the ship slides down the slipway to the cheers of the builders and enters her natural environment of the sea. This is the birth of a ship in its delivery from land to sea. The ship now has a name and a nationality. The death of a ship is also recognized as such by sailors, as in facial expressions depicted in paintings and films as their ship goes down. The European mariners who came to the Pacific instinctively knew that the cruelest way to punish recalcitrant island people was to destroy their vessels on which they had lavished years of building and care with such reverence.

It was the custom in several places for vessels setting out on long voyages to be further protected against loss by figureheads, usually gods, saints, heroes, beasts, or handsome women (figure 1.1). The Chinese and Vikings adopted dragonlike figureheads, and the Solomon and Trobriand

FIGURE 1.1. The figurehead and the sailor were survivors of a shipwreck on Penrhyn Island. The sailor is described in 1890 by Fanny Stevenson in *The Cruise of the Janet Nichol* as "a gentle, soft-eyed youth from Edinburgh" who settled as a trader on the island with his "proud lady." (Courtesy of the Writers' Museum, Edinburgh)

islanders had symbolic predatory birds and carved heads mounted on the prows of their canoes.[29] Apotropaic eyes were painted on the big trireme ships from the fourth century BC in Greece and are still painted or carved on wooden boats in China.

In Catholic countries it was thought prudent when a vessel took to the sea to seek the protection of saints, and many ships that went on voyages of exploration and conquest, such as the Santa Maria of Columbus in 1492, were given the names of patron saints, just as Pacific sailors had patron spirits such as Dakuwaqa, the shark god of Fiji. In offering up prayers to the saints, sixteenth-century mariners came under the scrutiny and suspicion of the Inquisition as to whether they departed from official dogma toward "pagan flavor." Their prayer to St. Elmo, fire of the night, was one such: "Holy Body, true friend of mariners, we want you to help us, and always appear at night before us." These sailors got into even more trouble when the inquisitors searched their ships, looking for paintings in which male and female saints appeared "not with their true decency."[30] Sailors then, as now, have images of women on cabin bulkheads and as body tattoo decorations.

There are many more unusual and unexplained beliefs and rituals held by seafarers. It is bad luck to sail from a port on a Friday; a knife stuck in the mast, or whistling, or throwing a broom overboard will all bring the wind. A strong favorable wind would be acknowledged with "the Judys have got us in tow," meaning it was the girls pulling them to port. Less esoteric expressions and metaphors have entered the English language from the sea heritage, including the "ship of state," "keeping on an even keel," and so on.

Taboos

In contrast to their favorable images on bulkheads and ship figureheads, women on board ships have been regarded as taboo, as bringers of bad luck. There were many forms of sexual taboos. During early European contacts in the Marquesas, women were seen swimming out to the vessels while the men came on canoes; the canoes, it was explained, were taboo for women.[31] In present-day Kiribati, women would not normally be welcomed on deep-sea fishing canoes, and they have never as yet been enrolled at the Marine Training Centre, even when they were perfectly well qualified. In Rotuma, "on the night before a deep sea fishing expedition the fishermen were supposed to sleep alone."[32] In the fishing villages of northeast Scotland it would even be considered unlucky if a crew member on his way to the boat spoke to a woman who had "a bad reputation."[33]

Women have in practice always sailed on vessels and, in the Pacific, carried goods for trade and presentation. There is also some history of women as navigators in a few places, which are referred to in the next chapter. Captains of Pacific whalers and traders from Europe and America sometimes had their wives with them, but sailors were not always happy. Women are seen as people of the land; in the Pacific they have traditionally looked after the children, the pigs, and the gardens. They have made mats and sails for vessels, but they were considered sedentary whereas men were nomadic. This viewpoint is changing (see chapter 10), but some Melanesian sailors still say women are welcome on board only in port when there is, in sailor pidgin, "pati long sip" (party on the ship). Working at sea has in fact always been an occupation reserved for men in most societies. This practice still prevails, as less than 2 percent of the 1.25 million merchant seafarers in the world are female, and those are mainly in catering and cleaning.

Words likewise have symbolic meanings, bringing bad and good luck by their utterance. Jocelyn Linnekin says of preliterate Pacific society: "Words have power: to cure, to curse, to provoke wars, to invoke the divine. Once uttered, their effects cannot be undone."[34] Consequently certain words of the land have been taboo at sea. Ed Knipe relates an experience during a trip on a Scottish fishing vessel in 1980: "I mentioned the word 'pig.' Their reaction was first to look at each other, then laugh. They made it clear that I should not say that word on board or the skipper might get angry enough to steam back to port and put me ashore."[35]

Reference to a minister of religion also had to be avoided. It has been regarded as even more unlucky if a clergyman actually sailed on a ship. Why this should be is uncertain. Perhaps it is because a minister of religion has close contact with death and is a somewhat mystical authority in the community on land. Any such intrusions of alternative status on board make life uncomfortable in the normal hierarchical structure of a crew, their sets of beliefs, and the bonds between men of the sea. A Pacific *palu* (navigator) says, "If a chief sails with me he is considered a member of the crew and not the leader. When we arrive at an island, I will go ashore first: the chiefs of that island will wait for me in their canoe house, will listen as I tell them of our voyage and give news of other islands. Why? Because the chief is of the land, but the palu is of the sea."[36]

Living on Board

When Pacific sailors began serving on foreign ships in the late eighteenth century (see chapter 6), they would have encountered unfamiliar rituals of the sea. Some of these they frighteningly associated with their own spirits of the deep; others were simply puzzling at first. A new sailor or a crew newly brought together will go through a subtle process of testing and bonding. Swapping yarns of experiences of past ships, mates, storms, accidents, ports, and so on is seen by Eric Sager as a ritual "affirming ties with the brotherhood of man."[37] On a long passage, boredom would be relieved when new sailors were required to attend the court of King Neptune on crossing the equator. If the ship hove to, the king and his guards and priests, all in bizarre costumes, would appear out of the sea and make the newcomers pay the price for brotherhood in a wet and boisterous rite of passage.

In the eighteenth century it was still the practice on naval ships to haul a new man to the yardarm in a ducking chair and drop him into the sea, to be pulled on board half drowned. A ritual on merchant ships would take place when sailors had worked off the costs of the cash advances they had received before sailing. This was the "old horse" ceremony, when a made-up wooden horse was hauled to the yardarm and dropped into the sea. Often it was accompanied by sailors' songs, including the sardonic line "After hard work and sore abuse we'll salt ye down for sailors' use." They were now earning pay, no longer flogging a dead horse on board. The bonding and reliance these rituals may have achieved for mateship and mutual help could be matters of life and death: "You'd be slithering about a deck, you know, and a hand'll catch you and pull you up, and something like 'By Christ you were bloody near for it there weren't you?'"—and the incident was over and done with.[38]

When they are bonded together in the closed confines of a ship, there are also unwritten rules of social behavior. Hill, writing about British sailors, observes, "The seafarer tends to develop a highly skilled way and ability to make quick jovial temporary relationships with those with whom he sails."[39] Similarly, writing about Pacific sailors from Anuta in the eastern Solomons, Richard Feinberg says that "on the ocean, the crew adopts a spirit of easy camaraderie, with much relaxed conventions, singing, joking and even banter."[40] There is often a tacit avoidance of controversy in this behavior. Bonding within a crew meant that someone thieving from another sailor would be dealt with summarily by the crew. On naval ships this could mean the culprit would run the gauntlet between lines of shipmates who would hit him with rope ends. Conversely, on boarding an enemy ship, "pilfering" of anything not part of the ship or cargo was allowed, a custom not unlike some in the Pacific toward foreign vessels and shipwrecks. Broaching cargo on their own ships and stealing officers' alcohol were not regarded as crimes by European crews, and no one would tell on another.

The term "broaching cargo" was used also for having, or hoping for, sex with passengers. On most voyages there was in fact little opportunity for sexual relations while at sea. It was still primarily a male society, and in the past "unnatural acts" in the Royal Navy could carry the death sentence. In practice such activities were often tacitly ignored when crew was short and the sailors were reliable and skilled in their duties, unlike the ridicule and persecutions met with ashore. On merchant ships homosexual liaisons tended to be unobserved or, when overt, treated with nautical humor by most sailors. The staid society of New Zealand in the 1950s, for example, was shocked when foreign seamen from ships in the port of Auckland turned out for the "wedding" of two male stewards from the British vessel *Largs Bay* as they were paraded down Queen Street with their burly "bridesmaids." Polynesians, in contrast to the New Zealand press, would have no problem of fitting this with the more tolerant island cultures of *fa'a fafine* and other descriptions of transvestites in their societies.[41]

Going Ashore

When the sailors' celebration of the *Largs Bay* event was in full swing at Ma Gleeson's hostelry, the Auckland police dared not enter. In the past there many such special places in the "sailor towns" around the world.[42] News would be exchanged between sailors from ships in port: "What's the mate like? What's the food like?" Barmaids and crimps were able to pass on information about who was on which ship, when it called, and where it sailed for. Herman Melville describes such a gathering of seamen in the 1840s: "Presently a rioting noise was heard without. Starting up, the landlord cried, 'That's the Grampus's crew. I seed her reported in the offing this morning; a three years' voyage, and a full ship. Hurrah, boys; now we'll have the latest news from the Feegees.'"[43] Even in the remote island of Rotuma in 1874 it was observed, "It is no rare thing to find men who have visited Havre, or New York, or Calcutta, men who can discuss the relative merits of a sailor's home in London or Liverpool."[44]

It has always been easy to recognize sailors ashore in port towns.

Robert Louis Stevenson, a keen observer of seafarers, had his character Jim Hawkins say with some wonder, "I saw, besides, many old sailors, with rings in their ears, and whiskers curled in ringlets, and tarry pigtails, and their swaggering, clumsy sea-walk."[45] Stevenson did not comment here on their tattoos. This characteristic was a gift to sailors from the Pacific islands. All over the Pacific, chiefs, men, women, and children were tattooed. It was a long, painful process, and there were many complex meanings to the decorations. From the time of Cook's arrival in 1769, foreign sailors underwent this ritual, possibly to show they had been to the South Seas. Later it became a universal means of tribal identification as a sailor. Tattoo parlors appeared in most of the sailor towns around the world; and sailors, often after a visit to a hostelry, awoke the next day with tattoos of girls, mermaids, ships, anchors, and the word "mother" on arms and chests. Stan Hugill says the reason for the once-popular tattoo of a crucifix on the arm of a sailor was that "if their bodies washed up on some foreign heathen shore, they could expect a good Christian burial."[46]

In the mid-1970s an old British bosun coming ashore from a newly paid-off ship would hardly be missed from "the cut of his jib" as a seaman. He would be weather-beaten, have tattoos visible on hard hands, and carry a canvas bag with "homeward bound stitching," and he would show an independent swagger, have money to spend, and probably be slightly inebriated when he called for a dockside taxi. By this time he was already a threatened species from the old world of western European crews. Teuea Toatu, writing in 1999 about the new seamen from Kiribati working on foreign ships, observed, "One can easily recognise these seamen with their long hair, long trousers, shoes (for in Kiribati it is rare to see people wearing shoes) and brand new motorcycles."[47]

Home from the Sea

When the modern Pacific seafarer finally makes it from an overseas port to his home island after a year or more away, he often feels greater culture shock than at the many ports visited during the voyage. Daily life in a village in the outer islands of Kiribati, for example, still revolves around fishing, copra making, church services, and listening to gatherings of old men in the *maneaba* (meeting house). The local store would carry only basic goods, such as biscuits, cigarettes, tinned meat, and possibly beer. It is a quiet relatively insular society, traditionally male dominated, but because so many young men go to sea, it is now in practice partially matriarchal. Inevitably a gulf develops between the seafarer and his wife and family in consequence of the enormous disparity in their respective experiences over the year or so he has been away. Generally the returned sailor will reconform to and enjoy island life for a time. He tends not to recount adventures in New York, Hamburg, or Sydney, except in the secretive presence of young admiring boys who want to go to sea.

This difficulty of readjusting to home life when on leave is not confined to seafarers of the Pacific islands. Francoise Péron describes the reception of sailors returning to the Isle of Quessant off northwest France.[48] The women lay down in no uncertain terms how they are to behave: "They can do what they like in their boats but here they have to sing Hail Mary." Members of the Overseas Seafarers' Wives Association, based in Tarawa, and the regional Pacific Women in Maritime Association (PacWIMA), also have views on the behavior of husbands and partners (discussed in chapter 11). The concern is that sexually transmitted diseases, and especially the dreaded AIDS, from the ports around the world will spread in this small population. Seafarers down the ages have always been the victims and carriers of contagious diseases. It was partly because of this that shipwrecked sailors were in danger on some islands in the early days of contact. They had "salt water in their eyes," meaning they had come uninvited to the island out of the sea.

A Sea People

This brief review of some seafaring myths, traditions, and lifestyles shows considerable commonality extending across time and national and ethnic boundaries. It is these values of shipmates, understanding each other and using a common nautical language, together with professionalism toward the dangers of the sea, that allows multinational crewed vessels under any flag to function with an equanimity beyond that of many ethnically mixed societies ashore. Pacific Island young men adapt extremely well to life at sea; women until very recently have seldom had the opportunity.

When they come together on board, Pacific sailors carry with them components of their own culture but conform to shipboard society. When they return home, they carry elements of shipboard identities as sailors, along with foreign port town values, which have an impact on their societies.

CHAPTER TWO

The First Pacific Seafarers

THE PEOPLES OF the Pacific have a history of early long-distance seafaring unequaled anywhere in the world. As far as can be determined, their ancient ancestors were the first ever to make use of the open sea for large-scale migrations. Sometime before 40,000 BC they entered the western region of the Pacific from Southeast Asia. Sea levels were rising in this period of the late Pleistocene ice age, but still stood about fifty meters below those of today. This exposed dry areas of continental shelf, reefs, and islands, interlaced by waterways.[1] The migratory Asia-Pacific hunter-gatherers followed these stepping-stones and channels and settled in New Guinea and possibly northern Australia. Some moved farther eastward over successive generations, following the coast of New Guinea until they reached open water and sailed to the near offshore islands of New Ireland about 40,000 BC, and the Solomons around 30,000 BC.[2]

The islands of the late Pleistocene were larger and had a different coastal morphology from their equivalents today. Sea passages to many offshore potential human habitats could be achieved by sailing between what were intervisible high landforms. This involved crossings of less than fifty miles, although on reaching the Admiralty group and the northern Solomons, people would have lost sight of land for a short time. It is not certain what the weather conditions were like during these Pleistocene voyages. Geoffrey Irwin agrees with other researchers that at least in this equatorial zone the winds would have been little different from what they are today.[3]

The Pleistocene-era migratory hunter-gatherers may be the most direct ancestors of the New Guinea highlanders and the Australian aborigines. Little is known about their material culture; their vessels were probably dugouts, bark boats, and bamboo rafts. The eastward migrations of these first seafarers apparently ceased when they encountered the open-sea horizons extending outward from the Bismarck Archipelago and the Solomon Islands. They established interisland trading systems in this area of "near

Oceania," which included the carriage of obsidian by sea. Patrick Kirch points to the importance of the archaeological evidence of oceanic trading seafaring some 18,000 to 20,000 years ago that covered over 350 kilometers by boat, much of it beyond visual landforms.[4]

Open-Ocean Migrations

Many centuries after the initial settlements of near Oceania, a more technically advanced seafaring society moved from Southeast Asia and emerged in the region of the Bismarcks. These were Neolithic cultivators, fishers, and rearers of livestock. Already by 4000 BC they appear to have possessed large sailing craft with affinities to those of Indonesia. From possibly 3500 BC they sailed by interisland passages to Santa Cruz, then through Vanuatu. From there it was more than 450 miles to Fiji, and from Fiji 650 miles to Samoa (ca. 1000 BC), with possible en route islands. These routes are marked by their distinctive Lapita pottery.

Straight-line distances are not very meaningful, since actual miles covered could be three times greater, due to set and drift of currents, leeway, and tacking. Simply as a basis for comparison, the Polynesian descendants of the Lapita people in Samoa later sailed much greater passages of 1,000 miles of open sea to Tahiti (arrival about 1000 BC) and 700 miles to some of the Cook Islands. Furthermore, in this easterly sector of the Pacific the southeast trades are strongest, and unless El Niño was prevalent, chances of westerlies would be minimal but not impossible. The onward voyages from Tahiti to the Marquesas through the islands of Tuamotu would entail only 300 miles of open sea, but from there to Hawai'i, nearly 2,000 miles (ca. AD 400), and from Mangareva possibly to Henderson Island, 380 miles, and from there to Rapa Nui, 1,000 miles (after AD 1000). Eastern Polynesia clearly presented formidable challenges.

It was several centuries following the colonization of the eastern Pacific that the southern periphery of what became the Polynesian triangle was completed, with voyages of over 1,600 miles assumed from Rarotonga to Aotearoa.[5] These passages appear to have been undertaken about AD 1000 to 1300.[6] There is no evidence of the great Polynesian voyages reaching Australia, although vessels did return northwestward from Western Polynesia into Melanesia and Micronesia, reaching Nukuoro, Tikopea, Anuta, and other islands, which are known as the Polynesian outliers. Polynesian seafarers also reached Norfolk Island around AD 1200; from there Australia is about 800 miles, well within their capability.[7] Similarly, there is no firm evidence of the Lapita descendants sailing from the remote east Pacific islands to South America. This would have been a more difficult but not impossible voyage of 2,000 miles from Rapa Nui. The sweet potato has origins in South America and was subsequently diffused throughout the Pacific.[8] There were obviously some early links between the American continent and the Pacific islands, but the extent of those links is still uncertain.

The Micronesian island groups of the northwest Pacific received seafarers direct from the Philippines into the Marianas. Others came from the Lapita of the Solomon-Vanuatu region. Yet other related groups came from the Bismarcks to Yap Islands. The probable dates of various island settlements in Micronesia, including the Marshalls and Kiribati, range between 1500 BC and AD 500. All the dates so far alluded to may be subject to future changes as DNA research progresses.

As it stands, DNA indicates that the migrants who entered the remote Pacific were not genetically homogenous. They had progressed through Melanesia and mixed with preexisting non-Austronesian populations. The research also confirms Fiji as pivotal in human dispersions. These voyagers carried commensal animals, including pigs and rats. Pig bones found in middens reveal a single genetic inheritance over several routes. The bones of the Pacific rat *(Rattus exulans)* are unique and are proving valuable in tracing the origins and routes of their seafaring hosts. So far the DNA analysis show general west-to-east movements. Of fundamental interest are the bones of the Pacific rats as proxy for human migrations in Rapa Nui, the very extreme eastward position. These rats do not have the complexities of human genetic data, which are open to interpretations. Excavations by University of Hawai'i teams in 2004 at Anakena beach on Rapa Nui have revealed rat bones in early arrival strata at about AD 1200. These rats are not native to North or South America, and this confirms a founding Polynesian population.[9]

The great Pacific migratory voyages were the basis for identifying the ethnographic stamp which the diaspora of 2000 BC to AD 1300 has put on the Eastern Pacific in particular. During this period, generations of seafarers visited every island in the vast Pacific Ocean, and they transferred thousands of people, plants, and animals to occupy most of the island world. Much of the flora, fauna, cultural, and human physical inheritances that are there today were the products of these voyages. In the course of time more locally distinctive cultural characteristics of people emerged in various island regions according to environmental challenges, levels of insularity, and later colonial impacts. Although there are many differences, overlaps, and transitional zones between islands and peoples, there is a broad basis for the accepted geographical classifications of regions, and somewhat tenuous groupings of related human characteristics, into the divisions and boundaries of Polynesia, Melanesia, and Micronesia. This geographical classification was initially made by Dumont d'Urville in 1831 and remains a useful generalization for some Pacific divisions, as indicated by map 2.1.[10]

The Ships

The great migrations from west to east and subsequent voyages were made on a variety of vessels. Unfortunately the European misnomer "canoe" for these seagoing ships of the Pacific is misleading but has persisted over centuries and would be difficult to displace. There were, and still are to a much reduced extent, many types of vessels indigenous to these islands. They range from single dugout canoes—some with outriggers, like the Fijian *takia,* which is still extant—to the substantial ships that made the great oceanic voyages of the past but have long since disappeared.

The generic term for island vessels is *"wa"* and its variants. It is frequently a prefix indicating the type and function of Pacific craft, as in the Fijian *"waqa ni koro"* (boat of the village) and *"waqa tabu"* (sacred, or chief's, vessel). In Samoa it is expressed as *"va'a"* (often indicating a large vessel) and *"va'aalo"* (small outrigger). Likewise in Tahiti and the Marquesas *"va'a"* is used as *"va'a motu"* (small vessel), as well as the term *"vaka."* The latter word is common in Tonga and the Cook Islands, and *"waka"* is also used in the Cooks. In Hawai'i it is *"wa'a,"* in Aotearoa *"waka"* (as in *"waka taua,"* or war vessel). This is also a boat word among the northwest Pacific Polynesian outliers. In Kiribati the term *"wa ririk"* is still in use for small outriggers,[11] and in the Marshalls it is *"wa lap."* There are many other descriptive terms for vessels, but the occurrence of *"wa"* over a vast area of the Pacific is one of the many indicators of a common maritime inheritance.

Little has remained of the actual vessels used on the ocean voyages of exploration, migration, or early long-distance trade. The teredo worm and the hot, humid conditions of the Pacific effectively put an end to most of the ancient littoral and underwater cultural heritage. Excavations on Huahine in the Society Islands have uncovered some ship artifacts circa AD 800, including a carved steering paddle 3.8 meters long and two adzed planks that are "believed to have been part of the platform of a double canoe about 24 meters long." Among other small but vital finds

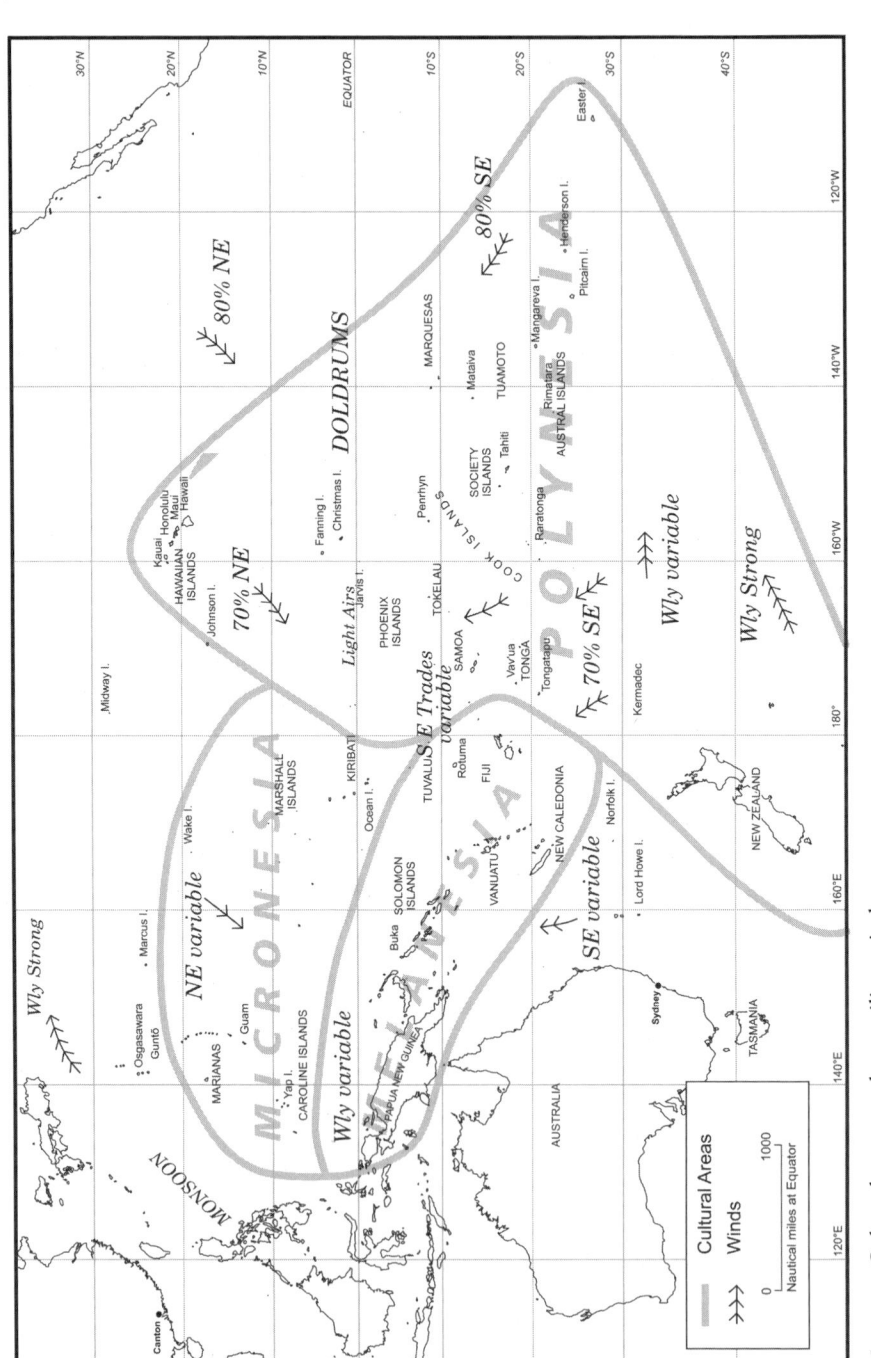

MAP 2.1. Cultural areas and prevailing winds.

were hand clubs similar to those being produced in Aotearoa at the time of Cook.[12]

The Pacific oceangoing ships took many years to build, often on an island that was within a group with suitable timber and specialized in shipbuilding. The whole community might be involved in divisions of labor, including carpentry, caulking, sail making, and cordage manufacturing. Food to provide for this specialized labor force would sometimes be brought from other islands.[13] Such ships were undoubtedly the most advanced achievement of the Neolithic Pacific.[14] They were highly valued and prestigious, had spiritual connotations, and were venerated and protected by ceremony and taboos. Many were also objects of art and had names that were both functional and poetic, such as the warship *Rusaivanua* (Fijian: destroyer of the land).

In summary, Micronesian vessels were built from planks and had single hulls, outriggers, and lateen sails. As the outrigger had to be kept to windward, coming about required the sail to be shifted fore to aft. In Fiji and Western Polynesia, long-distance vessels were mainly double hulled, with lateen sails, which likewise had to be shifted to come about. In Eastern Polynesia, including Tahiti and Hawai‘i there were double hulls, but with sprit sails on fixed masts, so that tacking was achieved by bringing the bow round to the wind. Melanesia is characterized by both double-hulled outriggers (east coast of Papua) and lateen and sprit sails of various forms. These and other differences in vessel technology were responses to available materials and wind, sea and coastal conditions, and to diffusion and adaptations of successful solutions for sailing and survival—all reinforced over generations by taught skills and memorized rules and rituals.

The ship construction techniques, all without metal, relied on the use of fire, wooden mallets, and adzes of basalt and obsidian, either local or obtained by trade. Other tools included adzes from the shells of giant clams, shell scrapers, shark-tooth- and coral-tipped drills, and sharkskin and sometimes pumice for smoothing the hulls. The vessels had to be big enough to carry viable family groups and broad for stability, with minimal draught for reefs and lagoons. They needed space for the crew, passengers, livestock, tools, weapons, plants, seeds, fishing gear, spare sails and spars, and possibly an alternative mast, as well as food and water for the voyage.

A vital first stage in ship construction was to choose the correct wood for various components of the vessel. All the parts had to respond intrinsically to incessant wave motions, sudden winds, and shocks of periodic heavy pounding. The natural shapes of trunks and branches were vital.

Mifflin Thomas describes the long process in Hawai'i of selecting trees for hull timbers. The party would be guided by the *kahuna kalai wa'a*, the specialized builder, who would follow the elepaio (a flycatcher species) in the forest over many days and observe its tree-pecking patterns until its behavior signaled a tree in the best condition. The forest god would then be placated by a pig sacrifice before the wood was transferred from a land to sea domain.[15]

John Twyning of the whaling brig *Minerva* (captained by Thomas Lewis), which sailed from Sydney in 1829 and was wrecked in Fiji, describes the process of building a large ship at Lakeba in the Lau Islands, where he and others in the crew were given refuge. After a tree of the hardwood vesi was felled under the directions of the Matia shipbuilder, it was split in the middle and each half reduced to the proper thickness. It was, Twyning wrote, "surprising to see the accuracy with which these planks are joined to each other; a piece of very thin tapa cloth with a kind of gum, made from the bread-fruit tree and laid between the two pieces to be joined, after which they are sewn together with threads of sennit, and made perfectly tight by small wedges driven between the threads and the wood." He went on to say that the design and building of the ship would have received "the admiration of even the most skillful and scientific naval architect in Europe."[16]

The ship seen by Twyning was most probably the Fijian *drua*, the building of which was usually directed by Tongans. Over one hundred feet in length, the *drua* had two hulls with length differences for hydrodynamic purposes, set about seven feet apart, over which an athwartship deck was laid. It had hatches for entry to the hulls, a deckhouse, and a platform erected above this from which the captain gave orders to the crew handling the sail and the massive steering oar. The single sloping mast of the *drua*, made from strong, flexible wood, stood about fifty feet above the deck and supported a massive lateen-type sail, contained between two flexible yards extending over the whole length of the ship. J. Glen Wilson of HMS *Herald* painted a scene of a fleet of *drua* sailing off Levuka in 1855.[17]

The Tongans and Samoans had vessels somewhat similar to the *drua*, including the *tongiaki*, which had two hulls of equal length, a sail like the *drua*'s, and two massive steering oars but was considered more difficult to handle in bad weather. A painting from the Schouten expedition shows a double-hulled vessel west of the Tuamotus in 1616 (figure 2.1). An impressive Tongan craft for speed was the *kalia*. Thomas West describes his 1865 trip on a *kalia*:

Up went the huge sail, down went the great steer-oars splashing into the sea, and away we shot like a race-horse. . . . Every timber of the canoe creaked again; while the mast bent like a reed, and cracked in its socket as if it would split the deck in two. . . . [T]he sea was like a hissing cauldron on either side of our course, and the kalia, instead of having to mount over the smaller waves, cut its way right through them.[18]

In Hawai'i the *wa'a kaulua*, a particularly fast and elegant ship, was double hulled and had crab-claw sprit sails and steering paddles.[19] The *pahi* of the Society Islands was unlike the other indigenous vessels in Polynesia. The *pahi* had a near-European type of keel, ribs, and knees and was full bellied, and its stem and stern posts were high and elaborately carved. It had two masts and unique sails. Robert Langdon, in his *Lost Caravel*, sees this vessel as possibly an adaptation of technology from sixteenth- and seventeenth-century Spanish ships.[20]

FIGURE 2.1. The Le Maire and Schouten voyage provided inspiration for the first image of a double-hulled canoe. The incident depicted in this painting took place off the Tuamotu Islands between 9 and 13 May 1616. The Dutch fired a warning shot from the boat of their ship, the *Eendracht*, but the crew of the canoe refused to stop. The Dutch then fired on the vessel. (Courtesy of the Pepys Library, Magdalene College, Cambridge)

In Micronesia the Kiribati *baurua* was a large, fast, slender vessel with an outrigger. The hull was more V-shaped than other ships in the Pacific, reducing the effects of leeway, and was also asymmetrically curved to compensate for the drag of the large outrigger.[21] People of the Marshalls and Carolines also built outrigger craft with lateen-type sails. These were characterized by a lee platform on which the captain stood to direct sailing and steering; in some atolls these vessels were kept small because of timber shortages and difficult reef passages. The vessels of western Melanesia such as the *puka* of Santa Cruz were outriggers and used the crab-claw sail.[22] On the New Guinea coast the Motu trading *lakatoi* was double hulled and had similar sails.[23]

Only a few types of large sailing craft were noted in Aotearoa by the first Europeans.[24] A general view is that after possibly multiple voyages from and to the original homeland of Hawaiki, the Maori Polynesians started to build mainly single-hulled vessels from giant kauri logs.[25] These *waka tana* were ornately carved, powered mainly by paddles, and used for coastal trade, and the *waka taua,* with its high stern and elaborate carvings, were used for warfare and were propelled by a hundred paddlers.

Weather and Climate Variables

The planetary wind systems of the Pacific are generally predictable in direction and force. These northeast and southeast trades blow from about 30° N and 30° S toward the equator, vary a few degrees in latitude over winter and summer, and are most consistent in the remote easterly zones. In higher latitudes beyond a zone of variables, the westerlies are on average fairly constant (see map 2.1), and hurricanes in the tropical latitudes have well-defined seasons and prevail in the westerly zones. In detail there are periodic and reasonably predictable departures from the prevailing planetary wind systems in several areas, which vessels on west-to-east voyages across the Pacific could take advantage of. The ocean currents in the main migratory zones would, however, often be adverse (map 2.2). Navigators in the eastward voyage from Samoa to Tahiti in the *Hokule'a* wanted to test this replica of an ancient Polynesian voyaging canoe by driving close-hauled in the southeast trade winds. The result surprised them: "Instead of the anticipated hard struggle to reach Tahiti, an embarrassment of favourable northwesterly winds sped the *Hokule'a* eastwards." In his account of the passage, Ben Finney says of the old voyagers, "Seafarers had to learn how to exploit spells of westerly winds to

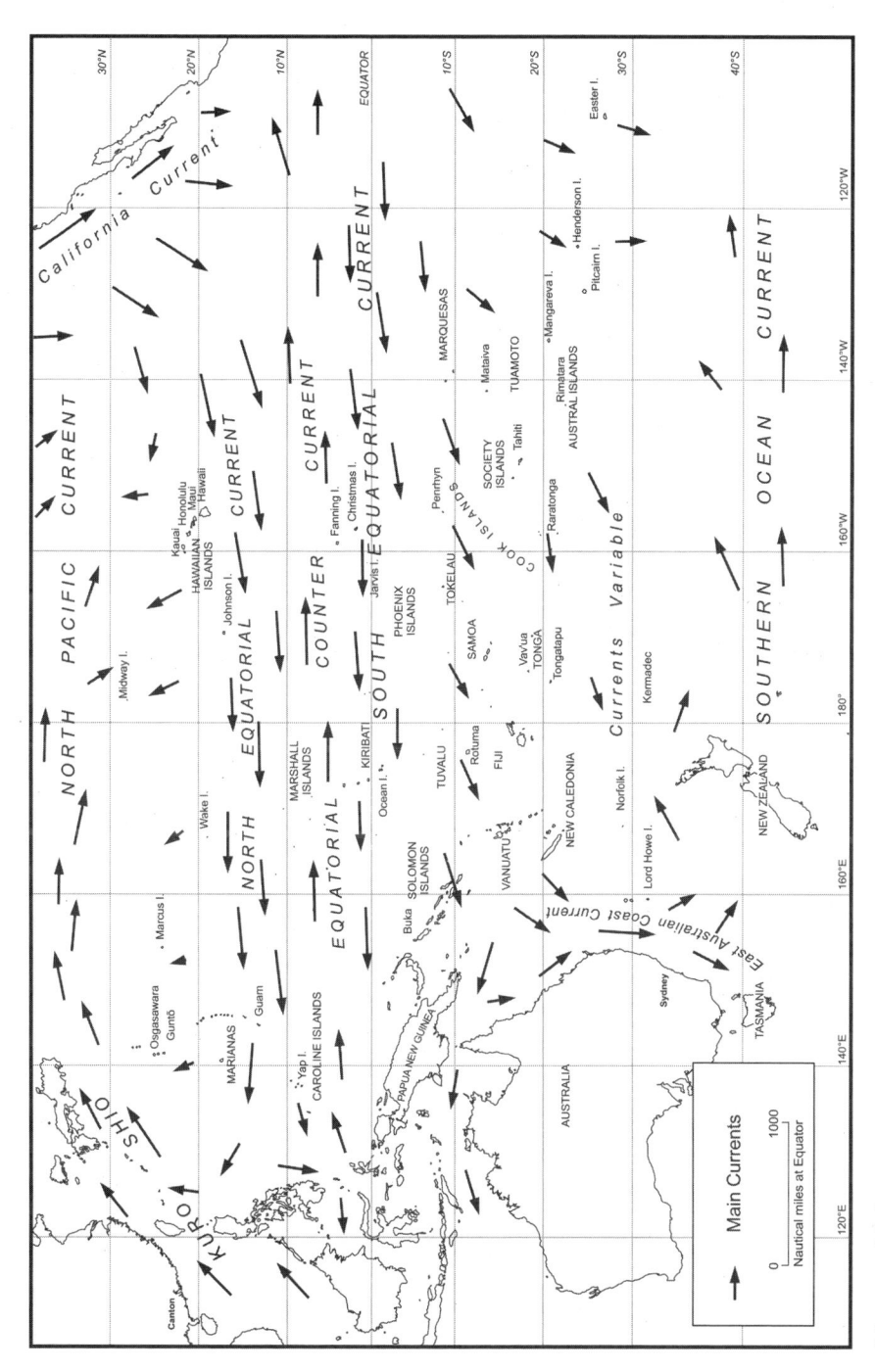

MAP 2.2. Main ocean currents.

keep pressing eastwards against the direction from which the trade winds often but not always blow."[26]

In Kiribati, predictions of winds were guided by the star calendar. Stars rise four minutes earlier each day, so that a rising morning star becomes an evening setting star in six months. When Antares (Rimwimata) appeared over the eastern horizon just after sunset, it marked the beginning of the best distant-sailing season (June). When it was replaced by the rising of the Pleiades (Nei Auti), dangerous westerlies could be expected (November–December).[27] In latitudes farther south the hurricane season was also often avoided. Hocart notes that canoes in Fiji were beached during December to March.[28] But this period of summer was, and is, often preferred for local voyages. It is called *draki vinaka*, when there are long periods of fine weather more comfortable than the boisterous winter season, which can be cold and wet on deck before dawn. Decisions about voyaging were a matter of keeping a weather eye open for signs of hurricanes.

The weather was not the only variable. There were changes in climate during the long periods of human migrations. These are recognizable in detail in the latter part of the migratory era.[29] During the final migrations of the Polynesians, which took them to Aotearoa, there is evidence that the weather was favorable. This period from AD 800 to 1250 is identified as the "little climatic optimum," with clear skies and fewer storms, which may have allowed seafarers from around the Cook Islands to extend their exploratory voyages beyond the trade wind zones, sail through the zones of variable winds, and work through the barrier of what are now strong westerlies to reach Aotearoa. Similarly this more benign climatic period extending into the thirteenth century may have allowed long-distance two-way voyages to take place. Later climatic change into the fifteenth century may account for deteriorations in weather, especially in the higher latitudes, that seem to have brought two-way links between Aotearoa and the original homelands to a close.[30]

Seamanship

The designs and materials of hull, sails, rigging, and steering gear were the strengths and maneuvering assets of Pacific vessels. This system was successful only when competent seafarers were in the loop. The ship had to bear variable loads and respond to a wide range of conditions at sea and on the coast. She would roll and pitch in a seaway and be subject to squalls and sudden shifts in wind force and direction. The vessel had to survive severe storms without capsizing, foundering, or suffering irreparable damage. This meant expert seamanship was required.

The captain of an oceangoing Pacific vessel would undoubtedly be an experienced seaman and have status and authority. He would probably have selected the crew and decided on the time of sailing from weather and astronomical observations. As the principal navigator, the captain would determine positions and courses during the voyage and maintain discipline and morale. As with all seagoing vessels, a captain of a Pacific craft would for safety reasons have been regarded as the equivalent of "master under God," with no one reigning above him while at sea.

The seamanship tasks would start from ensuring correct loading of the vessel for its stability and trim. Passengers would be distributed, livestock penned, and ship-handling areas kept clear. Among those on board a range of skills would be found in addition to those of the sailors. Possibly they would include fishermen, sailmakers, carpenters, divers, and specialists in traditional medicines, who could all contribute to safety.

Long west-to-east voyages, frequently into the prevailing trades, would inevitably involve extended periods of exhausting tacking or reversing lateens, as these vessels could sail no closer than about 75 degrees to the wind. When running free with a strong following wind and sea, a heavily laden double-hulled vessel required competent handling in adjusting to combinations of wind and sea. Twyning observes that the sea has to be kept on the quarter, for if a high wave was allowed to run between the two hulls, it could part them.[31] Scudding before a gale could also make any of these craft difficult to control, and there was the danger of being overtaken by waves and pooping a heavy sea, which could wash over the length of the vessel. It is likely that experienced seamen would in such weather pay out a long line with buoyant material, such as wooden spars attached to act as a sea anchor, and ride out the storm or drag it astern to slow down, but there is no evidence of this in the Pacific. Some vessels carried a heavy stone on a rope for anchoring. This could be hung in the water over the bow, then weights shifted aft and the vessel kept nearly head-on to the sea, assisted by expert use of a steering oar.[32] Morrison also observed in Tonga that "when taken by a squall they luff head on to it and shake it out—if long they jump overboard and hang her head to windward till the squall is over." He added that bringing the sail down on very big vessels could be dangerous, but they carried plenty of cordage and masts to repair damage.[33]

Calm weather could bring other problems, particularly where strong ocean currents were encountered (see map 2.2). The equatorial current can set in a westerly direction at thirty to forty miles per day, and under fresh trade winds at about three and a half knots. The easterly countercurrent has a rate that reaches over one knot. These currents vary seasonally, with the equatorial countercurrent extending just south of the equator in June and July. Captain G. H. Heyen, who commanded the brigantine *Alexa,* the last sailing vessel to operate regularly out of Sydney to the Pacific Islands in 1929, recalls becoming becalmed twenty miles west of Tarawa on the fifty-fifth day out of Sydney and drifting away; the *Alexa* did not reach the Gilberts again for another one hundred days.[34]

Navigation

The systems of determining direction and position finding varied in detail in different parts of the Pacific. There were many common features, but most of the local knowledge was closely guarded and passed on through hereditary channels. This process also included formal training onshore and long periods at sea under the instruction of leading navigators. Father Ernest Sabatier describes how the *maneaba,* the great social meeting house in the islands of Kiribati, was built north-south and was used for teaching astronomy and navigation. The ridgepole of the *maneaba* represented the meridian, the thatch between the parallel rafters conceptually contained various constellations and positions of individual stars in their diurnal transits throughout a year, and the eaves marked the horizon.[35] Grimble describes how outside under the changing night sky, the *uma ni borau* (roof of voyaging) would be the main school where names and passages of stars were identified and memorized, visualizing them within lines of rafters. Of particular significance would be the succession of "guiding stars," which rose and set in the direction of known islands. The navigator initiates also learned those zenith stars that reached their maximum altitude in the vicinity of the home island and other islands known to them.[36]

The Jesuit missionary Father Juan Antonio Cantova, writing in 1722, says of navigational training in the Caroline Islands that "young men received lessons in practical astronomy and navigation";[37] and Gladwin, writing of the same islands in 1970, records: "Formal instruction begins on land. It demands that great masses of factual information be committed to memory. This information is detailed, specific, and potentially of life-or-death importance. . . . Often they sit together in the canoe house. . . . The pebbles usually represent stars, but they are also used to illustrate islands."[38] The Marshall Islands stick charts are yet another type of teaching device. These simulate how swells bend and interact with patterns of distant islands—represented by cowry shells—below the horizon, thereby allowing navigators to establish approximate positions by the nodes of swells and courses to be adjusted.[39] It was not until the development of satellite imagery that these intricate long-distance swell patterns used by Pacific island voyagers (and to a more limited extent Shetland fishermen) could be fully appreciated.[40]

The process of navigating would begin on departure by setting a course for a known group of islands on the appropriate wind. At the low island of Arorae in Kiribati there are transit stones providing initial departure directions to specific islands. Transit stones have been identified also on Atiu, giving the direction to Rarotonga. By keeping the leading stones in sight from stern observations, a navigator could maintain a course and estimate the current set and drift. When the marks went below the horizon and the guiding stars appeared, the course could be adjusted to those stars, offset from the destination to allow for current and leeway. The sky was now one big compass, and the feel of the wind could also act in this way.[41] The departure from a high island is similarly described by Raymond Firth. The mountain peak known as Te Uru Asia, at one thousand feet above sea level on Tikopia, is the highest of five marks that, by relating vertical and horizontal scales, allow a series of first estimates of distance run.[42]

Gladwin details a voyage process of departure to arrival using the concept of *etak*. The disappearance of the island shore marks would show the end of the "*etak* of sight," the second zone would be marked by the "*etak* of birds." The third would be a series of *etak* distances in the open ocean. Then the navigator has guiding stars ahead in line with the destination, while another reference island, real or imaginary, was offset from the course. He would now visualize himself as stationary, and as successive stars came in transit with the reference island, the island of destination would move closer. Gladwin analyzes this system in detail and describes as a system for conceptually bringing together raw information and converting it into a solution of the essential navigational question, how far is our destination?[43]

Guiding stars—the sun and those stars close to the cardinal points of north (polestar), south (Southern Cross), east and west (Orion's belt and Altair), the latter two on rising and setting—plus allowances for currents and leeway, would enable skilled navigators to keep courses with some certainty throughout a voyage. There is also significant evidence that the

Pacific navigators could establish approximate latitudes in relation to the wide spread of an island group to which they were heading, providing they knew the zenith star of or close to these islands. When, for example (in the present period), Sirius is directly overhead, its approximate declination of 17° S corresponds to the latitude of a navigator at 17° S. This includes the south of Vanua Levu in Fiji. Similarly, Arcturus (declination 19° N), when reaching its zenith directly above the navigator, indicates that the vessel was in the latitude of the southernmost island of Hawai'i. The navigator of old would not know with certainty if he was east or west of the destination, because he had no way of establishing longitude. However, having made a directional allowance on departure and during the voyage for a windward approach to the destination, he could, when in the latitude of the islands, run downwind to pick up islands and would be guided in this by seabirds and other seamarks.

These indigenous systems of navigation have been well tested by David Lewis.[44] They were undoubtedly no less accurate than the European methods used before the mid-eighteenth century, when longitude at sea could not be established with certainty. This problem came to a head in 1707 when four British warships were wrecked on the Isles of Scilly, with the loss of two thousand men. The ships were sailing in reduced visibility with an estimated longitude by dead reckoning, which put them farther west than they actually were.[45] One of the purposes of Cook's second voyage to the Pacific in 1772–1775 was to test the accuracy of Harrison's timepiece for determining longitude by chronometer.

By this period of the eighteenth century, Europeans had some appreciation of the possible competent navigational skills of the Pacific islanders, primarily on the basis of their detailed geographical knowledge. Tupaia, the Ra'iatean priest-navigator who came from a family of famous seamen, proved invaluable to Cook.[46] In 1769 Tupaia named and gave sailing directions from Tahiti (the center of his world) to Fiji and to virtually every island group of Polynesia for more than one thousand miles north-south and three thousand miles east-west, with the exception of Hawai'i, Rapa Nui, and Aotearoa. Similarly, Cantova in 1722 was able to draw a map of Micronesia, based on information from local informants, that, Hezel observes, "reveals a surprisingly complete knowledge of an island world that, stretching over fifteen hundred miles of ocean as it did, must be considered large even for a seafaring people."[47] This map remained the best available of the region into the nineteenth century. The intellectual process and remarkable feats of memory involved in navigation are all the more impressive when one recalls that Pacific mariners had no written language and no mechanical timepieces.

Cook, during his first voyage, expressed admiration for these Pacific navigators, although he probably could not find the time to understand their systems in detail. On his return to the eighteenth-century society of land-based astronomers in England, this very practical navigator deferred to their views; as G. S. Parsonson expresses it, the English astronomers found it difficult to accept "that ignorant savages had long ago achieved the mastery of the sea which navigators in the old world had scarcely yet attained."[48]

This account of navigational skills has referred only to men. There are very few references in the Pacific (or other regions) of women in charge of navigating ships. Women have led trading parties on voyages, and often canoes with female crews can be seen on short passages in archipelagos. But, as indicated in chapter 1, on deep-sea vessels there were, and sometimes still are, prejudices and taboos. An oral account of a woman navigator was given to Father Sabatier in Kiribati during the 1930s.[49] It is also an interesting recollection of one of many minor wars between islands in the 1780s, and how the conflict between Abemama and Tarawa was amicably settled for a time in the traditional way. The account contains some ambiguities, as well as conflicts between gender, status, and skills. He entitled the account, "La vengeance d'une femme," which can be summarized as follows:

> A Tarawa fleet attacked Abemama. It was beaten, and an Abemama fleet sailed to Tarawa to reinforce its victory. Tarawa paid tribute of feasts and gifts to Abemama. The Abemama fleet was led by a "general," a "soothsayer," and a "navigator." The latter was Baintabu, a daughter from a navigator family without sons. At the feast she was ignored and did not receive a share of the gifts. On the seventy-mile return voyage to Abemama, Baintabu "sulked" and lay at the bottom of the leading boat, giving no instructions for tacking. She was eventually rolled up in her mat and thrown overboard. Fortunately for Baintabu, the last vessel picked her up. She navigated the boat to Abemama, and the other vessels were never seen again.

The questions is, was she "sulking," or was she actually on her back, feeling the swell or looking for the zenith star? At the Tarawa feast and on board the vessel, however, she certainly did not have the prestige ordinarily accorded to a navigator. There is another rare example of a woman navigator recorded about 1900. She was called Libe and was a teacher in the Ebon school of navigation in the Marshall Islands.[50] This is quite possible, for in Britain during the early nineteenth century some wives of captains ran private navigation courses.

Nutrition

There is no doubt that skilled navigation, while prestigious, was not hard to come by on the long voyages by Pacific seafarers. Lewis concludes, "The special problems of the longer journey concern such factors as food supply, manpower, motivation, and strength of the vessel—not navigation."[51] Passage could be extended in time, and with fifty or so people on board, food supplies could run out. The voyagers would then have to depend on food from the sea. This would not have been a major problem for Pacific island seafarers, with their detailed knowledge of the marine environment.

In contrast to Pacific people, some of the European sailors who came to the Pacific were too far removed in perception and suitable marine technology to exploit the diversity of food resources available from the ocean. When, for example, stores ran out on Magellan's ship *Trinidad* in 1521, the crew arrived at Guam ill with scurvy and starving, having been reduced to chewing cowhide and eating the last of the rats during the ninety-nine day crossing.[52] On the 1740–1744 voyage to the Pacific led by Commander George Anson, some 1,400 seamen out of 1,900 on his squadron of six ships died mainly of "disease and starvation." Unfortunately for Anson, who was a competent and caring naval officer, the seafarers that the British Admiralty provided him were of poor quality, and the northeast trade winds he had relied on to carry them across the Pacific proved to be very weak in the low latitudes he followed in May, thereby greatly increasing the length of passage.[53]

William Bligh was a little more successful in obtaining food in 1789, when he made a remarkable voyage of 3,500 miles in forty-eight days while in charge of eighteen men on a seven-meter launch with little freeboard. These castaways from the *Bounty* set off with food and water for about only five days in normal conditions. They managed to make a brief stop at nearby Tofua in the Tongan group and obtained some breadfruit and coconuts before one sailor was killed and they were driven off by hostile islanders. Bligh then safely navigated to the northern barrier reef of Australia en route to Timor, and the men were able to obtain large quantities of mollusks. Otherwise the boatload was able to collect rainwater and live on boobies, seabirds that they caught by hand. Bligh reported seeing plenty of fish, and although they had hand fishing lines, they did not have the skills.[54]

Even less successful in terms of living off the sea were the survivors of the whaleship *Essex* in 1821. The ship sank, and the three whaleboats eventually lost company with one another. When their meager supplies were exhausted, the castaways did what seafarers in lifeboats have done before and since: they agreed to cast lots and kill and eat one another in turn, in the hope that at least some would survive to be rescued or reach land. In the event that only one sacrifice was needed before they were rescued, the other who was eaten died of general weakness.[55]

If Pacific islanders had to resort to cannibalism at sea, which they did on other occasions on land, they would have been more conserving of related people by using only parts of someone who died, or of a voluntary victim, as bait to catch fish and birds. In practice, they would have lived off the sea. There are many contemporary accounts of islanders surviving very long voyages after losing their vessel or being carried away on small craft by the equatorial current. In June 2001, for example, four Samoan seamen lost their fishing craft northwest of Samoa. They took to the ship's boat without adequate provisions for a long voyage. Two of them survived and arrived at Normanby Island on the northeast of mainland New Guinea five months later, after drifting about 2,500 miles. The survivors said that they lived by catching fish and birds and drinking rainwater.[56]

The Pacific Ocean beyond the island fringes is not in fact very nutrient rich. However, all island mariners would recognize certain signs at sea that meant sustenance. Flurries of flying fish might indicate schools of pursuing skipjack tuna. Behavior of tuna might signal the existence of predatory sharks. The flight paths of certain birds would be known, and their behavior would indicate shoals of specific types of fish. It was also possible to use floating baited lines to catch birds that spend most of their lives at sea. The expert fishermen on the ships would be well equipped with spears, fishhooks (of shell, bone, and wood), dip nets, and trolling and deep-water lines for catching a wide range of fish, as well as torches for attracting squid and flying fish at night. They possessed, as they still do, a profound practical knowledge of marine ecology and fish behavior. They were aware of what is now termed fish aggregation devices (FADs). Their stationary wooden vessel would act as a FAD, and fish would congregate around and under it. They also knew how to use sound and vibration to attract fish from long distances. By beating rhythmically on the sides of the hull or using submerged coconut-shell rattles, they could attract certain species, including sharks. Pacific fishermen were using such methods centuries before modern hydrophone experimentation confirmed that fish communicate by sound and vibration over very long distances.

As fishermen, most Pacific islanders do not share the European fear and neurosis about sharks. They respect the shark, and they understand the habits of different shark species. They know when to remove themselves from aggressive or mobbing sharks but also recognize other forms of shark behavior that mean the islanders can safely share the sea with them. After killing a shark, fishermen in some of the islands of west Melanesia still release the spirit of the shark by sounding notes on a conch shell. Sharks would have been difficult to catch in early times with coconut sennit lines, which could be bitten through, resulting in the loss of precious shell hooks. R. E. Johannes has demonstrated a system whereby a noose is slipped over the head and gills of a shark, and then the big fish is speared and clubbed as it is held alongside the canoe. Johannes notes, "The Palauan fisherman had a special tattoo on his wrist. When holding out a flying fish to entice a shark to swim through the noose, he was not supposed to let go of the bait until the tip of the shark's snout reached the tattoo."[57]

The Pacific island migrants would not have starved on voyages led by experienced mariners. Fresh water might have been more of a problem, and on every crowded vessel during a long passage there would have been, as the British Admiralty terms them, the "sick and hurt." Greg Dening is realistically cautious of the view that "before the coming of the white man they [the islanders] had died only of old age, war and sorcery, that all the diseases that killed them came with the ships."[58] Undoubtedly the major epidemics and sexually transmitted diseases came from visiting ships, but on long voyages, as elsewhere, islanders may have suffered from intestinal, respiratory, muscular, skin, and skeletal problems, as well as accidents.

Ships would have carried stocks of island medicines, including those based on plants, possibly kava *(Piper methysticum),* seaweeds, coconut toddy and milk, and fermented pandanus and breadfruit would be taken or applied, as would the healing and cleansing properties of seawater and the ministrations of shaman healers.[59] Fresh water would no doubt be rationed; however, the vast pandanus sails of the ships could collect rain from periodic heavy squalls to supplement that carried in gourds and pottery containers. Other foods on board would be similar to those customarily stored on many islands in Kiribati: green nuts, pandanus flour *(te kabubu)*, preserved pandanus fruit *(te tuae)*, coconut toddy syrup *(te kamaima)*, pounded breadfruit and taro (kept in leaves), dried shellfish, live fowls, pigs, and rats. The rapid reproductive capacities of the rats would generate many young, providing a regular source of protein.

Arrival at the Beach

Having survived the ocean leg of a voyage, the flotilla faced other dangers before reaching the beach. All seafarers become more vigilant when approaching even a well-charted coast. When they sailed into an unknown but very likely reef-strewn archipelagic region, the dangers could be immense. Signs of the approach to land would be observed long before it was sighted. These would include the types and directions of the flight of birds, the characteristics of ocean swells and clouds, and the occurrence of floating vegetation. Night sailing would now become particularly hazardous. Most high islands have areas of fringing reefs along their coast, and several are characterized by offshore barrier reefs enclosing lateral lagoons, although some, like the Marquesas, present primarily beaches and cliffs direct to the sea. Atolls comprise a series of low islands (motus) standing on wide reefs on their weather side. To leeward they have a large, broad reef flat enclosed by barrier reef, within which is the lagoon. Low reef islands have only coastal fringing reefs and no lagoons. Dangers are encountered in the vicinity of all these islands.

The weather side of atolls is steep-to, and breakers can be seen and heard a mile or so offshore. Likewise, the reflection of lagoon waters on the base of cumulus clouds can sometimes be seen before the barrier reefs are sighted. If a vessel finds itself too close in on the weather side, and there are strong onshore winds and currents, it may be difficult to clear the long line of the barrier reef and avoid stranding. On the lee side of atolls the waters can be even more dangerous, with numerous sunken reefs extending seaward for many miles from the shore. The prudent navigator would lay off an island until the sun was up and behind him if possible. Then, with a masthead lookout, he would avoid the yellow and brown areas and follow the deep blue water toward the reef.

On the final part of the approach, deep and wide reef passes would have to be found to enter lagoons. On high islands, breaks in the reef occur on any side of the island where rivers carry fresh water and sediments, which inhibit coral growth. On low islands, reef passes into lagoons lie on the lee sides; through which water driven across the weather reefs circulates in the lagoon and flows outward through these passes. The currents in such passes vary in strength with the state of tide and wind. Depths also vary, but there can be shallow patches and reef spurs. Cook in 1773 nearly lost HMS *Resolution* in a reef pass,[60] and Tupaia in 1769 sent island divers down to determine clearance under the rudder on several occasions.

Clearly, in meeting the challenges of finding their way over vast distances to and from small islands, the Pacific islanders of the remote past were in practice quite close to European mariners in the application of some basic principles of seamanship. In navigation the latitude by zenith star was not far short of a latitude by meridian altitude, which was the method of the European seamen using a simple measuring instrument by the sixteenth century. The bearing of celestial bodies for course setting is still in a sense the ultimate safeguard of the modern navigator. He relies on a gyro compass, but the prudent navigator checks this mechanical device against the magnetic compass. In turn, errors of the magnetic compass are established by observing the azimuth of a star.

CHAPTER THREE

Settlements, Territories, and Trade

ONCE SHIPS, PEOPLE, animals, plants, and seed crops were brought to the beach of an unoccupied island, the accounts by explorers of bountiful resources would be tested. There would be plentiful water supplies on high islands, but low islands lacked surface water. On some islands there would probably be coastal coconut trees, the seed nuts having been carried there by winds and currents over many centuries.[1] Birdlife in all would be profuse. The variety of species decreases from west to east across the Pacific Islands, but the quantities of birds and eggs would be high everywhere in dense colonies that had lacked major predators. The lagoons, reefs, and adjacent ocean would similarly be full of an enormous variety and quantity of shellfish, mollusks, eels, fish, and turtles. As McGlone and colleagues noted, "The amount of accessible fat and protein per square kilometer on a Pacific island may have been unequaled anywhere in the world."[2]

The early colonizers would have lived quite well in their new home. There would have been time to establish yams and taro and to plant coconut and breadfruit trees, paper mulberry (for bark cloth), and *Piper methysticum* (kava)—all brought with them—and to start breeding the introduced pigs, dogs, and fowls and unfortunately to release rat families, which had arrived as stowaways. Like most migrant communities, they likely would have attempted to keep contact for a time with the original homeland to obtain further supplies of materials integral to their traditional way of life and to reinforce cultural cohesion and secondary migrations. The prevailing easterly winds would enable more predictable downwind voyages back to last places of departure. In the course of time there were increased cultural and social changes, particularly between high and low islands, partly in response to environmental conditions. Ultimately there would have been a decline in the more easily available birdlife and the spread of cultivation, including at some stage the diffusion of the sweet potato.

The original settlements would have many of the locational characteristics that have been retained in outer islands. The site values for villages on high islands would include shelter, freshwater streams, level land, and adjacency to a reef pass. Behind was higher land for clearing, terracing, and planting; in front, the tidal reef flats, lagoon, and sea reefs for marine resources. Villages would usually be nucleated, with coconut trees and breadfruit interspersed between houses and in garden clearings; inland, related dispersed hamlets developed. A chief's house in large villages would be raised by a stone platform, and, as in Fiji, there would be a ceremonial area *(rara)* and sacred structures elsewhere. On low coral islands, houses would be distributed more linearly, parallel to the lagoon. Above the beach, canoe houses would be situated; farther inland would be wells for fresh water and pits dug to reach moist layers for growing taro. High islands became primarily agricultural with some fishing, and low islands became fishing communities with some agriculture.

On both high and low islands, navigators and shipbuilders appear to have retained social status over time. The captains who brought the original communities to unoccupied islands were remembered in stories and family genealogies. In Aotearoa the names of the great vessels were retained in the Maori designations of people and places. In Vanuatu the ancient first arrivals were embedded in the social structure:

> The first canoes landed in different places at different times and their members were given power of primacy. . . . A society's symbols and structures often refer to the time of its origins and thus record the decisive act of social and political creation. Societies continually reliving their foundation express a dream of unity in the reminder of such earliest times. This is particularly clear in central and southern Vanuatu, where social organisation has modelled on the original canoe voyage and its group of seafarers.[3]

In the Carolines descent from a famous seafaring family likewise gave status, although not by right of birth only. Glen Petersen notes that birth by itself was not enough to be accepted as a chief; he also had to "undertake the long and rigorous schooling necessary to become a navigator *(pelu)* in order to enhance his status, [for] birth alone was by no means destiny and voyaging played a central role in the building of personal reputations."[4]

The doctrine of high status and primacy of "first arrivals" probably pertained in many places in the earliest periods. It was the basis of land rights and authority. However, as voyagers continued to arrive, conflicting claims would arise over land and sea resources, as well as territory. It is likely also that power shifts would occur within communities when there was greater population concentration on agriculture. It is in fact a feature of dual sea/land communities in most places, other than on small islands poor in land resources, that sea people (Fiji: *kai wai*), whose men spend most of their time fishing and trading away from home, have less potential influence in the community than the more sedentary land people *(kai vanua)*. Over the centuries, the leading mariners and boatbuilders would nevertheless have retained respect. They were vital in the geographical extensions of the spheres of influence of richer islands through their command of the sea in territorial competition.

Expanding Territory

Growth of population and environmental stresses would lead to many attempts by chiefs to extend their territories beyond their own villages and islands. They did so mainly by use of sea power. The early Europeans report that war fleets were operated by high chiefs in Hawai'i, Tahiti, Tonga, Samoa (Manono Island), Fiji (Lakeba and Bau), and the Carolines and by the Roviana in the Solomons, as well as by several Maori leaders in various parts of Aotearoa. The warships of the *drua* and *kalia* class and the great Maori war canoes, together with a breed of skilled mariners, allowed the transport of large numbers of well-provisioned warriors to move with speed and surprise and to threaten or inflict punishment on other islands and coastal areas. Many settlements in Fiji, Samoa, Tonga, and Aotearoa were fortified, and several were moved inland during these periods of strife.

Cook in 1774 was surprised to see a war fleet of canoes in Tahiti:

> Upwards of 300 of them all rainged in good order for some distance along the shore all completely equip'd and man'd and a vast crowd of men on the shore . . . their vessels were decorated with flags, streamers &c so that the whole made a grand and Noble appearance. . . . Besides these vessels of war there were 170 sail of smaller double canoes all with a little house on them. . . . These canoes must be designed for transport or victulars or both and to receive wounded men etc.

Cook judged that there were 7,760 men on 330 of these ships, all bound for sea and land action. These numbers greatly impressed him, since the men and vessels all belonged to only two districts. He would like to have spent more time with the admiral of the fleet before it sailed and regretted that he had "lost the opportunity of examining more narrowly into a part of the naval force of this island and making myself better acquainted how it acts and is conducted."[5] Cook saw this concentration of force as yet another disaffected chief challenging an existing ruler with a display of naval and military power. He commented on these struggles for primacy between islands in several groups without being able to fully understand the history, kinship, status, and rivalries involved.

In 1796, during the early contact time, Kamehameha I of Hawaiʻi also employed a massive fleet in an attempt to bring the linear group of islands under one rule. His power at sea was not sufficient. By 1798 he had built another eight hundred or so specially designed war canoes "capable of carrying many more men than the conventional double hull vessels" and with them "achieved the ambition of uniting the islands."[6]

Tonga was another archipelago that for a time experienced interisland wars. The chiefs of Vavaʻu, Haʻapai, and Tongatapu owned ships, many built in the Lau Islands. Several nobles attempted dominance, but it was the Tupou dynastic families that predominated and also revived some Tongan spheres of influence over hundreds of miles of ocean, including Samoa, parts of Fiji, Rotuma, and Wallis and Futuna.

The Tongan sailors were also sea raiders and mercenaries. The young William Mariner—a survivor of the British privateer *Port au Prince*, which was destroyed in Tonga in 1806—saw the return of the chief Kau Moala to Tonga after fourteen years of visiting and sea roving. He left for Fiji to, as Mariner says, "mingle in the wars of these people."[7] Destinations of his subsequent voyages included Fiji, Futuna, and Rotuma. Kau Moala returned in a newly built vessel with his crew of thirty-five Tongans, about fifteen of whom were women, as well as three Rotuman women and three men from Futuna. It is recorded also that a Tongan chief sent his two sons in turn on voyages seven hundred miles to Rotuma to exact tribute from this small island.[8] Tonga engaged in both conflicts and alliances with parts of Fiji. As late as 1855, R. A. Derrick records that ships from Tonga with "2000 warriors and many of their women folk" arrived in Fiji to support Cakobau, the paramount chief of Bua, in the civil war raging in these islands. On the way to Bua the fleet was joined by ships from Lau, a quasi-independent island group within the Tongan sphere of influence.[9]

The high fertile island of Lakeba in Lau had grown to an important center of sea power. It lay between Tonga and Fiji, and several islands in the region became subject to Lakeba, including Fuluga, which was rich in the hardwood vesi, used in shipbuilding. The sea region was also hazardous for navigation because of its reefs and many small islands exposed to storms. The province of Tui Lakeba thereby became the home of splendid shipbuilders and navigators. John Young writes that "*drua* and their forerunners enabled the chiefs of Lakeba to extend the area they influenced, and in some cases controlled, by their ability to collect tribute or to pay respect over long distances, in return for food supplies in emergency, alliance in war, or speedy vengeance in adversity."[10] The small island of Bua, which had a military alliance with Lakeba, dominated the coastal regions of eastern Viti Levu and the islands of the Koro Sea from the 1800s until near cession in 1874. Part of its power came from its location, which received foreign trade and foreign seafaring mercenaries, but most of all from the seamanship and ferocity of the Butoni and allied sailors of the island. John Jackson in the mid-nineteenth century describes sailing with a large fleet from all the islands of eastern Fiji, and vessels from Tonga and Wallis Island, to pay homage to the ruler Cakobau on the occasion of delivering a magnificent *drua*, which had taken seven years to build in Lau.[11]

Tribute was exacted by other chiefs from their neighbors. In the late eighteenth century the powerful rulers of Tahiti required the people of the coral islands of the Tuamotus to supply "coconuts, fish, birds, pearl shells, dogs and mats."[12] Tribute in this way from the smaller to the more powerful islands may not have always represented subjugation. In practice there would have been several forms of reciprocal benefits. This can be appreciated from the account below, under "Interisland Trade," of the relations in the Carolines between the high island of Yap and the linear groups of small coral islands extending a thousand miles to the east. The tribute from these islands seems dictated less by threats of punitive action than by the ability of Yap to offer, or refuse, assistance when the poorer islands suffered from famine as a result of hurricanes, droughts, or tsunamis.[13]

Sometimes the raiding of other islands was driven by famine. Such were the raids from Marquesas to the Tuamotus at times of drought, but these built up into general antagonism and suspicion of strangers. There is a record of people arriving at Kaikura in the Tuamotus from the Marquesas seeking food and all being killed by local inhabitants except for one woman.[14] Such hostile receptions were not unusual if sea raiding was remembered or island food resources were limited. Dening cites Edward Roberts, who describes how in 1798 in the Marquesas a strange canoe arrived and was "carried to the Marae [temple] with its contents of men and all, as an offering to the deity."[15]

In the traditions of some Melanesian islands, sea raiding by fleets of vessels also took more sinister forms, for headhunting, cannibalism, and slavery. The influence of the headhunting Roviana and Simbo sea raiders in the Solomons extended more than three hundred miles around their islands as they "raided far and wide for slaves, some of whom were set to work manufacturing shell money, while others were taken to serve as ceremonial sacrifices. . . . [T]hey became the terror of the neighbouring islands, especially Ysabel and Choiseul."[16] This was true also of parts of Fiji, including Bau. William Lockerby (1808), J. E. Erskine (1853), and many others describe raids in Fiji for *bakola* (human flesh for feasts), with "drumbeats announcing the taking of bakola [and] the pennants flying from the masts of victorious canoes signifying bakola on board."[17]

There were other groups of islands such as those in Kiribati where resources were so poor and virtually identical that there seemed few motives for interisland conflicts, or even a basis for trade. Periodic outbreaks of fighting nevertheless occurred between village communities on the same atolls and between islands, when they came under population pressures at times of drought or when leaders simply wished to enhance their status. Defeated people could then be driven off an island to seek asylum elsewhere. They could do so with certainty only if they arrived on an island where they would find an ancestral place *(boti)* in the *maneaba*. If they failed, there might be little prospect of *karokaro* (hospitality to a relative).[18] Sabatier records that there were more deaths at sea from populations being driven away from an island than by direct warfare. He also details several attacks. One was an attack on Tabiteuea South by a fleet of thirty-seven canoes from Beru, with six hundred warriors and some women. Sabatier also mentioned attacks on Tarawa by Butaritari, and a massacre on Tabiteuea of one thousand people in 1881, although the latter attack had some religious connotation. At this period of European contact, a *te booti* (European boat) was introduced to Kiribati, along with a crew of five Europeans with guns, all engaged by a chief of Betio Island in Tarawa lagoon. They conquered the rest of Tarawa and the islands of Abaiang and Marakei.[19] The Betio chief (Tokitaka) eventually killed the five Europeans and commandeered *te booti*. Wars then raged in Kiribati using European weapons, until a peace treaty was signed between chiefs on board HMS *Royalist* in 1892.[20]

Interisland Trade

While sea raids and wars between rival chieftains in several island groups were occurring, there was also considerable interisland trade, often based on kinship, and this was more regular than conflicts. It was evident in early contact times that every community in the Pacific Islands was engaged in some form of trade, and vast numbers of vessels and mariners were employed. Unlike the detailed observations made by visitors on indigenous wars and warships, the comments on the more peaceful sea trading activities give little indication of the geographical extent and the numbers of trading vessels involved. The master of HMS *Dolphin,* the first European ship to reach Tahiti, noted in 1767 the coming and going of great vessels with all streamers flying, but what they were carrying, and where they were coming from and going, he could not tell.[21] Erskine in the mid-nineteenth century wrote, "Feejeeans have a decided turn for commerce, a constant internal trade being carried on in their own canoes, which we constantly saw either arriving or sailing, heavily laden with bales of cloth, rolls of cordage, and quantities of earthen pots."[22]

What Robertson on the *Dolphin* saw in Tahiti and Erskine observed in Fiji was probably true of every part of the Pacific. Many of the networks of trade that have been historically documented, and those still extant, no doubt grew out of more ancient relationships. Such exchange activities between islands were based on multiple factors. There was a complementarity of natural resources, and many populations acquired specializations in production. But the actual directions and generation of movements involved kinship ceremonies and life crisis events, what Hocart has termed "the paths of feasts and gifts."[23] A good deal of exchanges were obligatory with immediate or deferred reciprocity and were often built around insurances against catastrophic occurrences. There were also systems akin to barter and currency-related transactions. None of these trading activities was mutually exclusive of others, and together they produced complex patterns of movements of goods, people, and services. There were in addition linkages from the maritime sector into the portage trading chains of inland communities, and by canoe along the great Fly and Sepik rivers in New Guinea and the Rewa and Sigatoka in Fiji.

In the webs of sea trading, nodal islands emerged where goods from several places were stored and ships called on a multilateral trading basis. These included the islands of Moce and Lakeba in Lau and the geographically central islands of the Siassi people in the Vitiaz Strait between New Guinea and New Britain.[24] Specific villages in turn had central place values that gave them prominence in trade, such as Kaduwaga in the Trobriand Islands, whose name means "water-land-place of boats."[25] A location adjacent to a deep-water pass into a lagoon was particularly valuable as a trading center. Such places prospered even more if they had tenure over the marine resources of these nutrient-rich passes, with, among other fishing assets, the giant clams that thrive in these channels. Many retained such locational advantages into the modern trading period.

The island trading systems were sometimes supported by specialists who engaged in the carriage of goods and people on behalf of several communities. Commander Charles Wilkes described the itinerant traders of Fiji as having no fixed place of residence,[26] and the Reverend Thomas Williams remarked on the seafaring Levukans who conducted much of the trade of central and eastern Lau.[27] Likewise the Siassi people of the Vitiaz Strait islands had rights over carriage and obtained their livelihood as seafarers and traders.[28] It has been shown for the Carolines that part of the reciprocity that the primary chiefs of Yap Island received for providing refuge and resources to distressed coral island people was the services of skilled seafarers and navigators of the small islands. They made voyages between Yap and Palau to obtain stone coin money vital for Yap as a store of wealth.[29]

Examples of Island Maritime Trading Systems

ESSENTIAL TOOLS

Sea trade was apparent from the earliest settlements of the Pacific. Stone tools, which were vital for the first sea migrants, are identified with their places of origin. Even on high islands the igneous rocks were not always suitable for toolmaking, which required fine-grained basalt and obsidian. The widespread finds of such tools in graves show that the sea trade in these items must have been plentiful and frequent in the near Pacific. Obsidian was also traded over open sea passages from New Britain to Santa Cruz eastward and Sabah westward, and as far as Fiji and New Caledonia via several islands over a distance of 1,500 miles. Farther east, vessels sailed from the northern Cooks to Samoa for basalt, and from the Tuamotus to the Society Islands to obtain stone tools. Trade in these essential implements was multilateral, as they passed between high islands and from high to low islands and between the low coral islands.[30]

ESSENTIAL LIFELINES

Maintaining linkages between islands was sometimes a matter of life and death. Gladwin describes these in the Carolines: "Dozens of islands stretched over a thousand miles of ocean from Yap on the west to Truk and the islands beyond on the east have been linked by their seafaring men and their sailing canoes into a network of social, economic, and often political ties without which they probably could not have survived."[31]

These small islands of the Carolines are vulnerable to typhoons, which cause island-wide destruction of trees and crops. Tsunamis occur periodically, and islands can disappear underwater for hours with, among other dire consequences, a loss of fresh water as well as food. Harold Weins quotes an old song from Ifalik Island:

Men are taking wing
Flying in all directions
To islands were there is food
and trees standing.[32]

The custom of providing hospitality and immediate refuge by each of these islands was built on trading relationships and intermarriage. All of the 550 islets and islands in the Caroline group were linked by many vessels and seafarers. The main islands had sea-lanes between them, each of which was named and whose sailing directions were memorized, including star courses and seamarks. With their fast outriggers, the highly skilled seafarers of the Carolines efficiently knit all these small islands into a single entity. The vast sea space was thereby as much a part of the homeland for the populations as their islands, lagoons, and reefs.

Of equal importance for mutual assistance between islands was the role of the island of Yap. Lying on the western periphery of the Carolines, Yap is a large, high, fertile island. The chiefs of the district Gagil on Yap had primacy in the island, and their influence extended eastward for about a thousand miles. All the small islands paid regular tribute to Yap and thereby acknowledged the status of the chiefs, but the island also served the purpose of trade and provided guarantees of food and shelter after a disaster. The annual *sawei* tribute, or trading system, saw vessels leaving from the eastward islands and following the sea-lanes to every other island in turn, where more vessels would join the fleet on the way to Yap. The flotilla would carry people, woven fibers, sennit, spondylus, turtle shells, and mother-of-pearl. At Yap they would received hospitality and leave with cargoes of turmeric, whetstones, and orangewood.

The *sawei* was regarded as not being entirely an act of submission. It was more a means of cementing bonds between vulnerable low islands and the richer high islands of Yap. In quantity, the exchanges seemed to be greatly in favor of the poorer islands. This gave prestige to Yap, but it also enabled the leading inhabitants of Yap, who became primarily land people, to receive as reciprocity assistance of the Caroline seafarers in making the three-hundred-mile voyage to Palau for the *fei* stone currency (comprising wheels of argonite). This was required by the dominant clan on Yap as a conspicuous representation of their wealth, as well as for redistribution by them to lesser chiefs to maintain peace and allegiances. At Palau the Caroline seafarers would load the yellow limestone *fei* disks, some weighing more than one hundred kilograms, onto large Yapese bamboo rafts *(fofoot)*, which they would then tow with skill behind their sailing craft through the Pacific swells to Yap.[33] As well as the reciprocal obligations to carry out these voyages, they would have been reminded that the renowned Yapese sorcery could devastate their home islands with storms and typhoons if their tributes were not met.[34]

The Caroline mariners made other trading voyages hundreds of miles northward to Guam and the islands of the Marianas and also sought kinship refuge there during periods of famine. In the eighteenth century they were employed by the Spanish colonizers in these islands as pilots, sailors, and traders and as carriers of government dispatches throughout the region. Hezel records, "By the time the French and Russian naval ships began making their calls at Guam, a flotilla of Carolinian outriggers in the harbor had become a familiar sight there."[35]

COMPLEMENTARY TRADE

Differences in resources and specialization in production gave rise to more naturally reciprocal trade between high and low islands. The former were often great yam and taro producers and manufacturers of bark cloth, sennit, and pottery, whereas the latter produced pandanus for matting sails and hardwoods for shipbuilding. In places such as Lakeba, with its political control of Lau, it was possible to combine resource inputs and skills from several islands to specialize in shipbuilding and to exchange these vessels in distant areas for other products. However, in most islands, craft specializations went beyond resource endowments. Buell Quain has described how the Fijian village of Nakoroko in Vanua Levu specialized in mat making at the expense of all else and depended on trade to maintain a balanced supply of goods.[36] The people of Vuna concentrated on the production of lampblack (for tattooing) and would trade this for nets on the island of Taveuni and exchange these for bark cloth from Lau.[37]

There are many such examples of local specialization that enabled islands producing craft goods to trade widely. Marshall Sahlins observes, "Moalan women make several kinds of sleeping and floor mats, but it is Gau that is known for the special double-thickness floor mats very much desired in other islands. Moalan women certainly have the material and skills necessary to make the kinds of mats imported from Gau. There are women from Gau who have married into Moala and who could practice and disseminate the techniques—yet they do not."[38] These traditions of specialization have the effects of maximizing local skills and achieving economies of scale, as well as giving many islands opportunities to trade widely in times of need. This process also generated very large volumes of vessel movements between islands in complex networks.

KINSHIP OBLIGATIONS

Many of the trading voyages were closely directed on a kinship basis, including long-distance marriage parties between Fiji, Tonga, and Samoa. There were even more frequent and bigger events within archipelagic groups. The Fijian *solevu* is typical of a range of such kinship-related gatherings and exchanges. It starts with messages being sent to an island or specific village by a related group of people to arrange a ceremonial exchange. This cannot easily be refused. Both sides start preparing the *solevu* over months or even years before the event.

Major *solevu* involved large parties on fleets of vessels carrying enormous quantities of goods. On arrival at the island, the boat parties would be welcomed and would arrange the piles of goods to be presented. The hosts would do likewise. After a feast, orators would declaim how they had worked day and night to produce all the cloth, mats, wooden bowls, and other items as "a means of cementing them together in eternal friendship."[39] These speeches would be accompanied by the passing backward and forward of whales' teeth *(tabua)* to each other. The women of the visiting party would present their mats and tapa, and the men their *tanoa*s, headrests, and other wooden articles, as well as pigs. The next day, the hosts would do likewise. Feasting, dancing, singing, and drinking yaqona would continue for several days, until the visiting party departed on vessels loaded with gifts. The party that showed the most generosity would win the greatest prestige. (Chapter 10 provides a detailed account of a modern *solevu* voyage).

On a smaller scale, but widespread in terms of reciprocal obligations between related people, there were, and still are, such customs as *kerekere* in Fiji, *kolo* in Tonga, *bubuti* in Kiribati, and *faka molemole* in Tuvalu. These are more hand-to-hand exchanges, as, for example, when sailors return with goods from elsewhere that are requested by relatives, or when a good fisherman unloads his catch and relatives *bubuti* parts of it. These traditions have an effect of achieving equality of food and material possessions within the extended family. The giver acquires status in this way rather than by the accumulation of wealth.

RELIGIOUS AND CEREMONIAL

In island societies before European colonization, long voyages were made to obtain articles of ceremonial significance. The art of navigation, skills in vessel construction, and tattooing were all practiced in combination with religious rituals involving exotic articles.[40] Of great significance for precontact religious observance were red bird feathers for the decoration of images in the worship of Oro, the son of the major sea god Tangaroa. Vessels made voyages from the Marquesas to Rarotonga for these feathers, and they were carried by marriage parties between Tonga, Fiji, and Samoa. In Melanesia, red feathers were a means of exchange in the Santa Cruz region.

Captain Cook was impressed by the importance of such religious and ceremonial articles sought for over great distances. When he was leaving Tahiti in 1774 bound for Tonga, the king, Cook said, "importuned me very much to take one or two [men] to collect red feathers for him."[41] During his third voyage in 1777, Cook was presented in Tonga with "cap[e]s covered with red feathers." He was very willing to accept these gifts, knowing they would be "highly valued at Otaheite."[42] He had already been surprised by the value placed on such ceremonial articles when he first arrived on Aotearoa in 1769. Among all the wonders on board the *Endeavour*, the Maori visitors to the ship wanted the bark cloth from Tahiti, which "they valued more than anything we could give them."[43]

The most documented account of voyages for exchanges of ceremonial articles that have survived into modern times is that of the Kula ring. This is conducted around the Trobriand and related islands of southeast New Guinea by outrigger vessels specially constructed and ornately carved and decorated for the purpose (although nowadays often by motorboats). Circular voyages are made in stages between two or more islands and village trading partners. Those carrying decorated shell armbands sail counterclockwise, and those with necklaces of red spondylus shell clockwise. The trading parties hold temporary ownership of the sacred items before passing them on to other partners as they move over limited legs of their respective sailing cycles. It is known that non-Kula utilitarian bartering also takes place during the Kula voyages but is subservient to the rituals of peace and relationships.[44]

BARTER AND CURRENCY

The Hiri trading systems in Papua New Guinea have a strong barter element, although not devoid of ceremony. The women of the Motu maritime people of the New Guinea coast in the vicinity of Port Moresby have traditionally produced clay pots for trade. Each October, under the prevailing southeast winds, men and women departed on fleets of twenty to thirty loaded double-hulled *lakatoi* vessels for the 180-mile voyage along the coast, westward to the Gulf of Papua. They traded there with the people of the Purari Delta and other rivers for sago, as well as for tobacco and betel nut. In this trade the Motu for centuries also carried stone axes, which they had received from hill people in their hinterland in exchange for sago. The Hiri trading system bridged several linguistic boundaries and gave rise to a regional seafaring and trading language that persists. The Motu would remain with the people of the estuaries, and there would be ceremonies and marriages, and during this time they would construct new *lakatoi* vessels for the return voyage when the westerly winds came in January.[45]

As well as barter, various forms of currency have been in use in Melanesia as the means of exchange and as stores of wealth that embody the values of other articles. The Yap Island stone disk was one such regional currency, as were porpoise teeth and cowry and other shells representing objects akin to money, which moved also from the coast to inland markets. In the New Guinea highlands pig tusks were a medium of exchange and bride-price, and in the Solomons strings of red and white shell disks were widely used. In Fiji, whales' teeth *(tabua)* accompanied ceremonial exchanges but could not be construed as currency. They were very symbolic and valuable in many other ways to the community.

WOMEN AS SEA TRADERS

Many of the articles of trade were produced by women such as pandanus mats, baskets, bark cloth, pottery, woven loincloth, sennit, and sails for vessels. Women sometimes led the trading parties on both sides and made sea voyages for marriage and mortuary occasions, and major ceremonies such as the *solevu*. They travelled as passengers, although the missionary Thomas Williams, writing in 1870 of Fiji, remarks that women had an important role as traders and ordinary seamen.[46]

Women often carried the items of exchange for presentation at ceremonials, as they do today in modern interisland exchanges (see chapter 10). Their roles in more precarious peace-maintaining exchanges between sea and land people on the beach were noted in 1886 by the British resident commissioner of the Solomon Islands Protectorate: "The actual bartering is done by the women, who advance one towards another, the island woman with the fish, and the bush woman with yams or taro, while the men stand on guard on either side with spears and rifles."[47] Matthew

Cooper, writing of the maritime Langalanga people of the Solomons, notes, "a Peace-of-the-Market and institutionalized trading partnerships persisted even in times of general hostility."[48]

These island trading systems were ceremonial and utilitarian. They helped maintain peace and promote intermarriage. Multilateral trade contributed to balancing resources and could respond to needs during times of crisis. The voyages were also a means of communication. On arrival, a navigator might meet with chiefs at a *marae*, a *maneaba*, or a canoe house and talk about the voyage, other islands, and general news. A small island that lay outside these networks of friendship, trading, and help could have problems of survival when meeting challenges of environmental, economic, social, or hostile shocks. Several such islands were occupied during the latter stages of the general diaspora across the vastness of the northwest and southeast Pacific.

Trade and Survival on Isolated Small Islands

Irwin has identified twenty-seven islands that were "empty at [European] contact but showed traces of earlier occupation."[49] Some of these were no doubt either way stations between major groups or simply temporary camps. Some others were nearly viable but were dependent on trade to balance resource requirements. An example can be drawn from the group of Mangareva, Pitcairn, and Henderson, which lie on average one thousand miles southeast of Tahiti.

Mangareva had quite good soil, reef resources, and trees but lacked vital quality stone for tools. Pitcairn, some three hundred miles southeast of Mangareva, was agriculturally poor and lacked coral reefs. It was also deficient in shells for deep-sea fishhooks but had excellent obsidian for adzes. The low coral island of Henderson, about a hundred miles northeast of Pitcairn, was well endowed with birdlife, reef resources, and turtles but lacked good land and quality stone. Excavations indicate these islands traded together from about AD 1000 to 1450. Mangareva, the largest of the three, was also periodically linked by long-distance sea trade with the Society Islands and Marquesas through the Tuamotu Archipelago.

For reasons that remain uncertain, Mangareva experienced adverse upheavals, which included civil war, deforestation, loss of shipbuilding, and consequently loss of trade. For the two small trade-dependent islands at the end of the line, that meant disaster, and they were depopulated by about AD 1500. The larger Mangareva population partially survived with difficulties. Henderson was never permanently reoccupied, and Pitcairn became settled again only after the *Bounty* mutineers arrived in 1790, attracted by its very isolation.

A more extreme case of isolation and loss of sea transport was Rapa Nui, which was colonized between AD 1000 and 1200. There is no evidence of any subsequent contacts from or to the island. The first known external link was the ship of Jacob Roggeveen in 1722. He estimated the population to be between two and three thousand. Cook arrived in 1774 and managed to obtain a few sweet potatoes and some sugarcane, but he described the water supply as brackish and stinking. The island, he said, was very barren, with few birds and no trees. He estimated the population as six to seven hundred. Rapa Nui is without coral reef. Its inhabitants could have engaged in sea fishing, but Cook saw only three very mean narrow canoes with outriggers.

Cook could not identify any evidence of sea transport by which the Rapa Nui people could reach such a remote place. A possible clue is found in his description of some of the houses as "low, long and narrow," with "much the appearance of a large boat turned bottom up." He measured one as sixty feet in length and eight to nine feet high in the middle.[50] What he possibly witnessed were symbolic remembrances in the landscape of the vessels that had brought the people to the island. The gunwale lines representing upturned boats *(hare paenga)* can still be seen on the ground, usually at the landward sides of the *moai* (stone statues). These boatlike structures are considered to have once been the houses of chiefly families, while the common people lived in cruder huts farther inland.[51] There are also a few very large *hare paenga* close to the sea at good landing places, the significance of which is open to interpretation (figure 3.1).[52]

How and why Rapa Nui people lost their seagoing ships and navigational skills have also been matters of research and speculation. Human destruction of the environment, and especially deforestation, rat consumption of palm nuts and bird's eggs, territorial disputes, and the diversion of resources and human efforts to quarrying, transporting, and erecting the statues, and then toppling them in wars are all postulated. Another possible factor is the effects of climatic change (AD 1300–1450), which saw the "destruction of elaborate terrace systems"[53] and related agricultural loss and social disintegration. However, prolonged isolation from social and economic linkages by sea, in what became virtually a cul-de-sac in Polynesian voyaging, must also figure in the apparent decline.

Another potential cul-de-sac, because of its distance of over 1,600 miles from the Polynesian heartland, was Aotearoa. The competent mariners who worked their vessels from the tropics through the adverse west-

FIGURE 3.1 A resident archaeologist on Easter Island, leading a party from the MV *Discovery*, anchored off. The site is the foundation of an ancient house structure designed along the lines of the inverted hull of a vessel *(hare paenga)* at a possible beach arrival place. (Photograph by the author, 2006)

erlies eventually arrived at a very different environment in temperate latitudes. The coconuts, breadfruit, and banana plants they may have carried would not have ripened. Return voyages to the home islands would have been equally difficult, although there is some evidence of such voyages being undertaken. The major differences with Rapa Nui were the size and diversity of Aotearoa, which, as with isolated Hawai'i, made it internally sustainable. Seasonal and environmental diversity gave rise to coastwise trade between various regions of Aotearoa, but there were also territorial competition, intertribal wars, and the building of fortified villages.

The fortitude and courage of the founding seafaring ancestors of Aotearoa were bred into traditions of *ihi* (fearlessness), as Cook learned from his very first contacts with the Maori in 1769. He wanted to stop two boats at sea crewed by young men. To impress them with gunfire and exert his naval authority, he ordered "a musket to be fired over their heads thinking that this would either make them surrender or jump overboard, but here I was mistaken for they immediately took to their arms or whatever they had in the boat and began to attack us."[54]

Cook and the other European mariners who arrived in the Pacific could not fully explain the similar cultural traditions of many indigenous societies, nor comprehend the size and complexities of their maritime trading networks. These new arrivals in the Pacific have been the subject of a substantial body of literature discussing the misunderstandings, violence, and subsequent agreements that took place with the island peoples. Without overduplication, it is necessary in this maritime account to reconsider the relationships between European sailors and local maritime communities.

CHAPTER FOUR

The Arrival of Foreign Ships

Until the voyages of Byron, Wallis, Carteret, and Bougainville, all in the years 1764–1769, and under Cook between 1768 and 1779, the arrivals of foreign ships at Pacific islands were few and sporadic. Some voyagers merely sighted islands, but when landings did occur, they were of short duration, although often traumatic for the inhabitants. The early European explorers were mainly naval. Most of them knew little about, and cared even less for, the cultures, religions, or achievements of the island societies they encountered. Their attitudes toward local people were, with few exceptions, imperious and predatory.

The First Encounters

Magellan, in his sixteenth-century voyage across the Pacific, was seeking an alternative route to the Spice Islands of Southeast Asia. On the ninety-nine-day passage from South America, he saw only two small islands until the landfall at Guam on 6 March 1521. On arrival, his ships—the *Trinidad*, *Victoria*, and *Conception*—were surrounded by local craft and the Chamorros clambered on board. In a confrontation of a type that was to be repeated in many parts of the Pacific, and that baffled and infuriated foreign captains, the islanders attempted pillaging anything they fancied before being driven back over the side.

The theft, as Magellan saw it, of his skiff from the stern of the *Trinidad* during the second day caused him to seek immediate retribution. A party of forty soldiers landed, burned a village, and killed seven men. After collecting fruit and vegetables, the Spaniards butchered the dead and carried buckets of intestines back on board to nourish the crew, who were suffering from scurvy and anemia. Such was the first encounter of Pacific islanders with European sailors.[1]

The *Trinidad* was eventually abandoned as unseaworthy and the *Conception* caught fire, but the *Victoria* completed the voyage to Seville loaded with spices. This Spanish commercial success provoked the Portuguese in the Moluccas to explore and colonize eastward, taking possession of islands in the Carolines in 1526.[2] In subsequent Spanish voyages local men at Guam were kidnapped to replace lost and sick crew, and in 1565 Guam was claimed for Spain and became the staging place for galleons sailing between Manila and Acapulco, although not before the islanders stoned the ships and killed seafarers ashore. To teach them a lesson, Admiral Miguel López de Legazpi burned villages and hanged several of the inhabitants.[3] The route from Guam to Mexico was northward under the trades until the westerlies were reached. For over two hundred years, this passage took the ships beyond the visibility of Hawai'i, while the more southerly return voyage passed through an almost empty area of the ocean.

During a more systematic search of the Pacific for new lands, people to convert, and gold, the Spaniards found the Marquesas Islands in 1595. On arrival the *San Geronimo* under Álvaro de Mendaña was surrounded, and people swarmed on board: "For a time there was merriment and a spirit of mutual curiosity, until the freedom with which islanders helped themselves to the odd gear about the ship became annoying."[4] The navigator Pedro Fernández de Quirós estimated that some two hundred Marquesans were killed during the two weeks they were there. Mendaña sighted Tuvalu and reached several Melanesian islands. He attempted religious settlements, with disastrous results for both the Spanish and the Melanesians.[5]

The Dutch in the Pacific were more secular and primarily in pursuit of trade. The expeditions of Willem Schouten and Isaac Le Maire in 1616 achieved little but are distinguished by being memorialized in the first painting of European mariners firing on a Pacific island vessel at sea (see figure 2.1). The Dutchman Abel Tasman in his voyages of 1642–1643 sighted Australia and Tasmania, called briefly at New Zealand, and sighted Fiji and Tonga. The major contacts with the islands came with British extensions of naval power and acquisition of territory following the Seven Years' War with France, which ended in 1763. Commander John Byron made a long and largely inconsequential voyage in the Pacific during 1764 with the frigate HMS *Dolphin*. This was followed in 1767 by Captain Samuel Wallis, also on the *Dolphin,* accompanied by Captain Philip Carteret on HMS *Swallow.* Wallis revealed Tahiti to Europeans when he arrived there on 18 June 1767. The ship anchored for five weeks, and Wallis proclaimed Tahiti as British territory and changed the name to King George's Island.

After the departure of Wallis, the French captain Louis de Bougainville arrived on 4 April 1768 with the frigate *La Boudeuse* and the supply ship *L'Etoile*. He declared the island French and named it Nouvelle-Cythere after the birthplace of Aphrodite, the goddess of love, presumably to mark the kindness of island women to his sailors. Bougainville sailed past Samoa, which he also proclaimed as French, and did likewise in Melanesia, sometimes passing and occasionally landing on a few islands. Following Bougainville's travels, the most eventful and wide-ranging voyages were those of Cook on the *Endeavour* in 1768–1771, the *Resolution* and the *Adventure* in 1772–1775, and the *Resolution* and the *Discovery* in 1776–1779, when Cook was killed in Hawai'i.

These voyages are so well known that they need not be detailed further. What is considered in this account are the perceptions and behavior of two seafaring peoples, Pacific islanders and the European mariners, during these first contacts.

Officers and the Perspectives of Law and Order

The statement that "a ship is a social system, a moving world in miniature that reflects and perhaps exaggerates the larger social system from which it is drawn," was never truer than on an eighteenth-century naval vessel.[6] Most European naval officers were drawn from "good" families and carried their class prejudices and virtues with them. They had a firm belief in the sanctity of private property and the maintenance of law and order, and in their society theft could be a matter of hanging or transportation. They originally joined the navy to serve on warships for glory, prize money, and patriotism. There seemed little prospects of attaining any of these goals on the exploration voyages; however, it was peacetime and such voyages were better than being ashore, at best on half pay, and they did offer prospects of promotion, providing they had some influential preferment and obeyed the orders of commanders. A number of masters of naval ships had their origins in the merchant navy, and several rose to naval officer rank, including Wallis, Cook, and Bligh.

The commanders of the naval exploration ships had specific orders throughout the voyage regarding necessary achievements under the authority of the monarch. The vessels were in effect floating parts of their nation-states as they moved around the world. The captains of British warships had awesome powers vested in them, underpinned by the articles of war. They were responsible for the application of law, order, and punishments; the safety of the ship and all on board; actions at sea under rules of engagement; and the conducting of diplomacy ashore.

One of the principles to be adhered to and maintained was freedom of the high seas, over which no single ruler could exert dominion. It was recognized also by customary law of the sea that a state could exert some jurisdiction over an area of sea bordering its coastline. This was ultimately acknowledged as the three-mile territorial sea, as determined by the "cannon-shot rule." Foreign vessels could traverse this area only if their passage was considered innocent by the adjacent coastal state. When a ship left the territorial sea and entered the internal waters of a state (estuaries, lagoons, bays, ports), it passed under the laws of that state. Often naval vessels, as distinct from merchant ships, would claim sovereign immunity from local laws while in internal waters, but such immunity would not extend to the ship's personnel ashore. They would come under the laws of the state they were in.

The customary laws of the sea have long antecedents and would have been respected at times of peace by European maritime powers during the eighteenth century.[7] However, it would not have entered the minds of any of the commanders of the ships in the Pacific that customary rules held by indigenous people over coastal sea tenure, reef passages, or lagoons could have any validity in the islands they had "discovered." These places were perceived as having no overall cohesive governments and therefore no civilized rules of law (other than when it suited the foreigners to create a monarch or exploit locally useful taboos). Furthermore, areas where there were no apparent fixed settlements or agricultural activities were considered terra nullius. It also followed that in all the countries of arrival the laws that pertained on board ship would be extended to the shore, not only to the ship's company but to the local populations.

The primary objectives of the Cook expedition were to observe the transit of Venus, to facilitate the scientific work of Joseph Banks, to search for Terra Australis Incognita, "and with the consent of the natives to take possession of convenient situations in the country in the name of the King of Great Britain."[8] Cook possessed sympathetic insights toward other cultures and was at the same time an able officer who paid strict attention to orders and the exercise of authority. He tried to reconcile the guidance of the Royal Society, the sponsors of the expedition, for humane behavior toward native people and the Admiralty requirements to take possession of their territory.

The president of the Royal Society, James Douglas, Earl of Morton, wrote among other things that the captain and others in charge of the *Endeavor* expedition should "check the petulance of the Sailors and restrain the wanton use of Fire Arms"; that "shedding the blood of these people is a crime of the highest nature"; that they are "the natural, and in the strictest sense of the word, the legal possessors of the several Regions they inhabit"; and that "conquest over such people can give no just title, because they could never be the Aggressors." And, the Royal Society continued: "They may naturally and justly attempt to repel intruders, whom they may apprehend are coming to disturb them in the quiet possession of their country, whether that apprehension be well or ill founded."[9] Cook ultimately expressed his own balance of views: "We enter their Ports without their daring to make opposition, we attempt to land in a peaceable manner, if this succeeds it's well, if not we land nevertheless and maintain the footing we thus got by the Superiority of our fire arms, in what other light can they than at first look upon us but as invaders of their Country." Cook adds optimistically and mistakenly, but possibly with an eye on the Admiralty scrutineers of his opinions, that "time and some acquaintance with us can only convince them of their mistake."[10]

Arrival of Wallis

The master of HMS *Dolphin* under Captain Wallis in June 1767 was George Robertson. He was typical in many ways of the normal run of career masters in the Royal Navy. Robertson was a good seaman who gave discreet guidance but showed suitable deference to the young gentlemen officers. He was also highly patriotic, with a firm belief in the rights of the British nation to take possession and rule over these "poor ignorant creatures," as he described the Tahitians. In one respect he was less typical than the average master in that he kept a journal of his voyages.[11] This is an important document recording the first relationships between sailors and Tahitians.

Robertson's journal describes alternating scenes of violence and friendship. At one stage a large canoe approached, and at a signal its occupants launched a storming of stone missiles. The *Dolphin* replied with a volley of grapeshot from its great guns. Noting that this "carried all before it and drove [the canoe] in two," Robertson added, "I believe few that were on her escaped with life." The carpenters were also sent ashore and "cut in the middle" some eighty canoes. The attitude of the master was clearly one of exasperation that these "poor creatures" would have the temerity to challenge sailors of the Royal Navy "and put us under the disagreeable necessity of killing a few of them." He was pleased that the Tahitians eventually recognized the error of their ways and that sailors and natives soon "walked arm in arm."[12]

The conversion to close friendships between the sailors and local people appears to have come about when the older men of the island discerned the obsession of the *Dolphin* sailors for women. The Tahitians were puzzled that the *Dolphin* had no females on board and may have assumed they came from islands with a dire shortage of women. In any event the Tahitians concluded that what they themselves regarded as normal relationships within society could be a means of obtaining iron from the *Dolphin*. For the sailors the availability of sex for payment was simply regarded as playing at, as Robertson puts it, "the old trade." They did so with such enthusiasm that it threatened the integrity of the ship as iron and nails were drawn from it. When the *Dolphin* left, Robertson described the sorrow and weeping of the people.[13]

Sailors under Cook

Cook had read the accounts of Wallis before sailing for Tahiti, and the crew of the *Endeavour* was no doubt regaled with stories from the hands on board who had previously served on the *Dolphin*. Cook knew what to expect and established rules, fines, and floggings for theft. The *Endeavour* sailors established their trade and close attachments ashore. These were sufficiently strong for Clement Webb and Sam Gibson to jump ship in 1769—as generations of sailors did subsequently. They had, said a Tahitian, "gone to the mountains and . . . got each of them a wife and would not return." Cook held a chief hostage until the Tahitians found and returned the deserters, although after meting out floggings, he expressed a wistful sympathy in his journal for these young men who preferred life on a Pacific island to that on a British man-of-war.[14]

Cook had the same problems in 1777. Sixteen-year-old midshipman Alexander Mouat of the *Discovery* declared that he had fallen in love with a girl and wanted to stay in Tahiti. He and the gunner's mate Shaw deserted. When the two were retrieved, the ship's company appealed to Cook against rigorous punishment, and the captain made concessions. He had been even more sympathetic in 1774 when an older sailor, John Marra, slipped over the side as they were leaving Tahiti and swam toward a prearranged canoe. Cook brought the ship about and sent a boat after him. Afterward he wrote, "I never learned that he had either friends or connections to confine him to any particular part of the world, all nations were alike to him, where then can such a man spend his days better than at one of these isles where he can enjoy the necessaries and some of the luxuries of life in ease and plenty." Cook later added, "I know not if he might not have obtained my consent if he had applied for it in proper time," [15] to which his biographer Beaglehole comments, "This is an unusual mood for a person commanding one of the vessels of the Royal Navy." [16]

The attachments of several sailors who spent longer periods ashore were deep and genuine, as were those of the women and children to them. After the mutiny of 1789, Morrison lived about eighteen months in Tahiti, along with sixteen other seamen from the *Bounty* who elected not to go with Christian to Pitcairn. Morrison described the scene when fourteen of them (two having been killed previously) were taken as prisoners on board HMS *Pandora* in May 1791: "[Their women,] several big with child[,] and four girls and two boys, cried and cut their heads until blood discoloured the waters." [17]

Most of the ordinary sailors one way or another integrated well with island people, and there were many pregnancies and surviving children. The sailors learned the language and conformed to local customs, including tattooing. However, they were not always aware of the cultural nuances. For many of them the material exchanges made for sex were the normal ways of a sailor's life, and there is little doubt that these more commercial transactions became increasingly adopted by some island women. A related legacy was sexually transmitted diseases. Several of the seven hundred or so sailors on the ships of Wallis, Carteret, Bougainville, and Cook who went ashore at Matavai Bay in Tahiti in 1767–1769 carried syphilis, gonorrhea, and other communicable sexually transmitted diseases, and some must have had what sailors term "a full house." When they left for other islands, many more were infected as the diseases passed around between sailors and their sweethearts. Cook wrote that "this distemper very soon spread itself over the greatest part of the Ship's company." It appears to have been the first entry of venereal disease into the Pacific Islands, and although Cook tried to contain it by keeping infected sailors on board, he realized that "it may in time spread itself over all the islands of the south seas, to the eternal reproach of those who first brought it among them." [18] The disease reached Hawai'i with the *Resolution* in 1778. [19]

There were both health and social impacts to the spread of venereal disease. Gonorrhea may have caused some sterility and miscarriages in women, and syphilis could mean dangerous long-term effects on men, although it is thought that the disease yaws, endemic on humid high islands, may have exercised a modifying immunity. The venereal diseases were new and feared by many people and soon carried a social stigma. Morrison records attitudes toward infected people in Tahiti: "No person will touch them nor theirs, no one will bath[e] near them in the river." [20] Possibly worse in the long term than the venereal diseases in morbidity were tuberculosis and other contagious diseases brought by the ships, for which there were no immunities in the populations. Lieutenant Zachary Hicks joined the *Endeavour* already suffering from consumption and died at sea; there must have been others that carried this killer to the islands.

The Scientists

The other members of the first exploration ships were the scientists and artists, whose perceptions were more politically influential. The second half of the eighteenth century was the age of the European Enlightenment, exploration, and science. The sciences involved in the voyages were primarily astronomy, botany, geography, and zoology. The period was characterized by systematically classifying plants in order to advance the universal botanical taxonomy developed by Linnaeus. During the first voyage of the *Endeavour*, Joseph Banks and the Swede Daniel Solander, a pupil of Linnaeus, collected thousands of plants, along with bird and marine species. These were accompanied by drawings and watercolors, mainly by Sydney Parkinson.

The classifying of flora and fauna was extended on a more speculative basis to the human species by Banks and others. The criteria they used to place people at various levels of civilization were highly Eurocentric and included skin color, physical characteristics, and cultural attributes such as morals, work ethics, clothing, and music; the eating of human flesh immediately relegated groups to the lower orders. Banks observed that "in the admirable chain of nature . . . Man . . . justly claims the highest rank." He considered that, because of cannibalism, the Maori as a race was "so infinitely below us in the order of Nature." [21]

The European scientists were so ethnocentric that they were unable to learn much from the skills and knowledge of Pacific people. When the Ra'iatea island priest-navigator Tupaia joined the *Endeavour* in Tahiti in 1769, Banks considered that he might well be useful and was certainly an interesting natural history specimen to take back with the rest of the collection. Banks thought Tupaia might even be worth keeping on his estate "as a curiosity, as well as some of my neighbours do lions and tygers at a larger expence than he will probably ever put me to." [22] This proud and intelligent Pacific navigator must have carried enormous indigenous knowledge, most of which remained unrecorded. He very quickly learned English, acted as interpreter, explaining customs and essential procedures;

saved the ship from grounding and the lives of parties ashore; and debated the ethics of cannibalism, which was not practiced in Tahiti, with the New Zealand Maori.

Banks, with his passion for collecting and classifying, seemed unaware of the extent of the science of marine ecology, which Pacific islanders had acquired and practiced for conservation purposes over many centuries. Island people knew the relationships between tides, currents, phases of the moon, spawning, fish behavior, and the webs of intricate relationships between living organisms and their physical and biological environments. Only in the twentieth century did this knowledge become more clearly recognized by Europeans as the essential basis of marine science. In the 1960s it was conceded by ecologists that "the Hawaiians of Captain James Cook's time knew more about the fishes of their islands than is known today."[23]

The Pacific island understandings of the marine environment also passed unnoticed by Banks' successor on the second voyage, the outstanding but prickly scientist Johann Reinhold Forster, who was accompanied by his seventeen-year-old son, George. The elder Forster continued the work on botany and zoology and also speculated on the causes of the physical and cultural differences between people in the Pacific region. He placed the Tahitians much higher than the Maori in his scale of humanity and formulated stimulating concepts of environmental determinism that were adopted and refined later by the German school of geography. Forster's son contributed to the 1777 observations and other joint publications and was particularly incensed by the perceptions presented by Europeans of the Pacific peoples.

Philip Edwards has identified and abstracted the views of George Forster from publications. Among his critical remarks, the younger Forster wrote, "I fear that hitherto our intercourse has been wholly disadvantageous to the natives of the South Seas; and that those communities have been the least injured, who have always kept aloof from us."[24] He went on to comment on the revulsion expressed by Europeans about those engaged in cannibalism, pointing out that "though we are too much polished to be canibals, we do not find it unnaturally and savagely cruel to take the field, and to cut one another's throats by thousands." On the condemnation of the immorality of Pacific women, he wrote, "It is the women who are the victims, caught between the brutality of importunate sailors on the one hand and their greedy men folk on the other—which are more guilty, those who make demand or those who provide the supply."[25]

George Forster took a jaundiced view of Cook, which was not justified, given that Cook expressed similar views on the degraded condition of women on his return visit to Queen Charlotte Sound in New Zealand in June 1773. Previously he had found these women "chaste," but on this second visit he noted, "Whatever favours a few of them might have granted to the crew of the *Endeavour* it was generally done in a private manner without the men seeming to interest themselves in it, but now we find the men are the chief promoters of this Vice, and for a spike nail or any other thing they value will oblige their Wives and Daughters to prostitute themselves whether they will or no." Cook went on to deplore the way "we debased their morals" and posed a rhetorical question regarding what natives "have gained by the commerce they have had with Europeans."[26]

The acts of debauching female morals in Tahiti by commerce in iron was echoed by the bosun's mate James Morrison when he reminded the more high-minded about corresponding effects of gold in his own country, where, he observed, "as fine a woman as any in Europe are said to prefer it to virtue."[27] George Forster continued to rage against European imperialism, which in his view was degrading and destroying the culture and well-being of Pacific people in the 1770s. Later his outspoken radicalism lost this talented young scientist his academic position at a German university, and he died in poverty at the age of thirty-eight.

Views from the Beach

Pacific island people would always have expected arrivals from the sea. Many knew there were other ships and beings, from the exotic timbers with iron nails found from time to time on reefs and beaches, especially in the Hawaiian Islands. Spanish galleons made at least 450 crossings of the North Pacific between the mid-sixteenth and early eighteenth centuries, and some 12 of these ships went missing. In addition, shipwrecked sailors may also have survived and been assimilated into island populations and folk memories.[28]

Stories of European arrivals spread among the islanders after initial sightings or landings were made. When Cook missed the island of Rarotonga, a chief on hearing of the calls of ships elsewhere prayed:

O, great Tangaroa, send your large ship to our land,
Send us a dead sea, send us propitious gale,

To bring the far-famed Cookies to our island,
To give us nails and iron axes,
Let us see these outriggerless canoes.[29]

Some recollections of the first arrivals were also preserved in Pacific songs. A Fijian song expresses approval of the careful seamanship of the foreigners:

A lookout man climbs aloft
To be quite sure how the ship must steer
Nairai lies right ahead
Koro is away to leeward
And the ship is sailing downwind towards Bua
The foreigner is a wide-awake person
And takes care to follow the open channel.[30]

In some islands there was still uncertainty about the origins of European ships, as well as the status of foreign sailors. Deryck Scarr writes of a Mangaian song as that expresses profound ambivalence in its verses "Tangaroa has sent a ship, which has burst through the solid blue vault," and the chorus, "A ship full of guests is here. What gibberish they talk."[31] The word "burst" relates to the appearance of the great white sails, as they topped the horizon. I. C. Campbell points to the Polynesian word for Europeans, *papalangi,* which means "heaven bursters," and to the Maori *pakeha,* which has a similar meaning. Soon the Europeans were recognized as mere human beings with accomplishments, but who sometimes were lacking in understanding and whose skills could be learned.[32]

Twist tobacco was the first item of trade to Kiribati. It is recalled in a song still remembered to this day, though its age is unknown. It shows also some ambivalence to new arrivals and trade, as it warns people, in vain, about the dangers of smoking:

AI TERA TE BAI AE E RAKA IAONABARA
(WHAT IS THIS THING WHICH HAS COME UP INTO OUR COUNTRY)
What is this thing which has come up into our country
We are dying for love of it
A thing with an odd sort of body
It is black
And what is its name
It's tobacco

How strong the love for smoking
We die if it goes away
A white man's thing which is black
And twisted round every strand
Go easy on this love of smoking.[33]

The island communities that received the foreign ships had their own well-established laws and customs, which, like their navigational and ecological knowledge, the Europeans failed to recognize, partly because they was transmitted orally. It was customary in places for communities to exercise rights to take possession of uninvited foreign vessels and anything else arriving from the sea. William Mariner records an example from the voyage of the Tongan chief "Cow Mooala." Variable voyaging conditions brought Chief Kau Moala to the islands of "Footona," where his vessel, property, and cargo were taken by the people. Mariner points out that this behavior was consistent with the laws of the islands. They nevertheless gave him hospitality and within twelve months built him a new ship. He then sailed for Fiji, loaded sandalwood, and returned to Tonga.[34] Attempts to confiscate the ships of strangers or remove material from the ships appear to fall within at least some indigenous customs. Underlying this may have been implied reciprocity.

Several island laws were less welcoming when it came to shipwrecks. When David Whippy, the part-Fijian son of a famous sailor, shipbuilder, and vice-consul for the United States, was shipwrecked on Vanua Levu, he knew that "by the sanguinary laws of Feejee the penalty of escape from shipwreck is death and conversion into food, he exerted himself to make it appear that he was but a casual traveller requiring hospitality." The people recognized he had "salt-water in the eyes," and he was saved only by a chief who was under obligation to his father.[35]

Where demand increased was for firearms and ammunition. Wars appeared to be common enough in most parts of the Pacific before the foreign ships came, but they increased in ferocity when the European weapons were acquired. The attack in 1806 on the British privateer *Port au Prince* at Haʻapai in Tonga was primarily motivated by an immediate need for guns. William Mariner, who was one of the survivors of the massacre of most of the crew, describes how he and fifteen other European sailors subsequently took part in a naval attack by Haʻapai warriors on the fortified town of Nukualofa on Tongatapu in 1807. The bombardment with four carronades was followed by the further slaughter of men, women, and children, and scenes of cannibalism.[36]

As more formal trade emerged, people began to recognize that they were losing their own things of value, which could not be replaced, and it was evident that the Europeans were insensitive to this. Nicholas, in his *Narrative of a Voyage to New Zealand,* describes his dealings with a Maori chief for a special comb worn by him, for which Nicholas offered a billhook: "The chief, it would appear, attached to the comb no ordinary degree of sacred importance; and fearful of incurring the guilt of profanation by parting with it in the same precipitate manner as with any other article of less awful attributes, he deemed it expedient to wait a certain time, and then transmit it to my hands with proper solemnities."[37] In this and other ways, innumerable parts of the Maori cultural heritage in greenstone and other materials disappeared from society before resentment surfaced in violence.

Other situations of stress arose when island people realized that the sailors did not understand the social complexities of sexual relationships. They could not distinguish between those females who were available to them, seemingly at a price in iron and tobacco, and those who were not, because of status and marriage. Cook began to discern these differences and warned of fatal mistakes. There were in various Pacific societies differences in levels of sexual freedom. In some traditional Polynesian societies, independent women of lower ranks were free to form temporary liaisons, not motivated by economic considerations, with men visiting their settlements. Also described were the "strolling players," who were, according to Beaglehole, the "less restricted young women of this social order who provided seamen with such advantageous entertainment."[38] These girls "toured the island group in fleets of consecrated canoes [and] were met with gifts and with joy; their god was the god of peace and fertility."[39] Morrison also shows some of the complexities of class and sexuality when he refers to the Areeuoy of Tahiti as "ladies of pleasure," of whom Queen Pbooraya was one.[40] These ladies were, like the *mahoo* (male transvestites), highly regarded in society.

The women of Micronesia as a whole were also given a reputation for prostitution by the commanders of visiting ships. They described husbands and fathers coming on board and offering their women for tobacco. In practice, chastity was valued in many parts of Micronesia, where "if the girl was not a virgin her parents would take her back and cancel the marriage." Those who came on board were in the traditional category of *nikiranroro,* "single women who are not virgins and married women who are not living with their husbands," women "who even in pre-European times supported themselves partly with gifts from lovers and were, in some measure, free agents." The men who were with these women were not necessarily related.[41] There were numerous instances, in several places, of sailors and traders being killed for illicit sexual transgressions.

The Exploring Ships—An Appraisal

The first encounters were full of ambiguities. Sailors were accustomed to going ashore in foreign places and forming temporary liaisons. For them a Pacific island was only another such place. Many of these British naval ratings and marines had experienced violent and victorious actions at sea. They regarded themselves as a superior breed entitled to take possession and to kill when necessary. Typically, when the Tahitians launched a surprise attack on the *Dolphin,* Richardson the barber penned a long, doggerel poem regretting having to kill them:

Poor simple men, to late you're taught
That Britons ne'er are easily caught.[42]

The officers and scientists shared this simplistic view, alternating with perceptions of Arcadian nobility and treachery, according to their mood and circumstances. Cook took a more balanced approach, while George Forster was outraged at the arbitrary shootings of people. The other scientists brushed aside the depth of indigenous knowledge of geography, navigation, and ecology in the belief that only Europeans could formulate scientific principles. Even Cook, who respected the information given by Tupaia, seems not to have inquired closely as to how he actually navigated.

Island people for their part had few illusions about the visitors. They valued the iron as a marked improvement on stone, shell, and wood and respected the firearms, if not the contagious diseases they acquired. The chiefs soon considered themselves at least the class equals of the ship commanders and regarded drunken and impolite sailors with "disdainful tolerance."[43] Tupaia as a chief made it plain that he was a cut above the European seamen on the *Endeavour.* Cook wrote that Tupaia "was proud and obstinate which often made his situation on board both disagreeable to himself and those about him."[44] Anne Salmond concludes that when the people of Hauraki first encountered the *Endeavour,* they "had no notion of these strangers as superior—quite to the contrary."[45] Several years later Captain Turnbull (see chapter 5) still got the impression that the Tahitians were "fully persuaded Tahiti is the first country on the face of the globe." He added that they "were persuaded that we have no other purpose in visiting them but that we are half starved at home."[46]

Several of the first foreign arrivals had concerns over their effects on the people. Cook was particularly worried by their introduction of venereal disease. By the time the *Resolution* and *Discovery* reached Kauaʻi Island, Hawaiʻi, in January 1778, he knew the disease had been spread widely elsewhere. He tried to keep infected sailors on board and women ashore for the fourteen days they were there. When they returned again to Hawaiʻi in November 1778 and lay off Maui, some young men came out on a boat and showed them the results of the new disease on their penis and asked for treatment. Lieutenant James King of the *Resolution* wrote in his journal that "the manner in which these innocent people complained to us seem'd to me to show they considered us the original authors."[47] There is no doubt that this contributed to a subsequent drastic decline in the population.

George Forster, and to a lesser extent Cook, also appreciated the longer-term social and economic effects of their arrivals on Pacific society. Philip Edwards discerned the perception of Forster to the introduction of iron. This undoubtedly was the beginning of a new iron age, with some advantages, but with related moral corruption. Forster emphasizes that the contact between sailors and islanders was most evident in the sexual coupling for which payment was made in iron nails. Iron took on mystical properties in some islands, and certainly in the long term this altered divisions of labor and reduced effort and time in the construction of vessels and other building activities. Forster saw the further portents of change in the acquisition of new luxuries by chiefs that would move the communities toward the more acquisitive inequality of a class-based society.[48] This became more evident with the adoption of European commercial practices by paramount chiefs, which are discussed in chapter 5.

CHAPTER FIVE

Pacific Commercial Shipowners

THE GOVERNMENT-SPONSORED voyages to the Pacific in the eighteenth century were motivated by European rivalry, scientific inquiry, and public appetite for the exotic. The expeditions were conducted by naval vessels whose commanders were given specific instructions on behavior toward native peoples and were required to report on the resource potential of island areas. They carried articles for use as gifts and as barter for victuals, but they did not carry goods of a commercial nature. Care had to be taken to ensure that firearms were not stolen, lost, or traded, although some were, and other items from the ship and belonging to the crew were bartered primarily for access to women. The periodic short bursts of violence between ship and shore were often due to misunderstandings, followed by retaliation and conciliation.

The subsequent encounters of island people with commercial shipping were different. The naval expeditions were followed by waves of privately owned trading and whaling vessels. They scoured the Pacific in search of whatever financial gains could be derived from sea and land resources. Not only did this change represent enormous increases in the quantity of ship arrivals, but it also heralded qualitative changes in the economic basis of societies and generated a class of Pacific chiefly entrepreneurs in shipping and trade.

The crews of the foreign commercial vessels comprised men from Britain, other parts of Europe, America, New South Wales, and occasionally Southeast Asia and China, and always with additions from the Pacific. The ships were commanded by independent, tough seamen who for long were beyond the reach of nation-state jurisdiction. These captains ruled on board according to "customs of the sea," which had passed between ships over centuries. The only recourses that the ordinary seafarer had in the face of violations of recognized customary law were sullen, uncooperative behavior, physical retaliation, mutiny, and desertion.

The captains of the merchant ships, unlike their naval compatriots, did not always resolutely pursue deserters. Some even drove seamen to desert and relinquish their wages, or discarded troublesome seamen and abandoned the sick and injured when and where they could. As a result, island societies received new seafaring and related skills as well as some unwelcome residents. These beachcombing populations were augmented by castaways from shipwrecks and, from the 1790s onward, by convicts escaping from the New South Wales colony. The latter were often carried to the islands by American whalers who held no liking for the British penal system. There were also convicts who with temporary permission from the authorities signed on to British ships at Port Jackson to make up a lack of crew numbers. They took the opportunity of "skinning out" in the islands and New Zealand. The Pacific was thereby soon crossed in every direction by commercial trading vessels and whalers. This left few islands untouched in the receipt of new goods, technology, and foreigners.

Ships that transported the convicts from Britain sought return cargoes. Those chartered by the British East India Company proceeded from New South Wales to China to load tea. Of six ship arrivals in the first fleet in 1788, two went on to Canton. The *Charlotte* under Captain Thomas Gilbert and the *Scarborough* under Captain John Marshall pioneered the Outer Eastern Passage to China. Sailing together northeastward to pick up the southeast trades, they called at Lord Howe and Norfolk islands and sighted Matthew Island to a longitude between Vanuatu and Fiji. From this position they proceeded northward, passing Anuta, and then through the variables and doldrums into the northeast trades (see map 2.1) and passages off Kiribati, the Marshalls, and the Carolines.[1] Knowledge of currents (see map 2.2) was uncertain, and the existence of many reefs and small islands unknown. Captains Gilbert and Marshall gave their names to these groups of Micronesian islands, many of which they suddenly encountered. Navigation was dangerous, and some populations hostile.[2] They and most subsequent mariners followed this route and engaged in a minimum trade with canoes offshore until the establishment of coconut oil commercial traders in the 1840s.[3]

Many other cargo ships, owned mainly by British investors, sought cargoes for China in the Pacific Islands. They sailed eastward from Port Jackson toward the North Cape of New Zealand, often calling there for victuals, and continued to about 150 degrees west, often under favorable westerlies. The ships then shaped a course northward for the Society Islands. The total passage from Australia to Matavai Bay in Tahiti could take seven weeks or more, depending on weather and any time spent in

New Zealand.[4] Some British convict ships also proceeded to Matavai Bay after Port Jackson and loaded for China.[5]

Some other speculative traders out of Port Jackson were unassociated with the China trade. These were small vessels usually owned in part by the captains, doing a round of the islands. In addition more regular commercial services developed. Ships from New England in particular were by the 1780s carrying furs from the northwest coast of America to China, calling at the Hawaiian group for provisions and sometimes supplementary cargo. Regular shipping was likewise established between Port Jackson and Tahiti for salt pork and to New Zealand for kauri timber spars, flax, and foodstuffs.

In the bigger Polynesian groups of Tahiti, Hawai'i, and Aotearoa the chiefly descendants of the great founding navigators admired these new oceangoing vessels. The Pacific island mariners recognized their advantages in having more freeboard and greater capacities for cargo and passengers. They appreciated the improved sails and the use of the rudder as superior to the steering oar. The disadvantages included deeper draughts unsuited to lagoon passes and submerged reefs. They also recognized the strengths and capacities of the rowed longboats and whaleboats carried by the foreign ships, despite their reduced speed compared with paddled indigenous craft. The chiefs in particular valued the facility to mount their new swivel guns on all of these crafts with strong gunwales.

Most masters of merchant ships appreciated that friendly relations with chiefs were essential to conduct trade. There were others who were cheats, racists, religious bigots, or drunks or had several of these traits. The resulting clash of cultures and personalities led to killings of island people and sailors. The attitude of "master under God" on board ship and the mana of chiefs underlay many of the conflicts. Pat Hohepa emphasizes the complex role of mana, with which chiefs were imbued: "Mana comes from the Gods, mana flows through the ancestors, mana flows from the sea and the land."[6] There is the mana of a warrior, mana that involves prestige, power, influence, authority, and many other attributes. The term could be ascribed to outstanding weapons or ships, as well as people.

The opportunities for misunderstanding and usurpation of status through words and actions between ship and shore were clearly considerable. Governor Philip Gidley King of New South Wales sensed this and was anxious to ensure a regular supply of provisions, as well as the development of wider markets for new products from the colony. He emphasized to captains: "At every other island some address and much circumspection is necessary in having any communication with the natives, which the momentary error either of a native or a seaman might destroy."[7]

For all the possible contradictions in values and acts of violence, commercial trade did emerge through trial and error. The emphasis shifted from tawdry trifles to a range of useful tools and on to guns and luxuries. The latter two were demanded and accumulated by the chiefly families, especially those in Tahiti and Hawai'i who controlled good harbors. They were already designated kings by naval commanders and continued to be recognized as such by the merchant captains and missionaries, to their mutual advantages. This gave the chance for some ambitious chiefs in Polynesia to enter into the new system of commercial trade and to become shipowners. This brief initial attempt to keep command of their sea trade in a new era ultimately proved unsuccessful for several reasons, but it was an important stage in the economic history of the Pacific.

First Commercial Ship-Owning Ventures by Polynesians

The entry into ship owning in Tahiti, Hawai'i, and Aotearoa represents the first large-scale participation in a significant sector of the capitalist global trading system by island people. Among other aspects, it was an attempt to bypass the foreigners in a maritime activity within which islanders were supremely experienced.

TAHITI

When Captain Wallis arrived at Matavai Bay in 1767, he assumed that the formidable woman Purea was queen. When Cook came in 1769, he also had the European predilection toward identifying a single ruler. He met with the Otou (Tu), who ascended to the chieftainship of the northwest of the island of Tahiti, in which lies Matavai Bay. According to H. E. Maude, "Cook seems to have been the originator of the myth of Tu's kingship."[8] Tu was accorded favors, gifts, and guns by all subsequent arrivals and from 1790 was acknowledged as King Pomare I.

Pomare was able to extend his territories. He recruited European sailors as mercenaries, including several *Bounty* mutineers during 1789–1791, and in 1792 the crew of the whaler *Matilda* wrecked in the Tuamotus, and the crew of the *Norfolk* grounded at Matavai Bay in 1802. In addition numerous ship deserters and many convicts who escaped from Botany Bay were available.[9] The relative political stability of Tahiti under Pomare I, the apparent abundance of foodstuffs, and the general friendliness of the people came to the attention of Governor King of New South

Wales. He studied Cook's account of the islands and received reports from missionaries who arrived in Tahiti during 1797, as well as from whalers calling at Sydney. The penal colony required regular provisions, and following a trial shipment, Governor King dispatched HMS *Porpoise* in 1801 to obtain salt pork under a formal contract with Pomare I.[10] The king imposed taboos on the consumption of pork by the common people and tried to concentrate all trade through royal channels.

In a short time Pomare I emerged as an astute business entrepreneur who recognized the forces of supply and demand in establishing exchange values. His son Otoo (Tu), under the complicated system of inheritance in Tahiti, ascended to power before Pomare died in 1803.[11] Pomare II was less efficient, but more ruthlessly dedicated to the nascent new economic order based on foreign trade. The journal of Captain John Turnbull of the brig *Margaret* provides accounts of the commercial milieu of the time.[12] The journal gives an understanding of the complexities of the trade and the hazards involved. It thereby shows the difficulties that the chiefly entrepreneurs faced when they entered the established shipping business, despite their strengths from the control of island resources and labor.

The voyage of the *Margaret* over the year 1802–1803 was, in brief, from Port Jackson to King Island in the Bass Strait to land a gang of sealers. From there the ship went to Norfolk Island for victuals that were unobtainable at Port Jackson. The seafarers arrived at Matavai Bay, Tahiti, on 23 December 1802. At this anchorage Turnbull spoke with Lieutenant William Scott of HMS *Porpoise*, who was on his second voyage for salt pork. He learned then of the internecine war raging in the group. On his first voyage in 1801, Scott had carried many iron tools and clothing, plus a few "old arms." In 1802 there were major changes in the types of goods carried for trade; he delivered a formidable array of muskets, pistols, ammunition, bayonets, and even military jackets,[13] reflecting something of the support that Governor King was giving to Pomare. When Turnbull started to trade his general cargo, which included domestic items and axes, he was ridiculed. It was made clear to him that hogs could be obtained only in exchange for armaments.

With few results after four weeks, the *Margaret* sailed for other islands in the group. At Ulitea (Ra'iatea) Island three of the Botany Bay convicts who had been allowed to sign on at Port Jackson deserted, along with an apprentice, the cooper, two seamen, and two Tahitians he had acquired. This group conspired with a deserter from the ship *Venus* and with a local chief to take the *Margaret*. They cut the anchor hawser and nearly grounded the vessel. Only after a running battle did the *Margaret* escape.

Everywhere Turnbull went, he found the recurring demand for guns. There was also the need to provide gifts to chiefs before any trade negotiations could commence. This he blamed on the previous naval vessels and commented wryly, "However well this might suit ships on astronomical pursuits, or voyages of discovery, it by no means corresponded with our commercial views." [14] He diverted requests for gifts to his tough armorer, who soon earned the accolade *"ahow tata"* (very bad fellow). Turnbull was a little more successful trading for a few hogs in smaller, more remote islands, and somewhere six Tahitians were added to the crew in place of the deserters. The ship then sailed on 21 January 1803 for the Sandwich Islands to load salt for Tahiti, where it was in demand for curing pork.

Turnbull found the terms of trade equally unfavorable for foreigners in Hawai'i. He blamed American fur traders on their way to China who were willing to pay highly for victuals. Some of the new Tahitian seamen jumped ship, as did his carpenter, attracted by opportunities ashore. Turnbull also encountered the monopoly on salt enforced by the royal family (discussed below in the section "Hawai'i"). On arrival of the ship at Oahu, a chief representing the king of Hawai'i boarded, and no cargo work commenced until goods were assessed and terms of trade established. Turnbull described how an old man dealt with him privately. When he was discovered by the inspector general, he "nearly expired with fright." [15] Turnbull managed to intervene on his behalf.

The cargo was loaded, and the ship sailed for Tahiti. During the southern voyage, Turnbull explored only a few of the seventy-seven scattered islands of the Tuamotu Archipelago and made the first European contact with Makemo Island. This was very hazardous navigationally and precarious in terms of contacts with the local people, some of whom were regarded as brigands.[16] Turnbull observed a chief wearing a pearl-oyster shell ornament, which signified valuable lagoon resources. He also noted a Pomare double-hulled vessel six months out of Tahiti, collecting tribute around the islands.[17]

On arrival at Tahiti it was agreed that Captain John Buyers take the *Margaret* to the Windward Islands (Tuamotus) and trade for hogs and possibly pearls and shells. Turnbull meanwhile was engaged in salting. He also enlisted several seafaring deserters and ex-convicts, along with the experienced beachcomber Peter the Swede and took boats around the coast to trade for hogs. On returning to Matavai Bay, he found that the *Margaret* was overdue. The captain and crew of eighteen were eventually sighted at sea on a makeshift punt. After their rescue a common enough tale unfolded of the ship's running on a reef and then being plundered of fittings, cargo, and armaments by local people. Having lost the carpenter in Hawai'i, they built a somewhat precarious punt of planks from the wreck of the *Margaret* to sail for Tahiti. The crew on arrival joined the forces of Pomare.

Wars led by chiefs against the despotism of the Pomares increased in Tahiti. In 1808 Pomare was forced to evacuate Matavai Bay with his forces and take refuge on Mooréa Island. The chiefs who now occupied Matavai Bay rashly raided the ship *Venus* from Port Jackson to obtain cannons. Unlike Pomare, they failed to appreciate that, in order to continue trading with the New South Wales colony, they had to guarantee the safety of vessels. Pomare reiterated such a guarantee from his base in Mooréa. This appeared in the *Sydney Gazette* of 5 May 1810, after the ship *Mercury* arrived from Mooréa.[18] Pomare also made the judicious decision to embrace Christianity in 1812 and obtain the support of the missions. The latter were not only engaged in religious conversions but also traded armaments for food at this time. Captain Thomas Hanson of the mission ship *Active* even exchanged two cannons for 126 hogs.[19]

With various levels of support ashore and afloat, Pomare in 1815 regained Matavai Bay and acquired other territories, including the Tuamotu Islands and Austral Islands, with their valuable resources. In 1817 he started a joint shipbuilding venture with the London Missionary Society. By 1819 their first ship, the *Haweis* (73 tons), is recorded as unloading salt pork and coconut oil at Port Jackson.[20] It had a Tahitian crew under the command of Captain John Nicholson, and by then was totally owned by Pomare. In 1820 Pomare sent his agent Captain Samuel Henry, who was born in Tahiti, to Port Jackson to purchase other ships in return for hogs and sandalwood.[21] The latter commodity had until then been shipped by European traders from the Fiji group but was now depleted in these islands. Pomare knew of the stands of sandalwood in his Austral Island domain, which had been found by the notorious Captain Michael Fodger in 1813 (see chapter 7).[22]

In order to obtain sufficient resources to expand in commercial shipping, Pomare required everyone under his rule, "including the lame and sick," to bring him a hog, or else "they would be banished from the land and go upon the reef."[23] The first of the ships purchased on this basis was the *Governor Macquarie* (136 tons), followed by the *Queen Charlotte* (110 tons) and the *Minerva* (about 80 tons). All of these, along with the *Haweis*, are recorded as trading to Sydney.[24] These ships collected cargoes of hogs and pearls throughout most of the Society Islands and Tuamotus, and sandalwood from the Austral Islands and later from the Marquesas.[25]

People were coerced under the Pomare dynasty to produce cargoes throughout their domains by resident officials and some complying missionaries and by threats of bombardments from Pomare's ships. When the *Queen Charlotte* called at the Austral Islands in July 1822, the Tahitian governor announced to the chiefs and people: "I have to say to you, give more hogs, fowls, yams, food and tioo (preserved sour bread-fruit), not a little, a great deal, in abundance and carry it down to the boat for the ship."[26] A rival missionary tried to get the Austral Island people to become shareholders in a vessel to compete with the ships of Pomare, which were, he said, "sent hither to strip them of all they possess without recompense."[27] Nothing apparently came of this venture, but the Reverend John Williams did help the independent-minded Leeward Islands chiefs obtain the *Endeavour* (25 tons) in defiance of Pomare. This ship is recorded as arriving in Sydney during 1825.[28]

The Pomare family had continued to enforce monopolies and trade after Pomare II died in 1821. In an attempt to raise finance, Queen Pomare (then acting for her brother, the boy king Pomare III, who died in 1827) ordered the seizure of foreign ships trading for pearl or pearl shells without paying a royal license. The Chain Islanders (Ana'a), who were regular buccaneers, accordingly took the chance to capture the English brig *Dragon* and stripped her of "every moveable thing." Pressures were also put on other vassal islands. In 1825 the Pomare ship *Minerva* is said to have bombarded Rapa Island in a demand for more sandalwood.[29]

Sandalwood and pearls were by 1825 becoming exhausted, and New South Wales was more self-sufficient in foodstuffs. The debts to foreigners now soared. Only coconut oil, introduced sugarcane, and a few other crops were producing cash. Expensive imports continued, although with peace fewer armaments were required. On the other hand, a wider demand for clothing existed with the insistence by missions that everyone became decently clad. This aspect added to the general ill health of the common people from introduced diseases.[30] For all these reasons it is unlikely that any of the Tahitian-owned ships ever made reasonable profits. By the midcentury there also were greater numbers of competing, privately owned, newly built ships trading from Australia.[31] These eventually put an end to what was by then an old, badly managed and maintained Tahitian royal foreign-going fleet. Having been supported almost entirely by the sale of natural resources that were now depleted, the fleet collapsed in a morass of debts. Local small craft crewed by Tahitians, and several owned by the Pomares, continued to operate between the islands of the group. Increasingly the overseas import and export channels fell into the hands of foreign merchant companies, many of whose agents were former beachcombers and their part-island progeny.

HAWAI'I

The processes in the development of commercial shipping by the chieftains of Hawai'i were in several ways similar to those in Tahiti. Commercial activities started soon after Cook's report on his third voyage was circulated in 1784. The report described the Sandwich Islands and the resources of the northwest coast of America. In 1786 there were seven British ships on that coast, two of which were commanded by men who had sailed with Cook.[32] The British ships on speculative voyages were disadvantaged by the official trading monopolies of the East India Company and the South Pacific Company. The Americans had been free of all such impediments since the end of the War of Independence in 1783. Ships from Boston in particular became the main traders in furs for sale in China and called at the Hawaiian group for victuals.

The chief on the island of Hawai'i was in control of Kealakekua Bay (Path of the God), which became the most important calling place for foreign vessels from the end of the eighteenth century. He acquired the title of Kamehameha I, and with this came wealth, armaments, and new ships for warfare and trade. The first European-type vessel came into his possession in 1789 as a result of conflict between a pioneer American fur trader and Hawaiians.[33]

The ship *Eleanor* under Captain Simon Metcalf was a well-armed scow engaged in the northwest America–China fur trade. In 1789 Metcalf was sailing around the islands, seeking provisions and any profitable items of cargo that could be picked up. While the ship lay off the village of Kohala on Hawai'i, a minor disagreement arose with the regional chief Kameeiamoku, and Metcalf had the chief flogged aboard the *Eleanor*. He then sailed to trade along the leeward coast of Maui. Here again he ran into trouble and lost a boat. In reprisal for the theft, Metcalf lured small craft from the village of Olowalu close alongside, ostensibly to trade, and then blasted them to pieces with cannon shot. About one hundred people were killed.[34]

Soon after the killing at Olowalu, the small schooner *Fair American* arrived at Kohala. She was owned by Metcalf and commanded by his son. In revenge for the flogging, the people of Kohala killed the crew of the *Fair*

American, with the exception of the mate Isaac Davis, who was spared to assist in grounding the vessel to facilitate salvage. When Metcalf returned to Kealakekua Bay on the island of Hawai'i, the *Eleanor* was arrested by Kamehameha and the bosun John Young held ashore. Sensing more problems, Metcalf slipped out of the bay, leaving Young behind. Young and Davis then joined the forces of Kamehameha. They operated the cannons of the refloated *Fair American* and were valuable additions to his navy and commercial ventures. Thomas notes, "Boatswain John Young and mate Isaac Davis were treated with great kindness, made chiefs, and given valuable lands. They became useful aids to Kamehameha and their skill in gunnery helped him win many battles."[35]

In the early 1790s, in addition to Davis and Young, several other foreign seafarers were living ashore. These included Ridder, the carpenter's mate off the whaler *Columbia*. They set to work building a vessel of European design. When the British warship HMS *Discovery* under George Vancouver called in 1792, he allocated his carpenters to help complete the ship. This was a political and goodwill gesture to the king from the British monarch. The vessel was named *Britannia* and came into use as a warship. Vancouver refused a request for armaments, saying they were taboo by King George, but he did promise to send Kamehameha another ship. Meanwhile Vancouver supplied Kamehameha with new canvas sails for the large royal double-hulled traditional vessel.[36]

With a shipbuilding industry established, a second European vessel, the *Tamana* (40 tons), was soon under construction, and conversions were made to traditional craft.[37] By 1806 more than ninety sailors, tradesmen, and ex-convicts were living ashore on Oahu alone where Kamehameha had a court. Honolulu, with its sheltered bay (as the name indicates), was by then the main port for interisland and foreign cargo vessels and whalers. Other places receiving foreign ships came under royal-related chiefs. They enforced the royal trading monopolies as described by Captain Turnbull, who noted that the king "was a master for any European in any bargaining and knew well his weights and measures." Turnbull saw some twenty vessels owned by the king in 1803. These ranged from 25 to 50 tons, "some copper bottomed." He also observed that the people were held in "abject submission."[38] Another English mariner, Archibald Campbell, who was the chief sailmaker to the king, reported thirty sloops and schooners of about 40 tons built in Hawai'i in 1809,[39] and his associate shipwright Boyle was then supervising the building of other vessels.

The payments for equipment, skilled labor, and the purchase of vessels were in money derived from sandalwood, which was exported from several of the islands by foreign and Hawaiian vessels from the 1800s. Sandalwood came to a peak in value in 1815, when Fijian supplies were worked out. The royal control of sandalwood included directing labor for cutting, hauling, and preparing the timber. Often the wood was obtained in remote and rough inland areas. The common people were burdened and exhausted by the work, and food gardens and fishing neglected. K. R. Howe notes that within two years of the sandalwood trade's operation the king had at least six ships to add to his already impressive fleet.[40]

Payments for ships were made by excavating a pit equal to the cargo volume of the ship to be purchased and filling it twice over with sandalwood. One of the largest ships to be bought was the *Lily Byrd* (175 tons). The American register of 1808 records that "worms had nearly destroyed her sheathing" and "her keel and sternpost were almost reduced to honeycombs."[41] After extensive repairs she traded to China with sandalwood. The brig *Forester*, purchased in 1816 and renamed *Kaahumanu* after a favorite wife of the king, also entered the China trade.[42] Other vessels did likewise, including the *Neo* in 1817. This ship was in a sorry state and was bought at an exorbitant price. In 1821 the *Neo* was carrying salt to Kamchatka and returning with furs. Another vessel paid for by sandalwood in 1817, the *Kalanimoku*, was abandoned as rotten in 1821.[43]

It was difficult for the Hawaiian-owned ships to enter the profitable northwest American fur trade. The American captains knew the business well and formed a ring, agreeing on terms of trade with the coastal Indian tribes. They also carried parts of each other's shipments so that one vessel could run back to Hawai'i with a full load and yet others load up for China in Hawai'i with their joint furs and sandalwood. These always carried some members of the crew who were owners of the cargo, to look after their interests. The Yankee captains had personal vested interests in these voyages, as they obtained shares of the proceeds. They were also allowed cargo space and some trading rights on their own account. Unlike the ordinary sailors, they, and more so several Boston families, became wealthy.[44]

By contrast the captains from Australia and Britain who commanded Hawaiian-owned ships were out of the oligopoly circle of the Yankee Nor'westmen. They often had to carry Hawaiian supercargoes on board to monitor cargo negotiations, while the captains mainly navigated and, with their European officers, ran the ship. These masters had little formal pecuniary interest in the cargo but probably managed to trade informally on their own account. There appear to have been only three Hawaiian-owned ships regularly on the very profitable northwest coast–China fur trade in the period 1800–1832. Those recorded were the *Kamolilani* and the *Tamaolani* in 1828 and the *Victoria* in 1832.[45]

The journal of Stephen Reynolds provides a picture of the life of the sailor and the commercial procedures in the Northwest-Hawai'i-China run.[46] Hawaiian sailors were often employed on these American ships and were encouraged to do this by Kamehameha in order to obtain experience and knowledge. Reynolds gives indications of the numbers of Hawaiian sailors and the hardships they experienced due to weather, and he also provides insights into seafarer relations with Hawaiians at ports of call in the period 1810–1813.[47] He was then a foremast hand on the brig *New Hazard* (281 tons) of Salem. The ship was owned jointly by five businessmen of Salem and four of Boston, a typical risk-spreading venture. The captain, mates, supercargo, and sailors were, on leaving Boston, all New Englanders, although the steward and cook were typically Afro-Americans. At the age of twenty-eight, Reynolds was one of the oldest on board.

The *New Hazard* loaded cargo in Boston to trade for victuals in Hawai'i and furs on the northwest coast. This included muskets, gunpowder, shot, clothing, India cottons, hardware, iron, paints, tobacco, sugar, molasses, and rice. They sailed on 9 October 1810 and arrived in Hawai'i on 26 February 1811. During this sea passage of over four and a half months, they sighted distant high land only once. The long, boring voyage was punctuated by crew illness and regular floggings—especially of the Afro-American cook and steward. A week before the ship's arrival in Hawai'i, the mate raised the morale with the order to clean the ship "for the reception of the Owyhee lasses."[48]

A Hawaiian pilot boarded with his wife, and on 26 February the ship anchored in Kealakekua Bay. To the relief of the crew, two canoe loads of girls, coconuts, plantains, and potatoes arrived. John Young also boarded and stayed with them. After the goods were stored, the girls went ashore and the ship sailed on 3 March. At Oahu the ship took on more fresh water and live hogs and signed on six Hawaiian sailors. On 8 March a much refreshed *New Hazard* sailed for the northwest coast.

After twenty-six days Vancouver Island was sighted, and trading started offshore with Indian canoes in the vicinity of Queen Charlotte Sound. By this period the valuable sea otter had been depleted, and beaver and other furs were obtained from inland. Several American ships were working the coast and exchanging muskets, molasses, rice, and bread for furs. Captains also picked up fish oil and skins from some tribes and traded these with others along the coast. They also bought and sold slaves, possibly on their own account. Reynolds notes that the captain on 17 June "bought two slaves this morning," on 20 June "sold one slave for five skins, one for three," on 25 June "sold a little girl slave for five skins," and on 1 August "bought four slaves."[49]

The American ships often met and exchanged news. The captains agreed among themselves on the quantity of commodities they should give per pelt to the Indians. They also passed information on navigational hazards and hostile conditions. On 21 May they were told that the third mate and a Hawaiian seaman from the *Lydia* were killed when they went ashore for water. This account, written on board the *Hamilton,* reads: "Received a volley of musquit balls from Sum natives consealed in the woods. Whitch unfortunately kill the islander ded on the spot and shot Mr Fox through the boddy."[50] On 15 July they received news that the ship *Tonquin* had been "taken" near Noodka. The ship at some stage exploded (possibly ignited by the captain), and about a hundred Indians and most of the mixed crew, including many of the twenty-four kanakas (Hawaiians), were killed, as were others on shore.[51]

Weather was yet another difficulty. Even in April and May it was cold, and the ship experienced snow, rain, and fog. Reynolds reports that five kanakas were sick. Trading went on until 8 September 1811, when the ship set sail for Hawai'i. The *New Hazard* arrived at Toahy (Kawaihae Bay) on 28 September and met with other American ships. On Sunday, 29 September, Reynolds notes, "Not much work done this afternoon being girls on board." The ship then proceeded to Oahu, where the time was spent repairing the vessel, unloading the skins, smoking the holds (against rats), and loading. On 15 October the *New Hazard* sailed again for the northwest coast. The crew now included at least four Hawaiian seamen. By this period the fur trade ships tended to ply the northwest coast in winter, whereas previously they had overwintered in Hawai'i. The *New Hazard* moved from place to place under ice and snow between November 1811 and September 1812.

There were about fourteen ships on the coast by midsummer 1812. The *New Hazard* loaded pelts from the *Lydia* to deliver to Hawai'i, where it arrived in October. The *New Hazard* then topped up with sandalwood, mainly at Honolulu, along with other American ships and the king's vessel *Lily Byrd*. The latter was not in a seaworthy condition for the voyage to China with sandalwood. The carpenter of the *New Hazard* was therefore detached to repair the *Lily Byrd*. The *New Hazard* also loaded skins brought from the Northwest by the American schooners *Albatross* and *Isabella*. On 13 November the *New Hazard* sailed for China.

On 19 December the ship arrived at Macao and then went on to Whampoa. Other vessels did likewise. They had tried, as was the practice for safety reasons, to make the ocean passage together. Reynolds notes that the *Lily Byrd* was then aground, presumably again under repair. The *New Hazard* loaded cargo of tea, nankeens, and chinaware, a cargo that was valued at $300,000 in Boston, and returned to Hawai'i on 30 June 1813 for victuals and crew changes.[52] They were there for the Fourth of July celebrations, when guns were fired from the American ships. King Kamehameha, Young, and others dined on board with several captains. The king was given presents, including "two bedsteads, nankeens, shoes, hats, and bread." These no doubt were added to the vast store of such things as clothes, silks, footwear, furniture, clocks, music boxes, and musical instruments, all decaying in the royal storehouses.[53]

Kamehameha died in 1819 at the age of about sixty-six. His fleet of foreign-going ships probably never made adequate profits, even though most of the capital and operating costs had been derived from the extraction of natural resources, with free Hawaiian labor ashore. Most of the voyages to China by his ships were ruinous, at least partly due to the unscrupulous agents and merchants in Canton, lack of care, recurring repairs and delays, and related payments of high port dues. His son Liholiho (Kamehameha II) faced increasing debts, as resources from land and sea, used for financing these ventures, had appreciably decreased.

Despite mounting debts the new king went on to purchase more ships. His first acquisition, at enormous cost, was the luxury yacht *Cleopatra's Barge* (191 tons), bought from the American millionaire shipowner George Crowninshield Jr. Renamed *Haaheo O Hawaii* (Pride of Hawai'i), the ship cruised around the Hawaiian group with the royal family and leading chiefs until 1825, when it was wrecked. It was reported that the ship at this time was "manned by a drunken, dissipated, irresponsible crew from the captain down to the cabin boy."[54] About the same time, the ship *Prince Regent*, which Vancouver had promised as a gift, was also wrecked after less than one year in service.[55] To add to the problems of the royal family, news was received in 1825 that the king and queen had died of measles on a visit to England during 1824. They were there to elicit British political support and in the process incurred considerable expenditure.

The family, now with a boy king (Kamehameha III), faced numerous creditors, and with sandalwood and pearls exhausted, a bold maritime venture was conceived to solve these financial problems. Governor Boki of Oahu and Chief Manui'a of Hawai'i were to sail for Erromango in Vanuatu and acquire the still plentiful sandalwood of that region for carrying to

China on Hawaiian ships. Chief Boki was in effect to occupy Erromango as ruler in a Hawaiian attempt at colonization.[56] They sailed on 2 December 1829. Boki was in charge of the royal warship *Kamehameha*, with a complement of 300 people, including 10 foreigners, Hawaiian sailors, soldiers, servants, women, and some other Polynesians. His navigators were Blakesly (a watchmaker) and Cox (a silversmith), possibly neither being qualified in navigation or experienced in seamanship. Manui'a was in charge of the *Becket*, with 179 people. His navigator was more sensibly a former mate of a whaler.[57]

Other merchants were also seeking Erromango sandalwood in 1829–1830 with Pacific Island labor. The *Sofia* carried more that 100 Tongans to the island in 1829. On a second voyage in January 1830 the *Sofia* recruited 200 Rotumans for Erromango. The *Snapper* in turn delivered another 113 Tongans for sandalwood extraction.[58] The *Kamehameha* never arrived in Erromango, and no trace was ever found of the ship. The *Becket* stayed there for six weeks, but Erromangoans were alarmed at the arrival of four European-type ships with 600 or so Polynesians, and there was much hostility, malaria, and many deaths. The *Becket* returned to Honolulu on 30 August 1830 with only a few Hawaiians and foreigners left alive.

The ownership of foreign-going vessels by the royal family finally ended in the mid-nineteenth century. Foreign companies and institutions had, since the early part of the century, made ingress into trade, shipping, and regulatory provisions. These moves were clearly connected. Caroline Ralston describes how American sandalwood dealers "engineered the appointment of their employee John Coffin Jones as the first agent of the United States for commerce and seamen."[59] Not only did Jones promote sandalwood interests, but, to support the flagging sale of armaments, he also spread concerns over the possible recurrence of civil wars.[60] Richard Charlton, as an employee of a British commercial firm, was appointed as the first British government representative in Hawai'i and likewise served national commercial interests. Similarly, various American and British justices of the peace and other quasi officials acted simultaneously in commercial positions and could control the information on trade and shipping opportunities.

The last foreign-going vessel independently owned by the Hawaiian royal family was the schooner *Kamehameha III* (116 tons), which sailed to California in 1848. However, the French Navy commandeered the ship in response to a complaint by its consul in Honolulu regarding unfair treatment of French business interests by the Hawaiian authorities. The

French took the ship to Tahiti, where the Pomares had already been coerced into becoming a protectorate of France. The *Kamehameha III* was never returned to Hawaiian ownership.[61] The royal ownership of vessels, along with ships of numerous chiefs in the 1850s, was confined to the interisland trades and a few whalers. Increasingly these became commercially privately owned, including a few owned by island communities. Government income from maritime activities was now virtually confined to pilotage and port dues.

AOTEAROA

The transition from noncommercial to commercial forms of maritime trade by the Maori of Aotearoa emerged from a socioeconomic environment somewhat different from that prevailing in the rest of Polynesia at the time of contact. There was less social rigidity in control by chiefs in Maori society, and individuals and families became willing entrants to various sectors of the commercial system.[62]

Maori ways of living varied within a diversity of physical environments over the nine hundred miles or so from north to south. Land transport was often difficult, and people in all of the coastal areas had seacraft. The largest were the elaborately carved war vessels *(waka taua)* under ownership of communities *(hapu)* and tribal leaders, and most families owned small vessels *(waka tiwai)* used by the *whanau* (kin) as a form of personal property.[63] Distant ocean voyages had long since declined by the time of European contact, but there were strong attachments to the sea and very skilled shipbuilders. Folk memories and tribal names recalled the great migratory voyages. There was pride in these and in the physical prowess of warriors, as well as deeply held mores involving status, mana, and taboos.

The period of commercial relations between 1800 and the 1860s was fraught with conflict between ship and shore due to violations of Maori status, and the application by the Maori of the principles of *ihi* (fearlessness) and *utu* (revenge). Imported arms likewise increased the extent and intensity of territorial conflicts between Maori tribes. But it was also a period of technological changes in Maori seagoing and the consolidation of Maori control over virtually all seaborne trade along the coast, as well as to some overseas destinations.

Maori seafarers readily assessed that their magnificent war canoes, propelled at considerable speeds by hundreds of strong paddlers, were not suitable for carrying cargo and passengers, especially in rough weather.

The technical revolution involved the introduction of cloth lugsails—in place of the triangular sails of local fiber—to the bigger wakas. Maori carpenters adapted some of the kauri paddled craft to rowing by fitting oarlocks to their strong gunwales, thereby reducing manning and providing more room for cargo. The whale boats and longboats carried by foreign ships were copied, and more purchased, as were numbers of cutters, ketches, and schooners. A. Murray Bathgate and Clifford Hawkins consider that these advances in Maori-owned shipping contributed significantly to the great increase, spread, and diversity of Maori agriculture by facilitating marketing.[64] The Maori not only supplied provisions to fleets of foreign whalers and trading vessels but also supported virtually all of the thousands of Europeans who began arriving in New Zealand.

As elsewhere in Polynesia the process of technical change was assisted by the assimilation of foreign sailors who deserted ships, especially in the Bay of Islands, or were shipwrecked on other parts of the coast. This happened early. While loading spars for China at Hauraki in 1799, Thomas Taylor and three shipmates left the *Hunter* and lived with the Maori as commercial agents.[65]

The New South Wales colonial authorities recognized New Zealand as a considerable source of foodstuffs, timber, flax, sealskins, and whale oil, as well as a market for future exports and settlements. Governor King sent presents to chiefs, and several were invited to Sydney to further these near-colonial intrusions. However, many captains and crews who constituted the main European presence in New Zealand showed little respect for the Maori in their own tribal homelands, and even less so on board ships. In 1807, for example, Captain John Glen of the *Parramatta* (102 tons), owned by Hullets and Company of Sydney, got into some difficulties near the Bay of Islands. He obtained assistance and supplies of fish and potatoes from the local Maori. After it was indicated that some reciprocity would be expected, Glen had the Maori party thrown overboard. The *Parramatta* subsequently grounded in a storm, and all on board were killed in retaliation.[66] There were many such incidences of injuries to Maori people and assaults on the mana of chiefs, which were usually followed by revenge. This also resulted in the cessation of foreign trade in parts of the New Zealand coast when news of what was depicted as Maori savagery and cannibalism was circulated.

The most widely reported of these conflicts and *utu* was that of the massacre on the *Boyd* (500 tons). In brief, the *Boyd* was under Captain John Thompson and had transported convicts from England in 1809. The

Boyd then loaded sealskins and whale oil in Sydney and was proceeding to Whangaroa to top up with kauri spars. Serving on board, after experiencing a long and financially unsuccessful trip on a British sealer, was Tara (signed on as George). He was the son of Te Puki, a chief of Whangaroa, and was taking the opportunity of returning home.

During the voyage Tara was falsely accused of stealing spoons (which the cook had inadvertently dumped over the side). For this Thompson had Tara flogged. When the *Boyd* arrived in Whangaroa, Tara showed his lacerated back to the people. In reprisal Maori warriors boarded the *Boyd,* and seventy of the crew and passengers were massacred on the ship and ashore. Only two women, a child, and the cabin boy who had befriended Tara during the trip were spared.[67]

The British ship *City of Edinburgh,* under Captain Simeon Pattison, was at Kororareka when news was received of the massacre. The chief of that place accused his rival, Te Pahi (not Te Puki, the possible culprit), of instigating the attack. Te Pahi was much favored in trade with the foreigners and had visited Sydney. Based on this false information, Captain Pattison brought together crews from six vessels and destroyed Te Pahi's village, wounding him and killing sixty of his people. The Reverend Samuel Marsden later vindicated Te Pahi.[68] However, trade was severely affected overall, and fewer ships called at the Bay of Islands for several successive years. These and other conflicts moved Governor Lachlan Macquarie to issue a general order in December 1813:

> Whereas many, and it is to be feared just, complaints have been lately made of the conduct of divers[e] masters of colonial and British ships, and of their crews, towards the natives of New Zealand, of Otaheite, and of the other islands in the south Pacific ocean : And whereas several ships, their masters and crews, have lately fallen a sacrifice to the indiscriminate revenge of the natives of the said islands, exasperated by such conduct . . . master of the said vessel, and the officers and crew of such vessel, shall each and every of them, peaceably and properly demean themselves, and be of their good behaviour towards the natives of New Zealand, or of such of the islands in the South Seas as the said vessel may touch at in the course of this her voyage.[69]

The order laid down conditions to be met, with a penalty of 1,000 pounds for noncompliance.

The problems in enforcing any of these orders were absence of authority and lack of reliable evidence to refute the shipmasters' accounts. Violence and fraud continued to be perpetrated on the Maori. A case that resonated throughout New Zealand and New South Wales was that of Captain James Kelly of the *Sophia* out of Hobart. There are mixed versions of the events. According to Kelly, the ship was engaged on a search for seals and called at Otago to barter iron for potatoes. An attack on a boat's crew was seemingly encouraged by a Tahitian beachcomber from the brig *Matilda*, which had been attacked in 1813. Two of the *Sophia*'s crew were killed in the attack, and Kelly was wounded. The boat was then forced to pull off, leaving a third sailor on the beach. Kelly describes the plaintive cry of Wioree—"Captain Kelly for God's sake don't leave me"—before he was "cut limb from limb and carried away." Another attack occurred when a Maori war canoe tried to come alongside the ship but was repulsed. Several of the Maori, including the chief, were killed in this encounter.

The next day (24 December 1817), Kelly thought from the noise on the beach that the Maori were going to attack in numbers to board the *Sophia*. He would have known that his merchant seamen would be no match for Maori warriors in hand-to-hand fighting on board once the first volley of muskets had been discharged. He decided therefore to launch a preemptive strike ashore to destroy their navy. The sailors cleared the beach with gunfire and then destroyed forty-two canoes. To press home his punitive measure, Kelly burned the settlement:

> This town consisted of about 600 fine houses, and perhaps a finer town never was seen in any part of New Zealand ... and in about four hours [it was] laid in a heap of ashes. ... On the 27th of December, 1817, at daylight, we weighed our anchor and left Port Otago, and sailed to Chatham Island. ... [H]undreds of natives came down on the shore to see us off; we fired a volley of musketry towards them.[70]

For decades after the *Sophia* left the coast, the people of Otago watched for the ship or any other vessel they thought belonged to Kelly. Several ships avoided the area, although seventeen years after the destruction of the settlement the *Mary & Elizabeth* was attacked in the belief that she was owned by Kelly.[71]

The balance of power in armaments between ship and shore became more equalized with the trade in muskets and cannon. This also enabled old insults and defeats to be revenged by one Maori tribe against another, with lethal results. As this arms race built up, it took over much of the maritime trading for kauri and flax. Pat Hohepa refers to the "one-ton rule," whereby one ton of dressed flax would purchase two muskets, and another ton would give sufficient powder and shot. He observes, "Carrying muskets and pistols became as natural as carrying traditional weapons of wood and stone."[72] Hohepa estimates that the number of Maori who died as a result of the "musket wars" between 1820 and 1835 was around eighty thousand.[73]

Another profitable trade related to warfare was the export of tattooed human heads. Reverend Marsden raised this issue with Governor Ralph Darling on 18 April 1831. Writing after killings in the Bay of Islands, Marsden gave the example of Captain Brind of the ship *Prince of Denmark:* "The heads of chiefs have been brought to Port Jackson by the Europeans for sale. When the chief who is with me went on board the *Prince of Denmark* he saw 14 heads of chiefs upon the table in the cabin. . . . The chief knew the heads; they were his friends; when he retired he said, 'Farewell my people, farewell my people.'"[74] Marsden went on to call for a naval vessel to go to New Zealand and check the conduct of masters and crews. The New South Wales authorities acted swiftly, at least on paper, to this appeal. On 25 April 1831 Marsden reported, "The Governor has issued a General Order prohibiting the importation of the heads of the New Zealanders into N. S. Wales."[75] It is satisfactorily noted by Harry Morton that "William Tucker a sealer involved in trading Maori heads to Sydney was killed by the Otago people along with two other sealers."[76]

As various conflicts subsided, thousands of settlers from New South Wales and England increased, as did the demands for Maori-produced food and raw materials. The Maori in turn built and purchased additional vessels, the latter, from New South Wales, rather old and in poor condition. These ships transported more cargoes of potatoes, maize, and livestock to the growing pakeha (non-Maori) settlements. Already as early as 1829, however, there was pakeha competition in shipbuilding in New Zealand. Thomas Raine, with British subjects employed, was building bigger craft at Hokianga in the northwest of the north island.[77] His first vessel, the *Enterprise,* was wrecked under the difficult navigational conditions of the New Zealand coast. Many Maori vessels of European design also went the way of the *Enterprise,* through failure of the expensive and unfamiliar imported material for rigging and steering gear.[78]

Despite financial and technical difficulties, Maori control of vessels for coastal and trans-Tasman travel was clearly valued, not only for support of the *whanau* and a facility to market their produce, but also as a bastion of Maori freedom and independence.[79] It had been agreed by the New South Wales authorities in 1834 that New Zealand vessels would have free entry into Australian ports. Maori chiefs also established a shipbuilding yard at Hokianga and achieved a shipping register, and their vessels flew a flag as a symbol of an independent Maori identity. The chiefs followed this in 1835 with a "Declaration of the Independence of New Zealand."[80] The 1840 Treaty of Waitangi rendered this faint ambition void, although there was continuity of Maori-owned shipping for another two decades.

It is possible from records to appreciate the large number of merchant ships owned by the Maori. According to the list held at the Wellington Maritime Museum there were by the 1850s some 177 Maori-owned vessels. Ownership was divided between 69 named chiefs and 108 named places.[81] An 1853 report shows 180 Maori-owned ships, including 37 schooners and ketches in Auckland alone, all built in New Zealand. Also trading to Auckland in 1852 were 1,792 canoes, "which landed 6235 male and 2542 female travellers as well as a great variety of foods and livestock."[82] Most of these Maori-owned vessels operating coastwise were crewed by *whanau*. Neil Atkinson notes that "the divisions of profits were determined by traditional tribal practices rather than European maritime custom."[83]

By the 1860s what had been flourishing Maori shipping enterprises virtually disappeared. The alienation of Maori land, the related wars of resistance, growth in agricultural production by the pakeha, and greater self-sufficiency in New South Wales all reduced the supply of and demand for Maori produce. The valuable timber resources of New Zealand in turn attracted capital and shipwrights from overseas in the establishment of major shipyards. The new ships, owned by commercial enterprises, were bigger and better rigged than the aging Maori craft. The scow in particular was a sturdy, flat-bottomed 150-ton ship designed for the difficult conditions of the New Zealand coast. New Zealand shipyards built many other types of wooden vessels for European companies and for some communities over most of the South Sea islands.[84] Maori maritime trade and related activities were reduced to mainly wage-earning carpenters ashore and sailors on foreign-owned ships.

Other Indigenous Commercial Shipping Ventures

Maritime commerce spread gradually and unevenly to all the Pacific islands beyond the three main groups of Polynesia, and few other places attempted to enter the business to any significant extent during the eighteenth and nineteenth centuries. Tonga would have been expected to do so, considering the skills and knowledge of Tongan seamen in voyaging to distant groups and collecting tribute. However, from the late eighteenth century the preoccupations of the chieftains of Tongatapu, Ha'apai, and Va'vau were in waging wars and the acquisition of armaments from foreign vessels for this purpose. In 1802 the schooner *Duke of Portland* was attacked in Tongatapu, and all the crew killed.[85] In 1806 the *Port au Prince* was destroyed at Ha'apai. Many of the sailors were killed, but William Mariner and others were spared and later took part in a successful attack with Ha'apai warriors on Tongatapu, using cannon from the *Port au Prince*.[86]

Samoa likewise had a precontact history of voyaging, including links with Kiribati. The massacre of the boat's crew of *La Perouse* in 1787 gave the place a reputation for savagery.[87] Nevertheless, civil wars in the nineteenth century did attract ships trading in armaments. The newly designated consuls of Britain and America promoted this by retailing muskets, powder, and shot to both sides. Ralston notes, "Had they refused to sell the instruments of war it is doubtful if any fighting would have taken place."[88] As a result of wars, commercial trading in Samoa was minimal.

In Melanesia the chieftain system in many places covered, at best, loose federations and alliances and was less conducive to operating commercial vessels on a large scale. Only in Fiji did unified rule extend over a wide region under King Cakobau I. He seemed still dedicated to traditional vessels but during the 1840s was seeking a schooner for prestige, and the Tongan Ma'afu, controlling the Lau Islands, already ran one, possibly for the same reason.[89] Erskine notes that in Fiji in the 1840s "one or two of the more civilised chiefs already possess small single decked craft."[90]

In Micronesia, Caroline Islands' sailors were engaged in carrying commercial cargo on traditional craft,[91] but unlikely on a profitable freight-charging basis. Later in the nineteenth century Marshall Islands chiefs "owned their own small schooners or brigs sailed by foreign captains."[92] These captains were often former sailors who had been beachcombers and then settled as traders on various islands. In Kiribati, "King" Tem Binoka (whose father, Tem Baiteki, as the ruler of Abemama and other islands had killed off all the European traders in 1851)[93] bought the schooner *Coronet* (95 tons). He employed the *Coronet* in interisland trade and made voyages as far as New Zealand. Relying on successive European supercargoes and captains to run the ship, he described each of three: "He cheat a litty, he cheat plenty, and I think he cheat too much," expressing no doubt the views of other aspiring island shipowners who adopted this system of management. It is said that for the first two classes Tem Binoka had perfect tolerance.[94]

Conclusion: First Taste of Commerce

The period of 1800 to the 1860s brought most of the main islands of Polynesia and several elsewhere to the edge of the capitalist system. This was carried to them by commercial ships, thereby linking the Pacific people with the vast world of commerce in Europe, North America, and China and the growing economy of New South Wales. The new system was, as far as it could be understood, embraced by Polynesian chieftains. It was primarily exploitative in the sense that production became geared to the dictates of remote, unseen markets with their institutions of finance, brokerage, law, and insurance. New wants were stimulated—some useful, some merely leading to hoarding and conspicuous consumption, and others dangerously feeding destructive arms races between communities.

The capitalist-related trading economy was based on ethics quite different from those of most Pacific societies. Much of indigenous trade was guided by kinship, life-crisis ceremonies, and locational specializations, which enabled trade to take place widely as a form of insurance against physical disasters. There were competitive exchanges, but these also were seen as inverted in comparison with Western modes. In effect, prestige in Pacific society was generally accorded to chiefs and others from the ability to distribute rather than accumulate forms of wealth. Meanness and hoarding were a social stigma. In the traditional society, chiefs did possess wealth, but even in the less socially rigid Aotearoa communities the chief was still, as Firth puts it, "a kind of channel through which wealth flowed, concentrating it only to pour it out freely again."[95] The facility for the chiefly concentration of resources and labor from time to time enabled major social and strategic requirements to be met in the interest of the community as a whole.

The introduced new economic system did not overwhelm all the mores of traditional lifestyles. New commodities were incorporated into indigenous channels of trade, as was cash. Indigenous trade likewise flowed between places, carried along by commercial trading vessels (see chapter 10). However, the principles of the commercial trading system, based on buying cheap and selling dear, and the accumulation of personal wealth for the prestige and power it gave were soon adopted by the now deeply entrenched kingships of Tahiti and Hawai'i. This change was detrimental to customary leadership obligations, redistribution, and the health and well-being of the common people.

The royal entrepreneurs who entered the commercial system found that, to begin with, they had decided advantages. They could control all of the resources demanded, and soon learned the power of monopoly. They were able to drive hard bargains with buyers, as Captain Turnbull found to his cost in Tahiti and Hawai'i. They also had power over producers through the traditional right of concentrating labor for social purposes. This they now utilized in the interests of production for the market. The new labor regime meant continuous work and therefore the neglect of subsistence food cultivation and fishing. Further, the right to declare taboos was now exercised to prevent the consumption of pigs and other tradable foodstuffs. These abuses of customary rights and obligations led to the impoverishment of many communities nutritionally and culturally.

The market-driven ethos also brought about environmental degradation. Pacific societies in the early centuries no doubt destroyed elements of the natural environment they inherited, but by the time of contact they were basically conservationists. Those in the coral islands had little choice; they were bounded by finite ecosystems.

For the mass of ordinary people in Tahiti and Hawai'i there were few positive returns from hard labor and the rapacious attitudes to natural resources. Nor did the chiefs benefit in the long run from their partial adoption of the capitalist ethos. They failed to follow the necessary economic component of the system that required investing accumulated profits in the maintenance and renewal of vessels and other infrastructure. They tended to squander many returns. Maori owners were somewhat different; their primary motives in shipping and trade seem to have been to support families through the traditional redistributional mediums and to enhance community pride in their boats. But this may have led to contradictions within a plural society of being unable to save for investment while meeting traditional social pressures to carry people and distribute returns in the community. This left them exposed to the competition of profit-maximizing incomers.

From an inventory and examination of Hawaiian-owned ships, Peter Mills nevertheless cautions against undervaluing the contributions of these locally owned vessels and enterprises in the power struggles between indigenous and Western elements. He points out the indirect contributions of new related employment skills and technology.[96] One of the most lasting effects from this was the creation of a working class at sea and ashore. There was also an element to these maritime changes that went beyond the pressures of a new economy of capital and labor. Firth and Davidson in their seminal 1942 work said of the Pacific people in this period of change: "To them the ship was among the most remarkable of the material changes which Europeans had introduced into the life of the Pacific. They threw themselves into the task of building and handling these vessels with the same enthusiasm with which their fathers had perfected their knowledge of canoes."[97]

CHAPTER SIX

Under Foreign Sail

No man will be a sailor who has
the contrivance to get himself into jail,
for being in a ship is being in jail
with a chance of being drowned.
 —Samuel Johnson, *Journal of a Tour of the Hebrides*

The aphorism of Samuel Johnson reflected perceptions shared by people in Britain and America of life at sea in the late 1770s. Even in the reforming "rights of man" postcolonial United States, a new federal law of 1790 sanctioned the arrest of merchant seamen who deserted, and a law of 1835 still in effect conceded "beating, wounding, imprisonment, withholding suitable food and other punishments inflicted by the masters justifiable, if done with cause."[1] In 1874, a century after Samuel Johnson wrote, a surgeon in the US Marine Hospital Service was moved to complain: "No prison, certainly none of modern days, [is] so wretched [that] life within its walls [is not] preferable on the score of physical comforts, to the quarters and life of the sailor in the vast majority of merchant ships."[2] As for the safety of the ships, the British Parliamentary Select Committee on Shipwrecks in 1836 reported that many hundreds of lives were still being lost due to the following factors: "defective construction of ships, inadequacy of equipment, imperfect state of repair, improper loading, incompetence of masters and officers, drunkenness of masters and officers."[3]

Such was the maritime employment that thousands of Pacific seafarers entered in the eighteenth and nineteenth centuries. They were recruited, as going to sea was no longer appealing to many of the nationals in the traditional ship-owning countries, other than for the adventurous and the destitute. By first considering the reasons for shortages of European sailors, this account provides also a view of the rebellious attitudes engendered among crews and some of the conditions that then applied to newly employed Pacific sailors. Particularly discouraging for those in the maritime regions of Britain and America were the restrictions on the freedoms of merchant seafarers to join and leave their ships at will. Merchant ships arriving off British home ports during the many wars in the eighteenth and early nineteenth centuries could be met by armed tenders, and the most experienced seamen taken off and shipped out on men-of-war, causing enormous resentment. In such situations, the men also had to endure the loss of leave after a long voyage; the loss of pay, which "threw families on the parish"; and the loss of opportunities for earning the higher wartime wages on other merchant ships. Impressment violated the individualism of the sailor and turned "a youthful venture at sea into permanent bonding to the state."[4] It bred antiauthoritarian feelings, and there were many riots in British port towns. To avoid the press-gangs, British seamen sought other employment ashore, adopted false identities as foreigners, or joined foreign ships. The most popular of the latter were those of the American colonies.

Thousands of British sailors were already manning American ships, but they too were taken as "deserters" when these vessels were ordered to heave to by British warships. As a result there were even more riots in American ports against the authorities that were infringing the "rights and liberties" of sailors, and near-revolutionary ideas spread between ships and ports.[5] The press-gangs boarding both British and American vessels were usually met with resistance: "Any who ventured aboard a whaler, in particular, could lose his fingers on flensing knives or even have his head shattered by a harpoon."[6] These embittered sailors were in fact considered "prime movers in the American revolution."[7] The impressment of American seafarers did not cease after the War of Independence in 1783. It was estimated that in 1807 about six thousand American sailors were still serving in the Royal Navy against their will.[8] The searching of an American ship off New York in 1811 was in fact a major element in the declaration of war against Britain in 1812.[9]

For all their actions ashore against unfair administrations, the American and British seafarers found themselves little better off when at sea. Ships continued to be run under harsh and often brutal regimes. When on the high seas, merchant vessels were beyond the reach of national laws. It was only in the late nineteenth century that it was acknowledged that a merchant ship was governed by the law of the state under whose flag it sailed. Even then some of these laws simply legitimized the customary rights of masters to act as judge and jury at sea. They could flog and imprison sailors and make arbitrary deductions from their earnings.

It was in effect an already outdated, class-structured hierarchical society with no recourse to legal remedies open to the common seafarer (discussed further in chapter 7). Shore employment became more sought after, offering greater freedom and sometimes better pay. Thousands of British and other foreign seamen who had transferred to American ships took a further step to the burgeoning port towns of the United States and joined the migrations westward.[10] Even the disadvantaged American Indians were affected: "Native Americans began to find conditions intolerable. As a result the number of Native American seafarers gradually declined."[11]

As a result of continued shortages of crew, British and American ships frequently sailed shorthanded for the Pacific. The trips involved passages that were four to five months long, via the Cape of Good Hope or Cape Horn. American ships sometimes picked up a few sailors in the Atlantic Islands, but generally shipowners were not unhappy with depleted crews, which reduced labor costs during these unproductive legs of voyages. Not so for the disgruntled seafarers whose lives were endangered from shortages of experienced shipmates in bad weather and when beating around Cape Horn against strong headwinds.

Arrival in the trading and whaling areas of the Pacific entailed supplementing the crew, all the more necessary because ships would lose many of the original crew during the three to four years the men were employed in the Pacific. Most losses were due to desertion. John Turnbull, during his 1801–1804 voyage, observed "there does not occur a greater difficulty to all European ships in the South Seas than that of keeping their crew together, such is the seduction of the life of indolence, and carelessness, which the several Islands hold out."[12] It was not only the allures of the tropical islands that concerned shipowners. A group of whaleship owners in 1823 wrote to the colonial authorities, "The greatest evil we experience, and which we dread from our ships going to the settlements in New Holland, is that the convict women so demoralize the crews as to make them in a short time, from the best of sailors, become extremely mutinous, and we scarcely know an instance of any of our ships going there without greatly altering the conduct of the crew, many of whom desert."[13] Although the shipowners failed to recognize it, desertions could equally well be attributed to the conditions on board their ships.

There followed a series of memoranda to the British government advocating the formal annexation of New Zealand as an economic and strategic base, and noting the opportunities this would provide for the recruitment of Maori as sailors, "being very powerful, brave, and with strong natural abilities." To this was added that the Maori was "a docile race,"[14] possibly in the hope that this self-delusion would get rid of the problem of the so-called sea lawyers and bloody-minded European and American sailors. It was a view that the more brutal captains believed ultimately to their cost.

Other recommendations were also put forth at the time, such as these:

> A vessel bound to the Fiji Islands requires a large crew and it is best to touch at the island of New Zealand and take on 10 or 12 of the natives of this place, rather than take men from any other of the south sea islands or from Manila (except such as have been on this voyage previously), and they should be particularly careful not to take any men from the Navigator Islands [Samoa] as they are too treacherous and cannot be depended on.[15]

The cautionary note on the recruitment of Samoans as sailors reflected the persistent bad reputation of those islands, arising from the massacre of the boat's crew of *La Perouse* in 1787. Whalers by the 1820s were likewise returning with stories of treachery and savagery experienced in parts of Melanesia and Micronesia. Such tales led to more misgivings regarding taking crew from several of these islands. The situation was different in Tahiti and Hawai'i, where local seamen were encouraged by chiefs to serve and showed reliability even in difficult Arctic voyaging. Several Hawaiians are recorded to have been on that coast in 1788 under Captain John Meares.[16] The *New Hazard* increased her crew from twenty-four to thirty-three in 1811 for voyages to the northwest coast, additions that were simply designated as "kanakas" in logbooks and journals.[17] The ill-fated *Tonquin* had a Hawaiian crew of twenty-four when it was destroyed possibly by the captain after Indians boarded on the coast, and the fur trading ship *Beaver* took on ten "kanakas" in 1812, together with an experienced island sailor, bosun Tom.[18] American whalers subsequently obtained most of their crews in Hawai'i and Tahiti and also periodically at the Marquesas, the Carolines, and New Zealand.

The British colonial authorities responded to crew shortages by permitting ships to recruit convicts at Botany Bay and Port Arthur under a bond for their return. In 1833 the Tasmanian-based sailor Richard Copping noted seven to eight thousand "ticket of leave" men from the penal colony of Port Arthur serving on British and colonial ships.[19] These invariably included experienced seafarers, some of whom had been transported as troublemakers, strikers, and mutineers from the merchant service and the Royal Navy.[20] Many shipowners were not happy with the prospect of employing men they considered felons. Lord Sandwich also rejected the solution of criminal recruitment to overcome crew shortages in the Royal Navy, believing that it was more likely to increase "desertion and villainy."[21] In fact, convicts from New South Wales and Tasmania captured and sailed away on several merchant vessels, including the *Cumberland* (1797), *Harrington* (1808), *Trail* (1816), *Wellington* (1826), *Cyprus* (1828), and *Frederick* (1833).[22] Overall, the most favored solution to crew shortages was to attract more Maori and Pacific Island seamen.

Recruitment of Pacific Seafarers

The motives of Pacific men for joining foreign ships were no doubt similar to those of young men from New England and the traditional maritime regions of Europe. When John Jackson joined the *Joshua Carroll* in London during 1837 at the age of sixteen, he was "stimulated by the desire of seeing foreign countries and strange manners."[23] He arrived in Hobart in 1838, and so began a life of Pacific seafaring. Some islands readily responded with sailors, and some were particularly favored by captains. It was said of the young men of remote Rotuma, "They loved to visit foreign countries and great numbers of them shipped aboard English whalers."[24] In Melanesia the Loyalty Islanders were equally enthusiastic and were sought after.[25] In Micronesia, ships like the *Honduras,* after an attack in 1836 (see chapter 7), took on almost a whole crew of Ponapeans for the voyage to Honolulu.[26]

In addition to their enthusiasm for travel and love of the sea, Pacific islanders were attracted by the clothes and the apparent freedom and lifestyles of the sailors they saw ashore, as well as the prospect of accumulating wealth for returning home. Those who returned spread their experiences of distant voyages, good and bad, through the oral channels of communication between islands. Some of the Tahitians who sailed with Turnbull stayed for periods in Hawai'i, others met a Tahitian in Tonga who had been there for three years, and another in Norfolk Island, lately arrived from England on the ship *Albion,* looked resplendent as a sailor. In Sydney, Tahitians likewise encountered Maori seamen who had been to England.[27]

There were also some reluctant recruits, such as Marquesans who were kidnapped,[28] and in New Zealand victorious chiefs in the musket wars traded captives with captains.[29] Many did not return home. Some died, some deserted, and others were abandoned. Still more joined the transit populations of sailors, spending their money in new port centers and finding other ships outward bound. At these growing Pacific port towns, beachcombers established themselves as crimps and arranged girls and ships for sailors of all nationalities. Richard Copping walked off the whaler *Endeavour* in April 1840 at the Bay of Islands along with several other sailors and three harpooners, as "she was leaking badly." They sought other berths through the agency of a notorious lodging house in the Bay:

> Of all the orgies imaginable it was here. There were nearly 100 men, mainly deserters from different ships, drinking, singing and dancing, and fighting. The captains used to come ashore and get their men but dare not touch one. So when a ship wanted hands, two or three captains would come ashore and be hail fellow well met, call for a quantity of their detestable grog, get them nearly all drunk; and at night kidnapped as many as they wanted.[30]

Sailors would waken outward bound and in debt to the captain, who had paid the crimp. They would need to purchase more clothing, tobacco, and drinks from the captain's slop chest at inflated prices against future earnings:

> The next I remember I woke in the morn,
> On a three skys'l yarder bound south round Cape Horn,
> With an ol' suit of oilskins, an' two pair o' sox,
> An' a bloomin' big head, an' a dose of the pox.[31]

There were other, more open, informal ways of recruitment. Frank Bullen, who went to sea from England at the age of twelve, describes how at age eighteen he fetched up in New Bedford. Young Bullen heard a voice in the street "looking for a ship stranger," and he joined the whaler *Cachalot* bound for the Pacific.[32] So it was with many Pacific men in these port centers in the Pacific and beyond.

When the potential recruits presented themselves on board, the captain and mate made selections. The criteria were proven experience (no "sodjers"), good health, strength, and agility, as well as ready acceptance of the conditions being proffered, including the allocation of some clothing, food, and an advance in cash, all to be set against verbally agreed further wages or lays. They would be divided into starboard and larboard (port) watches and, on whalers, allocated to boats under the first, second, and possibly third mates.

Captains clearly preferred Pacific seafarers, who were used to compliance toward chiefs and thus unlikely to give captains trouble by demanding seafaring customary rights on board. The islanders were useful too as interpreters and understood the Pacific ways of trade. As sailors they were skillful at handling loaded boats through heavy surf when ships had to stand off and on. On whalers they acquired reputations as good harpooners and for boldness in closing on a whale. The keen eyesight of island sailors earned them the tobacco bonuses for spotting whales, and this, along with reading the signs of the sea for sudden squalls and reefs, made them invaluable as masthead lookouts.

Swimming and diving proved other important assets. Turnbull was impressed when, on approaching Hawai'i, he encountered people a mile offshore supported only by "a thin feather-edge slice of wood."[33] He refers also to Hawaiians diving from topgallant yards and swimming under the ship. This skill of deep diving was employed on pearling and bêche-de-mer ships, as well as for making underwater hull repairs and clearing fouled cables. The extent to which island men and women were at home in the sea is further alluded to in dramatic rescues. Copping describes how, when the *Harriet* of Sydney was totally lost near Te Puna in April 1840, "the crew would have been lost also if it had not been for the Maori women on board the ship swimming them ashore."[34] He relates also that when his own whaleboat broached to, and he was knocked overboard and trapped under the boat, a shark "lay hold" of his shoulder, but "my harpooner a Maori jumped overboard after me."[35] Similarly when James Bagley fell from the topgallant crosstrees, a Hawaiian seaman, John Mowhee, dived after him and told Bagley to hold on to his shoulder until they were rescued.[36]

For the shipowners a more compelling reason for employing Pacific seafarers was their lower costs in wages and victualing. The whaleship owner F. Parbury, who gave evidence at the British House of Lords Select Committee on the Navigation Laws, readily attested to this and expressed preferences for New Zealand (Maori) crews.[37]

Numbers and Ranks of Pacific Seamen Employed

It is not possible to establish with any accuracy how many Pacific seamen were employed on foreign ships at any one time. Often their existence can only be deduced in crew lists from the absence of a surname or the use of some comic names. More often there is simply a log entry of taking on kanakas or natives. The maritime press notices are no clearer—the ship

Charlotte, which arrived in Sydney on 24 June 1818, listed Paddy, Palmo, Moai, Boxho, and Dune.[38] Only a little more helpful was the entry for the *Endeavour* on 12 April 1817; after the names of Browning, Taganne, Tahee, Mairee, Pippo, Poona, and Jack are listed, "all Tahitians" is stated.[39] On Dillon's ship *Calder* in 1825 the multinational composition is periodically combinations of Chinese, Cook Islanders, Bengali, English, Irish, Tongan, Tikopean, Rotuman, Marquesan, Tahitian, and Maori, and the sailors' nicknames include "Governor Macquarie," "Major Goulburn," "Buckgarow Riley," and "Saltfish."[40]

In the course of a voyage there would be many changes of crew by dismissal, desertion, abandonment, death, and voluntary transfers. The whaling journal of Captain W. B. Rhodes of the barque *Australian* out of Sydney is typical. Of the original four officers and twenty-five men who sailed from Sydney in 1836, only three officers and seven of the others were still on board when she returned in 1838.[41]

Given all the uncertainties, a rough estimate would be that between 1830 and 1840 about five thousand to six thousand Pacific sailors were at sea on any one day on foreign-owned vessels. There could also be as many ashore in ports between ships and at home for long periods. In addition some two thousand or so manned commercial interisland and coastal vessels, and unknown numbers were on indigenous craft also engaged in carrying some goods. At best it can be said that a substantial commercial maritime population existed without which the fur trade, whaling, sealing, pearling, sandalwood, bêche-de-mer, coconut oil, labor transport, and even "blackbirding" could not have been effectively conducted.

The numbers of Pacific islanders that were engaged as sailors in the last-mentioned nefarious activity are particularly uncertain. Some were recruited voluntarily to man the boats for this activity, as Pacific sailors were very adept at handling the boats through the surf and onto beaches. This was the attraction for the blackbirders, who were engaged in deceptive recruiting and surprise kidnapping of young men, and some women, for the guano mines in Peru. The ships were crewed mainly by an admixture of Europeans.

The first vessel recorded in the Pacific Peruvian labor trade, which lasted for about three years, was the 151-ton barque *Adelante*. It called at Nukuhiva to pick up five Marquesan boat handlers. These ships raided small islands, including removing 1,407 people from Rapa Nui mainly during 1863. Some Pacific sailors were unaware when joining that they were to be slave traders. The 209-ton whaler *Grecian* signed on fifteen Maoris in Wellington in 1863 to make up the crew. When a European sailor and several others discovered at sea that the captain intended slave trading, they refused to sail farther and were eventually discharged in Samoa.[42]

A good port sample, showing crew numbers by place of origin, age, and rank, is that made by Susan Chamberlain for whalers out of Hobart from 1855 to 1879 and from 1860 to 1879.[43] Table 1 shows that there were still seafarers from numerous parts of the Pacific sailing on whalers out of Hobart as late as 1870–1879, after the height of the whaling era had past. Table 2 shows the age range of sailors. Most were eighteen to thirty years old, but some were as young as twelve, and twenty of them were over the age of forty, which seems unusual considering the dangers and lifestyles of whaling crews.

Based on these tables and other data in the Chamberlain study, some further details are also notable:

- The 183 Pacific boatsteerers shown represent about one-quarter of all boatsteerers on Tasmanian whalers. In rank order, boatsteerers

TABLE 1. Places of origin of Pacific sailors serving on Tasmanian whaling ships, 1855–1879

Period	New Zealand	Hawaiʻi	Tahiti	Melanesia and other Polynesian islands	Total
1855–1859	16	11	4	17	48
1860–1869	53	31	12	74	170
1870–1879	22	22	13	60	117

Source: Susan Chamberlain, *An Analysis of the Composition of the Tasmanian Whaling Crews Based on Their Crew Agreements 1860–1898* (Hobart, Tasmania: Crowther Whaling Archives, 1982).

TABLE 2. Pacific Island crews by age and rank on Tasmanian whaling ships, 1860–1879

Age	12–17	18–21	21–25	26–30	31–35	36–40	41–45	46–50	51–55	Total
Sailors	19	69	88	60	28	22	11	8	1	306
Boatsteerers	—	—	83	57	29	10	4	—	—	183
Officers	—	—	21	37	10	6	—	4	—	78

Source: Chamberlain, *Composition of the Tasmanian Whaling Crews.*

were drawn from Tasmania, the Pacific, Britain, and America. Most of the Pacific boatsteerers were aged twenty-one to thirty.
- The 78 Pacific men serving as officers are particularly significant. The total number of officers on Tasman registered whalers was 609. Ranked by national origin, they comprised Tasmanians, Pacific islanders, British, Americans, and Cape Verdeans.
- The ratio of Pacific officers to Pacific seamen in this sample is about 1 to 6, but the typical ratio of officers to other ranks on board is about 1 to 10. This confirms that, given the usual number of crew, Pacific officers had nationalities serving under them in addition to those drawn from the Pacific. It also signifies a fair degree of social mobility on whalers at this time.

There are only a few recorded instances of non-Europeans serving as officers on mixed-crew ships in the Pacific. When the English sailor Frank Bullen joined the American whaler *Cachalot,* he was confronted by a large black man who told him, "[It's] yes sir, when you speak to me, I'se de fourth mate of this yer ship and my name's Mistah Jones."[44] Harry Morton refers to a Maori who was chief mate of the Australian ship Francis, and a Maori second mate of the *Earl Stanhope* in 1837 who also became a chief mate. Morton adds that such positions disappeared with whaling.[45]

Most appointments as officers were made informally by captains. Until the mid-nineteenth century there was no legislation requiring certification, and not until the early twentieth century was this fully implemented in the Pacific.[46] Promotions during voyages were mainly for replacements. The captain would simply tell a senior apprentice or an experienced seaman to "get your gear aft" and act as a mate. Samuel Lang sailed from Boston as a foremast hand on the *New Hazard,* and in July 1811, in the course of the voyage, he became third mate, returning on the ship as second mate in 1813.[47]

Junior officers did not have to be very literate or very numerate. The chief mate would have required more education. On New England whalers he would have been young, possibly related to the captain and certainly to others on board. The position of captain was almost exclusively the preserve of the white Yankee Quaker. On other ships, captains would still usually be from the country of the owner and possibly themselves have investment in the ship. A combination of prejudice, limited education, and lack of capital combined to impede Pacific seafarers from reaching the senior officer level and excluded them from master.

The Social Environment on Board

Most Pacific seafarers in the mid-nineteenth century still came from a preliterate society. They could not write any personal accounts of their lives. This is not an absolute impediment to describing many aspects of their lifestyles and work. It was an ethnically diverse, polyglot, and predominantly male society on most ships, and there were a few literate sailors who left accounts of their experiences. They all faced the same dangers, shared the same food and sometimes the same girls, and communicated much of the time in the lingua franca of nautical pidgin. It was not a totally cohesive society even in the foc'sle (forecastle), but it was an isolated world separate from the land and had its own rules. These took precedence over many national customs. The Pacific youth who joined a ship as a deck boy could, when he learned the ropes, become an ordinary seaman. Men drawn from local vessels would soon obtain able seamen's rank (AB) and progress to foremastmen. Some would become petty officers in the ranks of bosuns and boatsteerers, and very occasionally junior officers on whalers.

The hierarchical structure of the personnel of a ship was replicated in the accommodations. Within the foc'sle the living spaces would be allocated by the sailors themselves according to work status. The foc'sle community represented the lower tier of an onboard class society. On a typical barque of one hundred feet or so in length and weighing two hundred to three hundred tons, the foc'sle would occupy tween decks extending about twenty feet from the bow. It would measure around twenty feet in breadth at the widest, tapering into the bow, and some five feet in height. Here fourteen or more men would be housed with their sea chests and bedding, although at sea about half could be on duty at any one time. The foc'sle was entered from a hatch on deck that had to be closed in bad weather.

Although there was legislation regarding the cubic feet of air in cells for convicts in the mid-nineteenth century, there were no such rules for merchant ships until the late nineteenth century. Consequently tuberculosis was added to the several ailments, including scurvy and venereal disease, considered to be sailors' troubles. When the sailor Richard Copping joined the Australian whaler *Caernarvon* at the Bay of Islands in 1842, he noted that the foc'sle crowd "appeared to be a mixture of all nations under the sun, and nearly every colour." The space he occupied was "about four feet and one half high" and as dark as a dungeon—"you had to keep on a sharp stoop to move about at all, and so infested with cockroaches and mice, that you could scarcely move without touching one or the other."[48] Frank Bullen describes joining the American whaler *Cachalot* in New Bedford: "I entered the gloomy den which was to be for long my home, finding it fairly packed with my shipmates. A motley crowd they were. I had been used in English ships to considerable variety of nationalities; but here were gathered not only the representatives not only of five or six nations, but longshoremen of all kinds, half of them hardly ever set on a ship before."[49]

Bullen's observation of longshoremen was related to the difficulties of getting experienced crews for whalers in America, Australia, and Britain. These ships spent months at sea hunting for whales and, only when they had to, called at remote places for water and firewood. When they obtained a sufficient catch, only then would they return home. Sailors never knew when they joined if they were on a voyage for many months or many years. They were unpleasant, slow ships that even on the open deck constantly smelt of blubber, blood, and smoke, and ships downwind knew they were whalers.

The well-built and more fastidious Pacific seafarers who joined the crowded foc'sles found these spaces particularly uncomfortable and stifling. They generally slept and ate on deck in the tropical Pacific. It was a different matter in colder latitudes. A wood stove and an oil lamp would be provided. These, along with perpetually wet gear hanging around and the normal habit of sleeping in working clothes or long underwear, did nothing to improve the atmosphere. The heating in cold weather was conducive to further infestations of lice, cockroaches, and other vermin in straw beds or mats.

The next class division on the ship was that of petty officers who were located in a deckhouse abaft the foremast. They included the bosun, the carpenter, the sailmaker, and on whalers the boatsteerer and the cooper, together with apprentice officers. The galley stood between the midships deckhouse and the mainmast. Nearby would be freshwater butts, casks for salt meat, and sometimes pens for pigs and fowls, all within sight of the officer of the watch at the after end. The cook would also have a berth near the galley, although he generally was of lower status than the others amidships. Some Pacific men cooked only on ceremonial occasions ashore, and they tended to look down on the cook on board as doing women's work or that of a slave *(kuke)*. On British ships the cook was usually a disabled or old sailor, and on American ships he was invariably black.

At the after end was the elite of the ship, either in tween-deck or raised poop accommodation. They comprised three mates and possibly, on British whalers, a surgeon. The saloon and pantry were located here and also the captain's cabin and dayroom. On this afterdeck was the steering wheel and main compass binnacle. It was the captain's personal domain and sometimes that of his wife. The only others regularly allowed on the poop were the officers of the watch, the helmsmen, and the captain's steward, as here also was the hatch to the lazarette securing the stores.

When at sea, the ship was a twenty-four-hour, seven-day-a-week society. All the sailors worked for at least ten hours each day. On watch there were spells as helmsman and lookout (when near land or whaling). Others on the watch tended the rigging and carried out routine work. Petty officers were mainly day workers, not watchkeepers. There was one easier period of two hours available to each sailor during the dogwatches at 1600–1800 or 1800–2000. Sundays, after the decks were washed down in the morning, were normally free, apart from helm or lookout duties and, on a few ships, a religious service by the master.

The free times on board were utilized for washing clothes, make and mend, and sleeping. These were also important periods socially for bonding in card games, telling tall yarns, and making music. On some ships alcohol was available from the slops (administered by the steward with profits to the captain), along with tobacco and other items. Popular instruments included drums, fifes, fiddles, melodeons, and ukuleles; the latter, along with drums, were familiar to Pacific sailors and adopted as their own. The men also contributed stories, dances, songs, and chants on Saturday evenings and special days. Turnbull remarks that the Scottish bagpipes animated Pacific islanders to rapture. Sailors also had other distinctive art forms based on life at sea and the tools they used. Stitching pictures with wools, painting sea chests, fancy knotting, and, on whalers, scrimshaw designs carved on whale's teeth with a jackknife and a needle and colored with lampblack as in Pacific tattooing.

New recruits were always the butt of jokes for entertainment. The Tahitians who joined the *Margaret* were terrified when their shipmates warned they would be harassed by infernal spirits rising out of the water as they crossed the equator. When the hilarity of crossing the line was experienced, the Tahitians were highly amused and ready to relate this, no doubt with embellishments, on returning home.[50] The rites of manhood in crossing the line were in effect a time when the hierarchy of life on the ship was turned upside down. Sometimes the ship would be hove to, and a sailor dressed as King Neptune boarded, took precedence, and gave orders. The uninitiated, regardless of rank, who were unwilling to contribute grog were suitably shaved and baptized. The court of King Neptune drank, and jostled and lampooned officers with antics and words. Captains generally stayed clear of these ceremonies while the brotherhood of the foc'sle established a brief republic, and even the sanctity of the poop deck was violated. Neptune was often accompanied by his wife, a bizarrely dressed hefty sailor, which brought another ambiguity to the masculine society of the ship.

The exclusively male composition and culture of a crew was also periodically challenged by the existence of a captain's wife. In 1853, for example, some 20 percent of masters of American whalers were accompanied by their wives.[51] How acceptable they were to the crew is difficult to say. Generally, in the folklore of the Pacific Islands, women at sea were considered to be in the wrong place. Some sailors felt, for good or ill, that women reminded them of home, others that women reduced their spartan isolation, while some hoped they might ameliorate the harsh behavior of the captain. Margaret Creighton contends that wives "more often underscored their own power and that of their spouse" and "they exacerbated class divisions." This was not just gender antagonism but "resentment of the privilege and power of the after cabin."[52] Sailors were also suspicious that the influence of the wife was such that the crew were serving under two masters. Certainly some of these women were formidable sailors and good navigators, and several kept journals.

There was as much ambivalence regarding all women in the life of a ship. Captain Turnbull had to allow the Hawaiian girlfriend of his second mate to join the ship for the passage from Honolulu to Tahiti, or else the second mate would have jumped ship and stayed with her in Hawai'i.[53] It was the practice on many Pacific-based ships from the time of Cook for women to accompany the crew between islands, to everyone's satisfaction. At other times women caused troubles. While the *New Hazard* was on the northwest coast, for example, "Mr Dork, an Indian, lost his slave girl; she went on board [the *Lydia*] to sleep with Mr Butler the second mate."[54] Dork had his revenge; he retrieved his girl, but in the process Captain David Nye of the *New Hazard* was shot in the arm. Similarly, on the *Cape Packet* in 1842 a quarrel "was occasioned by the presence of native females, [and] part of the crew natives of New Zealand, Bora Bora and Oahi deserted taking one of the ship's boats." The situation escalated in a very complicated way, resulting in several killings on the ship.[55]

There are a few instances in the Pacific of the nineteenth century of a woman actually being employed as a member of the crew (as distinct from females disguised as sailors). One unsuccessful occasion was when a woman steward was signed on the American ship *Golden Cross* in 1862. The log describes an altercation with the ship's officers on 5 October: "She hove a jug at the captain's temple (lacerating it) and left without liberty."[56] It is likely that she was exposed to the sexual tensions existing on board, a social factor that has contributed to the negative reactions of predominantly male crews in the past to a woman working on board during a long voyage.

There was also the possibility in the ship environment of conflicts over homosexual encounters. Such would not have been condemned in some Pacific traditional societies, although the missionary influences may well have permeated the ships. Certainly the puritan New England captains are unlikely to have tolerated "unnatural acts" on board. It was something they would try to deal with without explicitly acknowledging its existence. An item in the *Hobart Mercury* on 18 December 1858, which defended a captain who abandoned a man in an inhospitable shore stated, "The particulars of the man's conduct cannot be given in a public newspaper."[57]

The Working Environment

Most sailors were employed in hard and hazardous labor. The levels of work and the dangers involved depended on the rig of the ship, the weather, and the trades in which they were engaged. A common rig in the Pacific on long-distance trades during the eighteenth and nineteenth centuries was the three-masted barque of two to three hundred tons. Its mainmast stood about one hundred feet above the deck, the foremast around ninety feet, and the mizzen eighty feet. The main- and foremasts each carried four or five yards, on which were set square mainsails, topsails, and topgallants, and the mizzen carried a large fore- and aft sail. In addition there were numerous jibs and spritsails, giving a spread of over fifteen thousand square feet of canvas. All ships, large and small, had standing rigging comprising shrouds and stays, horizontal ratlines to facilitate climbing, and foot ropes attached to the yards to allow sailors to spread out athwartships. Elaborate running gear included halyards for hoisting and lowering sails, braces for training the yards, and numerous sheets, bowlines, and other ropes amounting to about thirty or so separate ends. These were all led through blocks and tackles and operated from on deck at each side of the ship.

For the Pacific sailor these rigs were different from their traditional vessels, on which the sail work was done from the deck. Most were used to heights and wind from collecting toddy or nuts on high trees and soon learned the ways of working aloft. The basic systems of rigging were similar on most ships of the same type (barque, brig, schooner, cutter), enabling recently joined sailors to find their places aloft or on deck at a given order. For those working aloft the adage of "one hand for yourself and one for the ship" was not always possible in bad weather and darkness. The reefing and furling to shorten square sails under strong winds and a heaving ship involved keeping feet tight on the footropes and using knees and elbows as leverage to free both hands for gathering up the sail. There had to be confidence between the men along the yard that all would work in unison, that their shipmates on deck would correctly tend the ropes, and that the helmsmen would keep the wind in the right place. Any negligence could mean falls from the high rigging and almost certain death. The sailors on deck were likewise exposed to hazards as they manned the ropes. Each watch would be led by an experienced AB, and all would haul together on a call, while deck boys at the end of the line took up the slack around the belaying pins. A sea breaking on board could sweep any of them over the side.

These operations of handling a big ship in bad weather depended on the combined skills of a few sailors responding to a single command of the captain or mate. Anyone proving incompetent or shrinking would, at best, be resented by the crew as a danger to all their lives. The Pacific sailors with experience on the larger indigenous craft, or who served on the recently introduced smaller interisland and coastal vessels, would not have been surprised at the intrinsic discipline of the crew. The differences were that the barque and other ships carried more sails, had complex systems of rigging, and had more hierarchical divisions of labor than they were used to.[58]

Samuel Leech, writing in 1812, was overstating the industrial analogy of the big nineteenth-century sailing ship, but he nevertheless provides a graphic portrayal of a vessel with organizational behavior new to Pacific society: "Each task has its man, and each man his place. A ship contains a set of machinery, in which every man is a wheel, a band, or a crank, all moving with wonderful regularity and precision to the will of its machinist—the all-powerful captain."[59]

On many Pacific Ocean voyages there were long runs under the trade winds when there would be little routine handling of ropes and sails. Then work tasks would increase in mending, scraping, painting, pulling oakum, caulking, splicing, and other not unpleasant individual sailorizing tasks on deck. In fine weather Pacific sailors, wearing few clothes and with coral- and tree-hardened bare feet, would work aloft, overhauling rigging.

It was a different matter in high latitudes under stormy and cold conditions. Pacific seafarers were hampered by wearing gloves, breeches, furs, oilskins, and boots, which must have contributed to accidents when working aloft handling stiff and frozen sails. They suffered also from chest complaints and frostbite. Nevertheless their Pacific maritime culture was such that they willingly shared the masculine bravado of their shipmates against the perils of the sea. The dangers of storms were, in the eyes of sailors, all in a day's work. Reynolds portrays this in his understatement of the near loss of the ship when homeward bound in the stormy higher latitudes of the Pacific, 550 miles west of Cape Horn:

> At five a sea came in on larboard quarter; knocked down the man at the wheel (the same who fell overboard when the topmast was carried away), cut a large gash over one eye and bruised him badly. Broke the wheel to pieces, necessary bulwarks, etc. Called all hands, set trysail and fore-topmast-staysail. At six shipped a sea upon larboard bow, knocked away bulwarks as well forward part of fore rigging and broke tiller. Set fore-sail. Kept before the sea which was most tremendous, but we made excellent weather all things considered. Set main-topsail; it one half tore from foot rope; unbent and bent another; raining most of the time. Spliced main brace twice!!![60]

Arrival

> We're homeward bound to the joyful sound
> With a full ship, taut and free,
> We'll not give a damn as we drink our rum
> With the gals of ol' Maui.
> —Stan Hugill, *Sailortown*

The tensions of a voyage were removed when the ship arrived at one of the Pacific sailor towns. These included Honolulu, Lahaina, Papeete, Kororareka, Apia, Levuka, and Kosrae. Here they had the company of thousands of other sailors of all nationalities, and increasing numbers of women. They were free of captains, the confined hard and dangerous life of the ship, and the constraints of traditional Pacific society.

They spent their accumulated earnings as described by Richard Copping in the Bay of Islands, until they shipped out again. Many Pacific sailors became dangerously independent. They had lived as equals in multinational foc'sles, and in overseas ports they encountered dishonest and immoral men and women of the same nationalities as the missionaries and others who preached European virtues in their home islands. There were sailors' riots in Lahaina in 1827 when the missions tried to get a ban on women visiting the ships,[61] and in Honolulu in 1852 as several thousands demonstrated and defied the authorities. These sailors were regarded as a necessary evil for the economies of the growing towns, not least in the transfer of money and goods to the thousands of women who arrived during the whaling season. Gavan Daws also describes how the women "returned home a few months later gaudily dressed, and in many cases infected with venereal disease, which they spread about the district."[62]

It was in the Pacific sailor towns that the stereotypical view of the drunken irresponsible sailor was formed by officials, missionaries, new settlers, and the leaders of traditional society. Their perceptions influenced subsequent legislation (see chapter 7). They saw the somewhat riotous ceremonies as multiethnic crews paid off and said good-bye to old shipmates, and when they joined another ship and bonded with new shipmates. William Giles uncomprehendingly describes the sailing day of the *Bobtail Nag* when he watched the "mixed crew of white men and kanakas sprawling about the decks in various stages of inebriation."[63] But many others went home to wives and families for long periods. Bullen writes about this aspect of the Pacific sailor when his ship picked up Tongan seamen waiting at Honolulu to ship out on a suitable vessel that would eventually drop them off at their home island of Va'vau.

> Being short-handed, the captain engaged a number of friendly islanders for a limited period, on the understanding that they were to be discharged at their native place, Vau Vau. There were ten of them, fine, stalwart fellows, able-bodied, and willing as possible. They were cleanly in their habits, and devout members of the Wesleyan body, so that their behaviour was quite a reproach to some of our half-civilized crew. Berths were found for them in the forecastle, and they stood their places among us quite naturally, being fairly well used to a whale-ship.[64]

CHAPTER SEVEN

Dangers, Mutinies, and the Law

PACIFIC SEAFARERS, in common with all mariners, faced dangers at sea. Many ships were lost with all hands in bad weather and on reefs. Sailors were also drowned when washed overboard, were killed by falls from rigging and other occupational accidents, and were exposed to violence and diseases in some trading areas. Periodically they were victims of physical and mental abuse under unscrupulous masters. Many of these situations were considered inevitable components of seagoing. These negatives were compensated for by the mobility and freedom of a temporary seafaring life, and if all went well, the accumulation of money by young Pacific men to obtain land, a boat, or a bride or to meet some other personal goals. Occasionally sailors rebelled against grossly unfair and brutal treatment by resorting to desertion or mutiny, as there was little chance of recourse to law. When modern legal provisions emerged, they were primarily for the protection of property. Seafarers did have residual benefits from this as related economic assets, although they were considered somewhat unreliable but replaceable.

The problems of determining the place of Pacific seafarers in this multinational matrix of life and death on foreign ships is the perennial one of statistics. The fact that there are no reliable statistics on mortality is not surprising, since it was only in the late nineteenth century that approximate returns of the deaths on board British merchant ships were published, covering the two years from 1875 to 1877.[1] It was estimated that during this period 12,408 seafarers died on British ships, yielding a mortality rate of 1 in 60 serving seamen. This confirmed work at sea as the most dangerous of all occupations. The statistics were actually gross underestimates, since no account was taken of seafarers who died ashore from injuries and disease sustained while serving at sea. As late as 1924, fleet surgeon W. E. Home commented on records of deaths on merchant ships in the medical journal *Lancet:* "If the figures referred to bags of coffee or tons of coal, that would be alright: it would be in the financial interests of certain people to keep a watchful eye on the returns. But deaths of seamen are nobody's concern."[2]

The only overall indication of deaths at sea of Pacific people is a Hawaiian newspaper item for the period 1841–1858, which reported more than 600 persons lost on Hawaiian interisland vessels.[3] It is safe to assume that the mortality rate among Pacific sailors on foreign-going ships was little different from the British 1 in 60 for serving seamen. The main categories of deaths would also have been shared, with some modification for Pacific conditions. In the case of British ships the causes of the 12,408 deaths were drowning by wreck of vessel, 34 percent; drowning by accident other than wreck, 25 percent; diseases (10 recognized), 20 percent. The balance included other accidents, suicides, and murder. Drowning from wrecks due to storms may have been less in the Pacific, but shipwrecks from running on uncharted reefs were more prevalent. There was also the factor of unseaworthy vessels, and there were plenty of these in the whaling and sandalwood businesses. In addition there were the hazards of attacks on boats and ships close to shore.

Shipwreck

A factor that increased mortality in all ships was the practice of sailors not abandoning a vessel to save their own lives until all hopes of the ship's surviving had been exhausted. The reason for such apparent dedication was the rule that wages ceased on loss of the ship, and any accumulated earnings were likewise forfeited. When a ship was lost, insurance was paid to the shipowners and cargo interests, but nothing to seafarers or their families. There were charities in Britain and America that gave some help, and for a time in the eighteenth and nineteenth centuries British seamen had sixpence per month deducted from their wages to support the Seamen's Hospital in Greenwich.[4] But the families of lost or injured Pacific seafarers could depend only on support from the community. The names and places of origin of Pacific seafarers lost were in any case not always known to the shipowners or authorities.

The ships most prone to loss were the whalers. They tended to range widely after migrating whales, and captains did not build up the detailed knowledge of specific sea areas as did those on regular runs. Charts were inaccurate, and even known dangers seldom carried marks. For example, the Minerva reefs in the southern sea area between Tonga and Fiji claimed unknown numbers of ships. With certainty those shipwrecked there in the nineteenth century were the *Minerva* (1829), *Libelle* (1848), *Caroline* (1859), and *Sir George Gray* (1866). The *Canton,* which ran on the reefs in 1855, was able to break free by a feat of seamanship.[5]

Whalers did have some advantages when it came to crew survival after foundering or grounding. They carried four or so stout whaleboats, each with a compass, oars, a lugsail, and water tanks, and the Pacific crews were expert at handling them. From ashore on Minerva reef, the crew of the *Caroline* reached Fiji, over three hundred miles away, in six days. The boats from the *Independence,* which grounded on a reef in 1835, made it to Tahiti, while the crew of the *Thule* of Nantucket, which ran on an unknown shoal in 1845, also reached safety in whaleboats.[6] Morton refers to a boat crew that survived only because a Maori sailor could make fire and catch and cook fish.[7] There are also records of survival when boats were not available. The schooner *Shaw,* belonging to Captain Bernard of Kaua'i, ran aground on a tiny island one hour before sunset when bound for Ascension [Palau]. They lived for four and a half months on coconuts, fish, and brackish water before being rescued.[8] On the other hand, when the *Canton Packet* ran ashore in the cold north Pacific in 1867, four of the five sailors who died of exposure were Hawaiians.[9]

Occupational Accidents

Numerous deaths and injuries occurred on board all vessels, but whaling once again heads the list. This was partly because of the hazards of the work, but also because of a built-in incentive to take risks through the system of lays. This system awarded each of the crew a share in the value of the oil landed at the termination of a voyage. The following is a typical distribution of gross oil profits: captain, 1/12; mate, 1/28; second mate, 1/40; carpenter and boatsteerer (harpooner), 1/90; surgeon, 1/90; and seamen, between 1/100 and 1/180. The earnings of sailors were thereby directly related to the catch, not to the time spent at sea. If few whales were caught over a voyage of several years, then once deductions were made for tobacco, drink, clothes, soap, and fines, there could be little, if any, payoff. Consequently every effort was made to catch whales, regardless of risks.

The dangers of whaling were present at all stages of the operations. On whaleboats men were carried overboard with the rush of rope after harpooning, and boats were also pulled down with a deep-sounding whale (e.g., those of the *Flying Childers,* 1852; *Highlander,* 1855; and

Asia, 1878). A boat could be taken away at high speed with a whale and never recovered, and many more were shattered by the tail flukes of frenzied whales (e.g., *Runnymeade*, 1849; and *Islander*, 1876). Smashed limbs were common; for example, the Tahitian mate Cocky died after both of his thighs were broken. Once a whale was towed alongside the ship for butchering, sailors could fall off the cutting stage and be taken by sharks scavenging around the carcass. Many more were injured by razor-sharp flensing knives and cutting spades. On the *Wallaby* in 1841 a young seaman had his leg severed by a spade and "took ten agonising days to die." Massive slabs of blubber being hauled on board from masthead purchases were dangerous—Captain Edward Copping was crushed in 1880 during this operation.[10]

In contrast to whaling, most of the deaths in sealing occurred ashore. Sailors were landed in remote locations to kill and process seals under a system of lays, while a ship went whaling or trading elsewhere. The young Maori chief Ruatara, who served as a sailor, described how he, two Tahitians, and ten European seamen were landed on Bounty Island in 1808. It was five months before their ship *Santa Anna* returned. They suffered from lack of fresh water and fed only on seal meat and seabirds. Two of the Europeans and one Tahitian died during this time.[11] Such circumstances were not unusual, and incidents of cannibalism among sealers left on remote islands were reported in the *Sydney Press*.[12] Loss of ships was particularly common in the interisland and coastal services throughout the Pacific. Dangerous surf, reefs, and missing stays on lee shores were causes, but also the degrading of navigational skills, overloading, and poor maintenance of the new types of vessels were contributory factors. Between 1845 and 1861 there were thirty-one shipwrecks on the coasts of the Hawaiian Islands alone.[13]

Attacks on Boats and Ships

The cutting off of whaleboats, which were operating close to the coasts of places like Bougainville and Buka Island, was a constant hazard. The boat of the brig *Inga* was cut off and attacked in the Carolines in 1852.[14] There was also the danger of boarding. In 1836 on the whaler *Awashonha* at Barings Island (Namorik) the captain, officers, and several sailors were killed by boarders who armed themselves with cutting spades; the Society Island sailors and others had to jump into the sea to try to escape.[15]

The most exposed to danger of attacks were the crews of sandalwood vessels. As on whalers, the lay system induced extreme risk taking. John Jackson in 1849 notes that sailors, "collected at Sydney or picked up among the islands," received 1/72 of the value of the wood. He also described the ships as "nearly worn out, and . . . unfitted for other branches of commerce."[16] Many of the crews on the sandalwood vessels were Loyalty Islanders of sixteen to twenty years of age. Sailors were drawn also from Erromango, Tanna, and Aneityum. The list of seafarers massacred on the *Star of Tahiti* at the Isle of Pines in 1842 included Polynesians from the Marquesas, Mangaia, Aitutaki, Rarotonga, and New Zealand, in addition to the captain (Thomas Ebrill) and nine Europeans.[17] Shineberg records 34 sandalwood vessels (out of 209 arrivals) attacked between 1842 and 1855. Most frequently such attacks took place on the coasts of Vanuatu and New Caledonia. Some 107 sailors and 9 passengers were killed, and 6 ships destroyed.[18]

The bêche-de-mer and shell trades held similar dangers. Everyone on the Hawaiian brig *Waverly* was slaughtered at Kosrae in 1835. Six months later the *Honduras* of Boston arrived, and all on board were killed, except the mate and a steward. These two survivors managed to slip the cable and remarkably sailed the ship for eleven days to Ponape. There they obtained a new crew of Ponapeans and returned to Honolulu. At the time that the *Honduras* was sailing to Hawai'i, other Ponapeans killed Captain Hingston of the whaleship *Falcon* and several of the crew. This resulted in joint retaliation by the crews of three ships, along with some beachcombers against the local community. The chief was captured and sentenced by Captain Charles Hart of the *Lampton* to be hanged. Hart arranged a grotesque pantomime for the seamen of the three ships, during which "demons" terrified the chief before he was hauled to the yardarm to hang.[19]

Pacific seamen stood by their European shipmates and were killed, although on one reported occasion, four were spared because of their color.[20] Attacks were sporadic and often carried out in revenge for mistreatment or theft by earlier ships. Other causes included insults to chiefs, violations of taboos, and the abduction of women. In the mid-nineteenth century the reason was no longer simply suspicions toward strangers. Andrew Cheyne said of an attack in 1852 that the boarders must have served at sea: "They appeared to understand the management of a ship very well. The moment they got possession of the deck, they put the helm up, and kept the brig away, right for the reef, with the intention of running her on shore."[21]

Exposure to Disease

The young men from the Pacific were probably initially healthier than most of their European and American shipmates. On the other hand, they were more susceptible to diseases, encountered during foreign voyages, to which they had no natural immunities. Conditions in the foc'sle were also conducive to the spread of infections from Europeans, such as tuberculosis, and they became victims and carriers of venereal disease from multiple contacts with women ashore and on board.

The health of Pacific sailors was undermined generally by poor nutrition. Basic victuals on foreign-going ships on long passages comprised salt meat and hardtack biscuits, to which was added dried peas and other storable items, along with tea, coffee, sugar, and sometimes beer, while fresh water was often noxious. For Pacific men this diet was alien and nutritionally inadequate. They were used to bulky starch food, together with coconuts, greens, fresh fish, and meat as the true food *(kaka-nidina)*, which was prepared and eaten communally as an important component of their cultures.

When the ships were around islands, fresh supplies were available to them. Pacific sailors were sometimes able to obtain fresh food by fishing and by trading tobacco (paid for out of future earnings) for fowls and other items ashore, but this was not always possible on whalers. As a consequence outbreaks of scurvy were common. In 1855 the whaler *Pryde* called at the Bay of Islands with scurvy on board, and several of the crew then deserted. In 1876 the *Runnymeade* reported that seven of the crew were ill, including a thirty-seven-year-old experienced seaman Sam Walwo from Hawai'i, and that another sailor had attempted to jump overboard. In 1878 the *Sapphire* arrived at Hobart with the majority of crew suffering from the disease, and two already dead. Dr. W. L. Crowther, who was noted for his dedication to recording whalers, wrote an outraged letter to the *Hobart Mercury,* saying the *Sapphire* crew were all close to death. For this, he was heavily criticized by the shipowners and the local business community.[22]

Venereal disease was less serious but more common. It was difficult for many sailors to avoid, and the remedies on board were ineffectual. On the *New Hazard* it was reported to Captain David Nye that a seventeen-year-old apprentice had "swollen testicles," who replied, "I'll cut him tomorrow," but this sort of treatment was more of a lesson than a cure. The captain demanded to be told of the girls and the sailors who brought them on board. The crew said nothing, although Stephen Reynolds ruefully records that the girls had also stolen their "allowances of pork!!!"[23] The pox was simply considered another occupational hazard.

Medical Care

Medical care for accidents and illnesses was always inadequate. The surgeons that some British whalers carried were variable in qualifications and status, as is reflected in their share of the proceeds from the lay, which was between that of an AB and of a carpenter. William Dalton, a surgeon on the whaleship *Phoenix* from 1823 to 1825 and the *Harriot* from 1826 to 1829, kept a diary. He qualified in 1821 at the age of twenty after paying for an apprenticeship of observing operations in London and obtained membership of the Society of Apothecaries. He went to sea to earn some money and for adventure. He notes that on his first trip to New Zealand he cared for another surgeon, John O'Brien, who died of tuberculosis. He also describes visiting the London whaleship *Francis,* lying offshore, and finding that all the crew were ill with scurvy. Only the captain and mates were well enough, as they had retained a store of potatoes. Had the weather turned bad, the ship would have been lost, as several undoubtedly were in similar circumstances.[24]

Like surgeon Dalton, the sailors were aware that fresh vegetables could avert scurvy, and they also knew there were substitutes. On the *New Hazard* while on the northwest coast the men made spruce beer as an antiscorbutic. In 1844 an act was passed in Britain that all British ships were required to issue lime juice, but it was many years before ships complied with the act. On most vessels the crew relied on the experience of the captain for medical attention. He had a medical chest that contained purgatives, potions, sometimes laudanum, an instruction manual, and simple surgical instruments. A captain who was bold enough to amputate to prevent gangrene could only stupefy an injured sailor with rum and provide a leather thong for the patient to bite on. Death usually followed from trauma, lack of antiseptics, or loss of blood. Morton points out that on whalers there was a "higher proportion of insane people than the normal population."[25]

Abuse of Seafarers

The dangers and hardships experienced by sailors were generally considered as "perils of the sea," which self-preservation and good seamanship could ameliorate. It was a different matter when seafarers were at the mercy of unscrupulous masters and violent bucko mates, against whom they had no protection while at sea. Most abuses were directed toward non-Europeans in the crew, although not exclusively.

Nor were all captains guilty of abuse; many were highly respected by crews for their fairness. Captain William Campbell of Sydney, who was part owner or full owner of several ships that he operated with Pacific crews, was well regarded, but he gave up the sea when his ship the *Harrington* was captured by convicts in 1807.[26] When the sailor Richard Copping and his shipmates decided not to sail on the whaler *Endeavour* in 1840, because they considered the ship unseaworthy, Copping nevertheless recorded how sorry he was to leave Captain Studley and noted that "he was always kind to me."[27] Nor was it always true that black seafarers were discriminated against. Many Nantucket whaleship owners held antislavery sentiments and hired ex-slaves, not simply as cooks. Edward Stackpole writes,

> On board the whaleships from Nantucket and New Bedford, early in the nineteenth century, the negro was a valuable member of the crew and his advance to an officer's berth was not unusual. When the *Loper* arrived at Nantucket on September 7, 1830, with 2,280 barrels of oil, after having made one of the shortest voyages ever recorded—fourteen months and fourteen days—the owners, including Captain Obed Starbuck, gave a dinner to the almost entirely negro crew.[28]

However, Spate notes that "there was a sharp decline in decency after 1825 as the Quaker element lessened."[29]

A general form of abuse of Pacific seafarers was the theft of their identities. They were almost all given a single European name or nickname when they joined a ship. This was not part of the Pacific tradition of exchanging names; rather, it was more akin to the practice of slave owners. It meant that those with indigenous names or titles signifying chiefly status were suitably put in their place below the Europeans.

When it came to remuneration, it was the rule that Pacific sailors received less than Europeans of the same rank. Samuel Marsden indicates that they were accustomed to this when he wrote in 1814, "I told the New Zealanders who acted as sailors, that I would pay them for their services, the same as I paid the Europeans according to the work they did—at this they were astonished and much gratified."[30] Some on other ships received no remuneration whatsoever for their labors. The case of "George," a chief of Whangaroa, is recalled. He spent about one year on the sealer *Elizabeth*, and partly because of the unfair lay system, he received nothing in return. After further abuse, he was avenged by the massacre of the crew of the *Boyd* in 1809 (see chapter 5). As late as 1877 W. G. Giles records that when the *Bobtail Nag* was supposed to be paying off its Efate sailors after a labor-recruiting voyage, Captain Inman simply said, "They are niggers[;] let them wait for their pay," pay that it seems they never ever received.[31]

In most ships the non-European sailors were beaten to a greater extent than others, as in the treatment of the black cook and steward on the *New Hazard*. Likewise, on this ship the Hawaiian sailors were unfairly treated. When the mate found a cask of molasses, the head of which had been gnawed by rats, he took his displeasure out on a Hawaiian: "Mr. Hewes struck one of the Kanakas with a large rope over the head so that he fainted."[32]

Some of the ill treatment on several ships was an attempt to drive long-serving sailors into deserting, whenever it was possible to find replacements. A sailor who deserted forfeited all his earnings and share of the lay he would be entitled to at the end of the voyage. The money then accrued to the captain. Treatment was so bad for the steward on the *New Hazard* that he voluntarily offered "all his wages" to the captain if he would simply permit him to transfer to another ship and "allow him to go home." The armorer of the same vessel tried to jump ship, but as there was no opportunity to replace him, he was caught and suitably restrained. The second mate, having trouble in shackling the armorer, was shouting for assistance to "knock the booger stiff with a stick or a hammer."[33] Some captains, from whatever causes, had continuous difficulty in keeping a crew. The whaler *James Steward* entered Sydney for repairs in 1847, and "as the original crew had given trouble a practically new crew was signed on and the ship left for the Gilberts." After whaling in the North Pacific, it arrived in Hawai'i, where once again all the crew deserted. Their desertion was attributed to news of gold finds in California.[34]

When seamen could not be driven to desert, or for other reasons were unwanted, they were simply abandoned and once again lost all their belongings and wages. In January 1813 while the *New Hazard* was at anchor below Canton, an offending sailor referred to only as Jack (who does not appear in the crew list) was ordered into the ship's boat and set ashore in a paddy field "without his being allowed to wait for his chest and bedding or money" (although his shipmates did slip him four dollars).[35] Similarly the captain of the *Roman II*, after flogging and confining members of the crew in irons, landed "seven troublemakers" on Nukunau Island in 1851.[36]

Very occasionally accusations of abandonment came to a court of law. The *Hobart Town Courier* reported on 19 July 1848 that Captain Hudespeth of the brig *Patriot* had been accused of forcing three men ashore on a remote part of the coast of Australia. Two of them died from starvation during a three-hundred-mile walk, but the third tried to bring a case against the captain, who was absolved because they were troublemakers.[37]

There are a few documented accounts of abandonment and related abuses. In 1811 Captain Michael Fodger of the *Trial* left a party on the uninhabited Palmerston Island. The group comprised four Europeans, one American, one Brazilian, and several Tahitian sailors who were to collect bêche-de-mer, pearl shells, and shark fins. The ship never returned for them. One year later Fodger passed the island on the *Daphne*. Even though one of the abandoned sailors swam out and reported that two of the Europeans were dead and one injured with a spear wound, Fodger refused to pick them up. The crew of the *Trial* offered to forgo wages to compensate for the time and provisions involved, but still Fodger refused. Later the same captain threw fourteen Rimatara Islanders over the side to drown and also abandoned sailors on an island in Tahiti, shooting one and recommending to the local chiefs that the others "have their brains beaten out with stones."[38]

Ruatara, a young Maori chief of the Ngaputi in the Bay of Islands, left a more detailed account of treatment on board a sequence of foreign ships. He told his story to John Nicholas and Samuel Marsden of the Sydney Mission, who befriended him. From this and other sources the main events are summarized as follows:[39]

> In 1805, at the age of eighteen, Ruatara joined the whaler *Argo* as a common sailor. The ship was commanded by Captain Baden, and Ruatara was allocated by him to one of the whaleboats. They went whaling in New Zealand waters for about twelve months before the voyage terminated in Sydney. Ruatara was discharged there but received no remuneration for his services.
>
> At Sydney, Ruatara joined the *Albion*, which was commanded by Captain Richardson and also engaged in whaling around New Zealand. After six months or so, Ruatara was paid off at the Bay of Islands with "various European articles." He stayed ashore for six months before joining the sealer *Santa Anna*, commanded by Captain William

Moody. The ship landed him and others on Bounty Island (the deaths of three of the sailors have already been mentioned). When the *Santa Anna* returned, Ruatara and the survivors loaded eight thousand sealskins, and they sailed for England.

The *Santa Anna* arrived in the Thames during July 1809. Ruatara was confined on board to assist with the unloading. He was then discharged without money or proper clothing. The captain told him to go aboard the convict transport vessel *Anna* and the owners would pay him his due when he arrived in New South Wales. He was in effect abandoned, sick and impoverished. He saw little of London and nothing of King George III, which was one of his life's ambitions.

When Ruatara eventually found the *Anna* lying downstream, the commander, Captain Charles Clark, described him as naked and sick. Clark managed to prevail on the captain of the *Santa Anna* to issue Ruatara with some seagoing gear before he would take him. There appears to have been no payment on the *Anna*, nor did he ever receive money due for sealing or work done on the *Santa Anna*. It was on the convict transport vessel that he met the missionaries who assisted him.

At Sydney, Ruatara joined the whaler *Frederick*. The captain promised to land him in New Zealand when the ship called there during the voyage. The ship did lie off the Bay of Islands at one stage, quite close to his home village of Rangihoua. He was not allowed to land, and the ship bore off for Norfolk Island. Ruatara was highly distressed, having been missing from his family for three years. The captain did promise that on the return voyage from Norfolk to England, he would be calling at the Bay of Islands and would pay him off.

At Norfolk, Ruatara and three Maori sailors were occupied handling workboats through heavy surf and nearly lost their lives. The captain then abandoned them without money, provisions, or clothing and sailed for England. Fortunately for Ruatara, Captain Gwyn of the whaler *Ann* called at Norfolk and found him in a distressed condition. The captain signed him on, and after five months he was paid off in Sydney. At Sydney, Ruatara was looked after by Samuel Marsden and the mission. He found work again on the *Anne* and eventually was landed in New Zealand. He gave up seagoing and took to agriculture. Surprisingly Ruatara remained friendly toward the pakehas, but not surprisingly he died at the age of twenty-eight.

Most other Pacific sailors who died at sea or were abandoned were never heard of again. They became what David Chappell aptly terms "double ghosts,"[40] both themselves and their memories having been lost forever. When Robert Louis Stevenson arrived on the yacht *Casco* at Nukuhiva in the Marquesas on 28 July 1888, he met "an old, melancholy, grizzled man of the name of Tari (Charlie) Coffin":

> He was a native of Oahu, in the Sandwich Islands; and had gone to sea in his youth in the American whalers. . . . [O]ne captain, sailing out of New Bedford, carried him to Nuka-hiva and marooned him there among the cannibals. The motive for this act was inconceivably small; poor Tari's wages, which were thus economised, would scarce have shook the credit of the New Bedford owners.[41]

Mutiny and Piracy

The maritime traditions of the Pacific included respect for the navigator who guided the ship through the dangers of the ocean. The crew could be relied on to follow his orders. In turn they expected the captain to show an unfailing duty of care toward the ship community and to consult on many aspects of the voyage, as is still the custom in the less formal interisland vessels (see chapter 10). They brought these social mores on board foreign ships and met with some similar views in the foc's'le on the customary rights of seafarers. The difference was resorting to the act of mutiny at sea, which was something new for Pacific island seafarers.

The tougher of the foreign captains that Pacific seafarers encountered on these foreign ships recognized only two responses to their orders, either "duty or mutiny"; there was nothing in between. A member of the crew who made a suggestion or a complaint would risk being accused of disobeying the lawful commands of the master. This was not mutiny, but captains could draw a fine line between complaints and mutiny in the legal isolation of a ship.

A mutiny meant the takeover of a ship at sea by its crew and was always a hanging offense. It was not a frequent occurrence in the Pacific, even if the most famous mutiny occurred there. More common was the expression of a personal grievance by an individual sailor, the representation by the crew of a foc's'le acting as a spokesman, or, less common at sea, a refusal to work. The latter strike action was traditionally resorted to by sailors in port. The very term "strike" emanates from sailors in its original warship meaning of stopping a ship by striking at its sails and masts, or striking the ship's colors as a signal of surrender.

Some of the more arrogant captains on both merchant and naval ships allowed simple complaints to escalate into strikes and sometimes mutinies. This even occurred in the British Royal Navy during wartime. Complaints over wages and food in the 1790s led to strikes in British ports, which were then classed as mutinies. Admiral Cuthbert Collingwood told the captains thereafter that "they would be unwise not to redress the first complaint or grievance" and perceptively added that sailors "should not be allowed to feel what power there is in so numerous a body." When this failed, it was customary to hang one or two mutineers (often chosen by lot), commute a few to transportation, and pardon the rest.[42]

Strikes and mutinies were usually a last resort planned and agreed to by badly abused foreign and ultimately island sailors. The Hawaiian sailors on the *John Little* mutinied in 1834 and threw the captain over the side. The crew of the *Thetis* mutinied in 1835 and killed the captain and mate while they were sleeping. The sailors of the whaleship *Planter* of Nantucket were so incensed by their treatment that on 18 December 1849 they assembled on deck and refused duties. The captain loaded a musket and "shot dead the ringleader" and then one other, after which "the rest submitted."[43] On the whaler *William Penn* on 6 November 1853, the crew of fifteen kanakas had come to the end of their tether. Led by the harpooner Henry, a native of Hawai'i, they armed themselves with whaling lances and spades and took over the ship. In the mutiny Captain Isaac Hussey was killed, along with the cook George Reed. The chief mate Nelson was wounded, as was the Chinese steward. Only two of the five Europeans on board were unharmed. The Hawaiian sailors said they had no wish to kill anyone or to take the ship; they clearly just wanted to get off. They took two whaleboats and landed ashore. The ringleader Henry was later shot, and the boats retrieved by the *Herald of Fairhaven*.[44] There are many such accounts in court and local records.[45]

These types of mutinies seemed to be unplanned spontaneous responses to brutal incidents. They were most likely to occur on a trochus shell and pearling vessel carrying large numbers of sailor-divers and enforcing dangerous deep diving by bullying. Not surprisingly, the tyrannical Captain Michael Fodger met his end in such a venture during the latter part of the 1812 voyage of the *Daphne,* mentioned above. The *Sydney Shipping Gazette* on 13 November 1813 gave the first account of this incident:

> Captain Fodger, having shipped 25 Tahiti divers proceeded to Palisers. On 29th August he was knocked down with a club on his own deck, and rose no more. Mr Marcus Vanderdyne, chief mate, was next assaulted and wounded, but ran below and making his way out of

the cabin window, was seen no more. Wm Gill seaman, desperately wounded, got below but after was brought on deck and deliberately killed. Three others were wounded and put on an uninhabited island without provisions, w[h]ither five of their unhappy companions had leaped overboard and escaped."[46]

The *Gazette* added the news that the *Queen Charlotte* (Captain Shelley) was also "captured at Paliseer Island by Tahitians who had been taken on as divers." They murdered "Leslie mate, Harris second mate and Watson Australian boy."[47] Both ships were later rescued and returned to their owners. In the case of the *Daphne,* Captain Theodore Walker of the whaler *Endeavour* repossessed her. He then acted as judge and jury and hanged one of the mutineers from the yardarm. This was an illegal act on his part, as a merchant ship captain, but he was never brought to account.[48]

There were several other mutinies that involved Pacific seafarers. Accounts of these appeared in the press of the time, drawn from evidence given in court against the mutineers and from horrifying stories then circulating. Little of this information is likely to have been objective regarding the conditions on board and the circumstances of the mutiny. Sailors, knowing the dire consequences that would result from such actions, would not have embarked on them lightly.

Other mutinies were planned in the foc'sle, and oaths of secrecy taken. Sometimes a paper was drawn up and signed by each of the seamen as a customary round-robin, on which there was no first or last signature or mark. The leader was usually one of the best seamen—a foremastman, bosun, or harpooner—well respected by the others. He was articulate and prepared to speak to the captain on behalf of the rest of the crew to avoid the more drastic measures. It is not known who the leader was who was shot by the captain of the *Planter* when the crew assembled. The Hawaiian harpooner Henry, who led the crew of the *William Penn,* also remains anonymous as a person, as do many other seafarers who spoke or acted against injustices and were hanged from yardarms.

Other mutinies were planned ashore by sailors before they joined a ship. Most of them were motivated, not out of grievances or desperation, but by monetary gain, and as such they were, in law, closer to piracy on the high seas than to mutiny. Some, however, may have been acts by embittered sailors at having been abandoned or forced to desert from other ships without wages and possessions. The mutiny on the whaleship *Globe* of Nantucket was probably an act of piracy. When the ship called at Hawai'i in 1824 after two years of whaling, it was deserted by six of its young sailors. The captain signed on a group of six or seven replacements led by a harpooner, Samuel Comstock, and including one Hawaiian, one of "Indian blood," and a black steward. Some had clearly planned to hijack the ship, and within one week they had killed Captain Thomas Worth and the first mate and thrown the second and third mates overboard. They then proceeded to sail the vessel to the Marshall Islands.[49] Most were subsequently killed by local people, including the Hawaiian, who, it seems, had not mutinied.

A similar instance was mutiny on the whaler *Sharon*. The captain needed to replace eleven of the crew who had deserted at Ascension Island (Ponape). Among those who came on board was a group of Kingsmill (Kiribati) Islanders. They were clearly experienced sailors, as they took over the ship while the rest of the crew and mates were away on whaleboats. They killed Captain Norris and others on board. Only because the ship's boy was able to signal a warning from the masthead to the returning boats was the ship recaptured by the rest of the crew, after a fight. Possibly also planned as a pirate act was the attack on board the sloop *William Little*. The Hawaiian leaders Napalac and Kaheniau, after killing Captain Carter and then ransacking and scuttling the ship, returned on boats to Honolulu with others of the crew, claiming to be castaways. They were eventually arrested and both ringleaders hanged on a yardarm of the king's ship *Niu* in 1834.[50]

Seafarers and the Law

Considering the neglect of legal rights and the conditions at sea until well into the nineteenth century, it is surprising there was not more violence. Most captains acknowledged that seafarers had rights to complain and to negotiate on certain matters under the "customs of the sea." Remnants of these customs were inheritances from the ancient rules of the Rhodian Sea Code of the eighth century and the Rules of Oleron in the fourteenth century. They originated in the medieval city ports of Europe, and while they were primarily for the protection of shipping and trade, embedded in them were some basic rights of seafarers that actually far exceeded the then legal rights of workers on land.[51]

In the course of time, separate states adopted laws on employment, including prohibiting forced labor, withholding wages, and protecting health and safety in different occupations. Seafaring was generally excluded from these, in the mistaken belief that ships were covered by inherited customs of the sea that had the force of law under the master. On occasions when incidents on board came to court, it was seldom that the actions of the master were ruled against.

Because of their legal isolation from national laws, multinational crews continually appealed to the customs of the sea, as preserved in their oral traditions that had been carried between ships. Before signing on a ship, they would negotiate wages and a scale of provisions and would assess what they considered to be a safe ship and safe manning. The success or otherwise of these efforts would depend on labor supply and demand. At sea in the absence of clearly defined safety rules, the crew would be vocal regarding who was capable of going aloft, how many hours they should work, the quantity and quality of food, and what constituted brutal treatment as distinct from acceptable punishments. Most masters recognized the rights of seamen to express opinions on these matters without being accused of mutinous behavior.

Pacific sailors would soon have assimilated these aspects of crew culture. In addition a few new laws that applied to Pacific seamen on foreign ships were introduced by the colonial authorities during the nineteenth century. Governor King of New South Wales issued a general order on 26 May 1805, prohibiting the "beating or ill use of Otaheitans, Sandwich Islanders or New Zealanders" and "it is to be clearly understood that such Otaheitans etc are protected in their properties, claims for wages, and the same redress as any of His Majesty's Subjects." The order also stated that "they should not be left in the colony without employment."[52] Primarily designed for the regulation of the labor trade generally, this legislation also covered seafarers.

In 1814 Governor Lachlan Macquarie followed with a Government and General Order stating that "no master or seamen of any ship or vessel belonging to any British port, or any of the colonies of Great Britain . . . shall in future remove or carry there-from any of the natives without first obtaining permission of the chief or chiefs of the districts." Similarly, masters could not leave natives in a district without permission of chiefs or magistrates. It was added that disobedience of masters would be prosecuted with the "utmost rigor of the law."[53]

These orders were not entirely paternalistic in their motives. King and Macquarie were concerned with reprisals against ships in the Pacific as a result of the abuse of crews by some masters, and they were nervous about the concentration of unemployed sailors in colonial towns, especially in proximity to recalcitrant convicts. In general the legislation was ineffective. In 1816 Samuel Marsden charged Captain John Martin with seizing canoes, kidnapping several natives from Santa Christina Island (Tahuata) in the Marquesas, and forcing them to leap into the sea, But "the bench was prepared to do no more than find the charges substantiated."[54]

Subsequent laws that were introduced ostensibly to protect sailors were influenced by the perceived behavior of riotous seamen in port towns, and there was much of that at times. These laws had an adverse effect on seafarers. Craig Forsyth correctly observes, "Since the early 1800s American seamen have had a very low status, which maritime laws and codes have caused and helped perpetuate."[55] The type of legal opinion to which Forsyth no doubt refers is that stated by US Justice Story in the case of *Harden v. Gordon* in 1823. In part this opinion states, "Every court should watch with jealousy any encroachment upon the rights of seamen, because they are unprotected and need counsel; because they are thoughtless and require indulgence."[56] In 1825 Lord Stowell, the leading British Admiralty judge, delivered a similar opinion when he compared the thoughtless improvident seamen with their prudent ship-owning gentlemen employers:

> On the one side are gentlemen possessed of wealth, and intent, I mean not unfairly, upon augmenting it, conversant in business, and possessing the means of calling in the aid of practical and professional knowledge. On the other side, is a set of men, generally ignorant and illiterate, notoriously and verbally reckless and improvident, ill provided with the means of obtaining useful information, and almost ready to sign any instrument that may be proposed to them; and on all accounts requiring protection, even against themselves.[57]

These apparently paternalistic views belied the professionalism of seafarers and reduced their credibility when they complained of bad conditions and abuses at sea.

The continued increases in the losses of ships led to further legislation, which contained a belated recognition that, in order to reduce losses, more improvements were required at every level on board ships. From the 1830s to the 1860s a plethora of government bills became law, including requirements for minimum space in the foc'sle, a scale of medical provisions, the issue of lime juice for the prevention of scurvy (in Britain), examinations for certificates of competency, articles of agreement, and much more.[58] There were still anomalies. The US statutes of 1857 prohibiting compulsory labor left seamen as the sole exceptions, and shanghaiing to obtain crews for US ships was not effectively prohibited until

1906.[59] The independent government of Hawai'i in the 1840s to its credit tried to secure bonds for the return of its nationals from foreign ships and also appointed a representative in Sydney to look after the interests of island sailors between ships.[60]

The subsequent improvements in living and safety conditions applied equally to all seamen on the multinationally crewed, foreign-going American, British, and other European and colonial flag vessels. When it came to remuneration, a negative differential usually continued to exist between Pacific seafarers and others. Improved pay, safety, and living conditions attracted more European, American, and Australasian crews. Attitudes of enlightened self-interest began to prevail on board that either Pacific island seafarers received equal pay with the European races or they should be excluded from national flag vessels, together with Chinese and other lower-cost crews. Many European seafarers supported equal-pay proposals, especially since shipowners were against them. Owners frankly stated they saw "restrictions on the employment of foreigners as the unnecessary blunting of a useful, tactical weapon in labour disputes,"[61] and Marion Diamond has noted that "the first occasion in Australia of the use of islanders as strike breakers" occurred in shipping during 1846.[62] These conflicts of interest became an increasingly common feature of Pacific seafaring in the age of industrialization and colonization, which is discussed in chapter 8.

CHAPTER EIGHT

Companies, Colonies, and Crewing

THE COMMERCE, TECHNOLOGY, and imperial politics of the mid-nineteenth century transformed seafaring generally and had major repercussions for the sailors of the Pacific. The period was one of increasing industrialization of merchant shipping in Europe and America. In contrast to the near merchant adventuring voyages of past centuries, ships now became parts of a structured world system for the distribution of manufactured goods from the centers of industry, and for the transportation of massive tonnages of raw materials and foodstuffs from peripheral areas of the world. In turn, ocean passenger ships of the period, in both sail and steam, moved millions of people between places in an enlarged global economy. Sailors in the ship-owning countries were similarly becoming more industrialized. They acquired new skills for mechanization on deck and for steam propulsion. They also faced, as they saw it, unfair competition in wages by crews drawn from less developed countries in Africa, Asia, and the Pacific, and they combined in defense of wages and conditions under new industrial trade unions.

The overseas trading areas of the industrial countries were increasingly being demarcated as spheres of interest through resident commercial enterprises, agencies, and consuls and coming to be served by national shipping. These commercial developments were precursors to political annexation. The actual processes of colonization of the Pacific region is beyond the scope of this study, but it had such significance for Pacific seafaring employment that it needs to be summarized before considering crewing.

The progress from informal trading to more structured shipping, and on to large company dominance, moved quite rapidly. In Fiji during May 1839 the missionaries Cargill and Calvert remarked that a few Europeans were based at Levuka: "These men lived with native women, built boats, made chests, planted food, and traded with the natives for biche-de-mar, turtle shell, coaconut oil and arrow-root, which they sold for articles of barter to vessels principally from America. Several of them chartered their small schooners, and hired themselves to these trading vessels."[1]

By the early 1860s around two hundred Europeans were more widely settled in Fiji as traders and planters. The British consul at Levuka reported on methods of trading, which had moved from itinerant buying and selling on board to serving small-scale island traders: "The masters generally make the tour of the several groups of islands, calling at each of the trading stations, and replenishing the stock of the resident traders as they may require to have it renewed. The cargo is seldom consigned to any merchant residing in the islands, but is left for the master or supercargo to dispose of to the best of his judgment."[2]

Already political intervention in these activities was emanating from distant foreign governments with no real authority in the country. The British consular record book of Fiji from 1863 to 1865 includes warnings to chiefs: "Now it is your duty as chief to keep your people in order and protect the property of the white traders. . . . [T]hink well over these matters and punish all evil doers."[3] By the late 1860s a wider dispersion of settlers had occurred, and it was necessary to have regular communication with bigger firms and overseas ships at the port town of Levuka. In 1874 a local fleet with Fijian crews owned by foreign traders and planters included "36 ketches, cutters, and schooners from 2 to 12 tons; 27 other vessels under 5 tons; and many larger ranging up to 60 or 70 tons."[4]

As island economies diversified, so did the volume and types of shipping. New craft were built in New Zealand and ultimately elsewhere in the region. They were designed specifically to meet the physical and economic conditions of the islands. Mainly these were three- and two-masted schooners between 70 and 200 tons (such as the *Samoa*, shown in Figure 8.1). They carried small square topsails and two or more fore and aft mainsails and had streamlined hulls for speed and low draughts for access. The topsail schooners could sail closer to the wind than the previous foreign-built traders and whalers, they were nimble at tacking, and seldom did sailors go aloft to shorten sails in bad weather. Crew sizes were reduced on average to a master, one or two mates, and six or so sailors.[5] This was a considerable economic advantage at a time of social and political pressures to recruit higher-wage sailors from the growing European populations at places of shipbuilding and ship owning in Australia, New Zealand, and America.

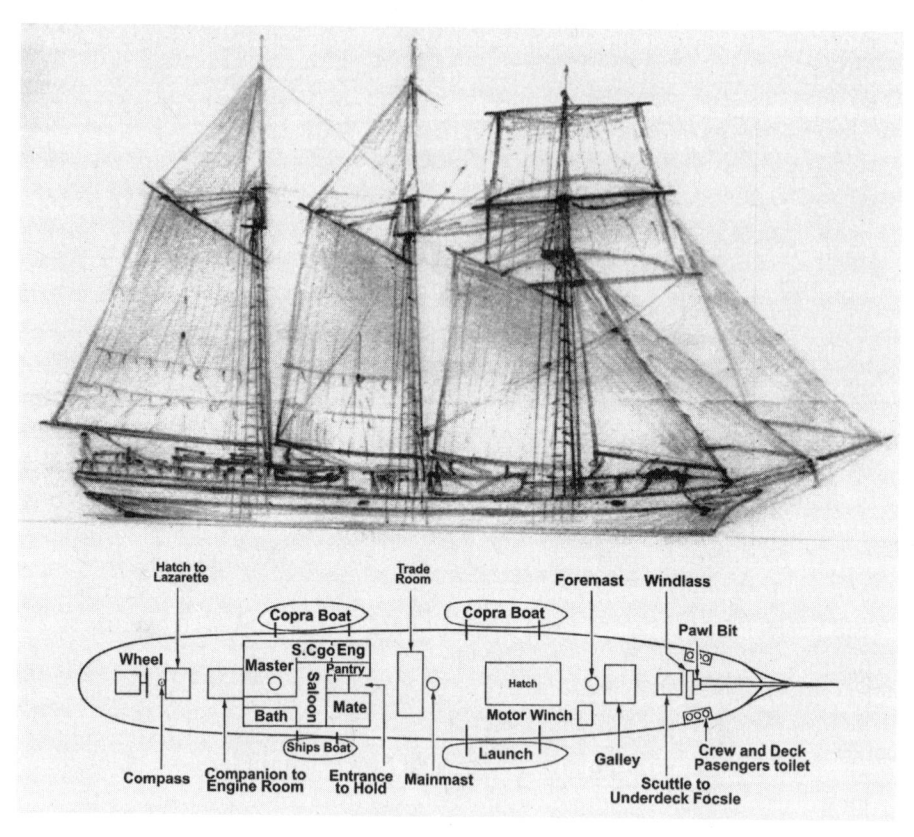

FIGURE 8.1. The *Samoa*, a typical three-masted auxiliary topsail schooner of 171 tons, measuring 106.8 by 25 by 11.2 feet. Built in Whangaroa in 1902, she plied as a German recruiting vessel in the Pacific. During 1922 she was acquired by Burns Philp for trading in the Gilberts. The drawings are by Captain G. Heyen, who was mate of the *Samoa* from 1922 to 1923. She was lost in 1924.

Major Merchant Shipping Companies

With the rise in the demand for island products and the profits to be derived from this, and even more from the sale of trade goods, there was greatly increased interest from large European trading houses. The company that established the model for future Pacific commerce was Godeffroy and Son of Hamburg. Its ships of the White Falcon Line were already engaged in passenger and cargo carriage to the American West Coast and to New South Wales. They entered the Pacific island trades from a depot in the Tuamotus in the 1850s and Samoa in 1857.[6] The company recruited local beachcombers or established new resident traders, irrespective of nationality, in networks over most groups of islands.[7] They purchased coconut oil and ultimately copra on commission, and the goods were then carried by Godeffroy's ships and chartered schooners mainly to Apia for onward transportation to Valparaiso en route to Europe.

A sequence of other foreign merchant companies followed that competed against each other but cooperated when it was advantageous against island producers. Most of the companies were financially supported by their governments as they consolidated commercial spheres of interest. The new companies built on the trading patterns of the schooner era. They went on to employ ships of increased tonnage and introduced technological changes from sail with auxiliary engines to fully powered steamships. Over this period British trading interests were served by vessels direct from the United Kingdom and through Australasian transshipments.

Merchant shipping companies operating from Australia in the 1850s included a Chinese firm in Sydney, On Chong, which sailed to the Gilberts, and Burns Philp, which traded to New Guinea in the 1880s and thereafter to most of the Pacific (except Tahiti). From New Zealand came McArthur and Company, Henderson and MacFarlane, and the Union Steamship Company, sailing to Fiji, Rotuma, Ellice, the Gilberts, the Cooks, Samoa, and Tonga. Henderson and MacFarlane had already taken over most of the Maori commercial coastal routes around New Zealand in the 1850s.

The German companies that followed Godeffroy included the Deutsche Handels- und Plantagen-Gesellschaft (DHPG), Jaluit Gesellschaft, Ruge, Norddeutscher Lloyd, Hernsheim, and the Capelle Company. They operated from Ponape, Yap, and Jaluit in the northwest and from Apia and Sydney, to New Guinea, the Solomons, Fiji, the Gilberts, the Marshalls, and Tonga.[8] The French Société Française, Ballande and Son, and Messageries Maritimes covered the New Hebrides, New Caledonia, and the Society Islands. Japanese merchant companies arrived in the 1890s, mainly the ships of Nippon Yusen Kaisha (NYK). They traded into the Marianas, the Carolines, the northern Gilberts, and Sydney but were effectively excluded from the Marshalls by the Germans. The Dutch vessels of Koninklijke Paketvaart Maatschappij (KPM) Line also operated from Southeast Asia to Sydney, calling at New Guinea. The French had services direct from France to New Caledonia and New Hebrides, from which large fleets of schooners belonging to settlers operated more widely.[9]

American companies, including Messrs. Crawford and Messrs. Wightman, operated out of Jaluit in the Marshalls and Butaritari in the Gilberts, and John Rothschild, sailing from Samoa. Several American sailing ships ran from San Francisco, calling at Hawai'i and crossing the Pacific to the Far East. These fast clippers dominated most of the long-distance routes until the Civil War in the 1860s. Smaller American schooners were very active in Hawai'i and periodically traded from there to Tahiti and to the Marquesas. During the 1830s about ten schooners were still owned by the Hawaiian royal family. By the 1850s these were sold to private investors. Of the sixty-five ships then registered in Hawai'i, only a few were owned by native Hawaiians; most belonged to Americans, many of whom were by then Hawaiian citizens.[10]

Colonization

The managers of the major merchant companies based at the main entrepôts in the islands were often ex-sailors. Several acted as consuls for their governments and supported the companies in many ways, including evoking gunboat diplomacy. A prime example is John Bates Thurston. He served at sea in the island trades, was wrecked at Rotuma in 1865, became British consul in Fiji in 1867, was highly influential in the negotiations for the ceding of Fiji to Britain in 1874, and became governor of Fiji in 1887. The companies, the new settlers, and their sympathetic consuls pressed for annexations. The French were the first to act and took Tahiti, the Marquesas, and the Tuamotus as French protectorates in 1842 and New Caledonia in 1853. These were declared colonies in 1880, and the Australs and Wallis and Futuna in 1887.

The British annexed Fiji in 1874 and established protectorates over southeast New Guinea in 1884, Gilbert and Ellice in 1892, most of the Solomons soon after, and Ocean Island in 1900. They agreed that New Zealand would exercise authority over the Kermadecs in 1887, the Tokelaus in 1889, and the Cooks and Niue in 1901. The Dutch took western New Guinea in 1848. Germany annexed northeast New Guinea in 1885, along with the Bismarck Archipelago and the northwest Solomons; took possession of most of the Carolines in 1885; and ultimately purchased Yap and other islands in the Carolines and Marianas from Spain in 1899. The Germans also acquired the Marshall Islands in 1884 and took over Nauru in 1888. Chile obtained Easter Island in 1888.[11]

America, after its disastrous Civil War, had not recovered a significant merchant fleet and showed little inclination for acquiring Pacific territory. American guano companies had already secured legislation in 1856–1860 that allowed claims over some small Pacific islands, and the US government went on to secure others, including Baker, Jarvis, Johnson, Midway,

Palmyra, and Wake. In 1893 the influential American maritime geostrategist Alfred Mahan wrote that it was "imperative to take possession, when it can be righteously done, of such maritime positions as can contribute to secure command."[12] In 1898, Hawai'i was annexed (US citizenships were granted in 1900), as was eastern Samoa with Pago Pago as a main naval coaling station, while Guam was captured from Spain by the US Navy in 1898.

The Pacific was now effectively divided between several colonial powers mainly by agreements. In the final carve-up, it was confirmed that Western Samoa was a German colony separated from American Samoa in the east. In turn Germany agreed to relinquish claims for Tonga. As a result, in the closing days Tonga appeared to survive as the only independent Polynesian kingdom, although not quite. It was declared a British protectorate in 1900, and in 1905 it was decreed mandatory for the king of Tonga to take advice from the British consul on all matters of importance.[13] Finally, in 1906 New Hebrides was divided as a condominium between Britain and France.

Technological Change

The companies secure within colonial territories made more capital investments in land, stores, and shipping. A major item was the shift from wind power to coal in propulsion and from wood to iron in ship construction. In many ways sail was still more suited to Pacific conditions. Distances were great—some 6,500 miles from San Francisco to Sydney. By then more information was available on favorable winds and currents for passage planning under sail, where calms had always been of more concern than storms. The early steamships, carrying around 1,500 tons of cargo, were disadvantaged, as they burned about thirty-five tons of coal per day to give a speed of seven knots. This meant coaling stations were required across the Pacific, including Honolulu (2,100 miles from San Francisco), Suva (2,800 miles from Honolulu), and to reach Sydney, another 1,700 miles away. Coal was expensive whereas wind was free. Bunkers took up cargo space and added weight, as did the engines, which required spares, skilled engineers, and technical maintenance. Coal in turn had to be brought to bunkering ports by other ships and stockpiled. By the 1870s there were bigger steamships with more efficient engines, requiring a coal consumption of fourteen tons per day at nine knots. Sail then focused internationally on low-value bulk but continued on some Pacific routes.

In the island trades the strategies adopted by several companies were to continue using sail for the long-haul supply ships from main ports, ultimately with auxiliary engines, and steam vessels for trading permanently around the islands, for a time with auxiliary sail (figure 8.2). The advantages of steam and diesel propulsion in the islands included improved schedules, greater maneuverability in reef areas, ability to work clear from a lee shore, and the facility to leave lagoons regardless of wind direction. On Chong employed the barque *Loongana* for the 2,500-mile passage from Sydney to the north Gilberts, and steam vessels such as the *St. George* for trading around the islands. It was such a successful division that when the *Loongana* was lost, she was replaced by the sailing ship *Alexa*, until she too was lost in 1924.

FIGURE 8.2. The ship's company of the *Janet Nicholl*, a 600-ton steamship with an auxiliary topsail. She replaced several Henderson and MacFarlane sailing vessels. There were nine European officers and a deck and engine crew of forty from the Solomons and the New Hebrides. The ship sailed from Sydney on 11 April 1890 on a round voyage via New Zealand to the Henderson and MacFarlane trading stations in the Pacific (and delivering Niue Island labourers home). On board were the charterer Harry Henderson, R. L. and Fanny Stevenson, and her son, Lloyd Osbourne (photographer). (Courtesy of the Writers' Museum, Edinburgh)

By the 1890s the more energy-efficient steamships of Burns Philp (BP) had made complete trading circuits from Sydney northward to the Solomon Islands and on to Jaluit, then south through the Gilbert and Ellice and Fiji groups and back to Sydney. The BP trading vessel in the German-controlled Marshall Islands dealt directly with island people through its trade room. Over six weeks or so, it called at twenty islands with some sixty stopping places, covering about 1,900 miles in the group.[14]

The original companies in the Pacific were still primarily merchants who owned ships for the carriage of their own cargos. They delivered "tea and sugar" to their island trade stores outward and loaded copra for sale on the world markets. Costs of carriage and insurance were added to the consumer goods delivered and were deducted from the prices paid to producers for copra. The resident traders of all nationalities who were employed in their island stores worked on selling and buying commissions. Many of them married local women, and some wives and offspring were great assets in the business; others believed there were too many obligations to relatives.[15] A normal procedure was for the vessels to anchor in the lagoons or to stand off and on at sea. Supercargoes would use workboats to reach each trade store. Where there was no company store, they would weigh and bag copra on the beach and issue a chit to the producers for the value of their copra. People would then go out to the ship and exchange the chit for an equivalent value of goods in the trade room.[16]

Government Support to the Companies

Shipping services were essential for the maintenance of the island empires in the movements of officials, mail, and cargo. Subsidies were provided by governments for these purposes and to support the competitive position of national companies. The P&O Line and the French Compagnie des Messageries Maritimes operated subsidized services from Europe to Australia, with connections and transshipments at Sydney. The German Norddeutscher Lloyd did likewise, and the Dutch KPM made onward connections to Australia and New Guinea from the East Indies under subsidy. In the late 1890s the Japanese government financially supported ships operating from Yokohama via Hong Kong to Sydney and calling at several Pacific islands. The transshipment services from Australia and New Zealand to and from the Pacific Islands were likewise subsidized.

Competitive subsidization, cargo reservation, and flag preferences were thus common between the imperial administrations. They favored the largest companies, which could maintain mail and passenger schedules and provide ships of the required standards.[17] But the demands of the schedules often caused problems. N. Chatfield of Burns Philp describes how in 1907 the schedule of the SS *Malaita* (929 tons) involved Sydney-Vila-Tarawa (where she met the BP regional vessels *Kerry* and *Titus*), then through the islands groups south of Tarawa and on to Vila. The ship made twenty-three calls in twenty-two days in the islands, the crew had little time to trade and on occasion refused to load copra from noncompany traders.[18]

These mail runs were important for administrators and they strengthened the power of the merchant companies, but they were unpopular with small-scale traders, and even more so with the people on several remoter islands that had lost all their resident traders by the early twentieth century. There were a few small unsubsidized companies, such as that of Captain Allen, that picked up trade in very small, distant places. His supply brigantine *Jeanette* ran from Sydney to Funafuti, and the SS *Dawn*, with a trade room, made the rounds from there. Similarly, small Chinese vessels, including the auxiliary schooners of Tiy Sang and Company, increasingly competed with the companies, as did their very small trading stores, which soon were the most prevalent in the remoter islands.[19]

The major companies operating from colonial territories gained other advantages from colonial policies. The administrators concentrated all overseas shipping at specific ports in order to levy custom duties, port and light dues, and control matters of security, health, and immigration. This reduced foreign political and commercial interventions in outer islands. In Fiji, Suva and Levuka were designated ports of entry in 1882, and all other ports were closed to direct overseas calls.[20] The German consul at Apia wrote to Bismarck: "In Rotuma the company monopolised the whole trade, until that island was annexed by England. Since then, vessels proceeding to Rotuma are obliged to call at a port of entry in the Fiji group; and this restriction necessitated a stoppage of the trade, and the company's buildings on the islands have recently been sold with great loss."[21]

As German trade to Rotuma receded, the High Commission in Fiji wrote to the major New Zealand firm of Henderson and MacFarlane:

> In the event of the *Archer* coming to Fiji there is no reason why your firm should not also resume trading at Rotuma, with which island there is very little connection with the outside world, of where there is every reason to suppose you might do a profitable business. As regards this

part of the question I am to say that the HC, as Governor of Fiji would make arrangements by which you would be relieved of customs duties leviable in respect of that island. The island you are aware exports about 600 tons of copra annually.[22]

The US government agreed to subsidies in 1867 for steam packets from San Francisco to Honolulu and onwards to Australia. The Australian and New Zealand governments did likewise for their ships to link with Hawai'i and the American West Coast.[23] Burns Philp complained that when an Australian ship called at Hawai'i, she was not allowed to take cargo to San Francisco or any other American port. The company complained also in 1904 that the German authorities at the port of entry Jaluit were charging 2,700 pounds for trading licenses to foreign vessels and 100 pounds to ships flying the German flag. The BP ship *Ysabel* was refused fresh water at Jaluit; and the Jaluit Gesellschaft tried to prohibit BP from trading in the Carolines and the Marshalls.[24] In New Caledonia, port dues were heavy on all vessels except those of the Compagnie des Messageries Maritimes. The Japanese trading in the Mariana and Caroline Islands imposed similar restrictions.

Displacement of Pacific Seafarers

The erosion of the seafaring skills and the reduction of crew employment by Pacific people were some of the results of these commercial and colonial policies. In this period seafaring became more nationally homogenous to the countries of ship owning, and elements of racism now entered into the relationships between multiethnic seafarers. This undermined the traditional unity of the foc'sle that had prevailed on most ships. There were several reasons for these changes, both intentional and unintentional. They may be summarized under three headings, as follows.

ADMINISTRATIVE RESTRICTIONS

The colonial administrators were from the start ambivalent about the movement of indigenous craft within their own island groups and across political boundaries between islands. They could not always grasp the extent or purport of the noncommercial exchanges, which had taken place for centuries. Sir Arthur Gordon, who became the first governor of Fiji in 1875, adopted at best a condescending attitude toward the great Solevu exchanges by simply tolerating them on the grounds that "they would form a substitute for commerce until the natives should become better accustomed to money as a medium of exchange, and it was inseparable from the quasi-communal institutions in which the race had been raised."[25]

By 1896 Gordon's successors had decided that *solevu* was a burden on the people, and in any case had "lost much of their native character," adding with disapproval that "at Rewa a cutter filled to the hatches with cases of kerosene formed the contribution of the Toga district."[26] Attempts followed to curtail large-scale interisland exchanges in Fiji.

It was much the same story in several other parts of the Pacific. In 1896 Telford Campbell, resident commissioner of the Gilbert and Ellice Islands reported that he had managed to obtain a check "on natives who formerly travelled indiscriminately on what were nothing more than predatory voyages."[27] Arthur Mahaffy, who carried out an official survey of the colony in 1909, commended this prohibition. He deduced that the equatorial current was too hazardous for native vessels and people, and that "the government has wisely declared that all interisland voyages save on trading steamers are unlawful."[28] This suited the shipping companies. However, it not only destroyed local vessel building skills and navigational knowledge but also negated a nursery for young men with a love of adventure and the sea, thereby keeping them from entering commercial shipping with experience in the future.

In Hawai'i there was already a considerable body of native Hawaiian seafarers serving on local commercial vessels. Some were captains and officers, but the majority were sailors particularly skilled under sail and in workboat handling through heavy surf. Soon after Hawai'i's annexation in 1898, American regulations were brought into force. All captains and officers were required to pass examinations for US marine licenses before they could continue serving at sea. The Hawaiian mariners had their own less formal practical training systems, and few could attend the new maritime training establishments. Other than on small vessels, their positions were taken by licensed men from the mainland Pacific coast who received higher rates of wages but had less experience.

Vessels were also subject to US survey standards of hull and equipment, and strict limits were placed on the carriage of cargo and passengers. It was necessary to refit ships, and although steamship companies such as Wilder met most of the standards, others went out of business. Along with the high rates of wages to mainland officers, these costs raised freight rates and fares, to the disadvantage of island people in agriculture.

To make matters worse, regulatory changes coincided with an outbreak of bubonic plague in Hawai'i. The indigenous population as a whole was already depleted, and the decrease was being compensated for by immigrants from Asia. Japanese in particular were now recruited as sailors from new arrivals to overcome shortages of crew. Like the officers from the mainland, they were unfamiliar with the difficult conditions on the Hawaiian coast, and especially at the fifty or so open boat landings. Consequently there were "many accidents."[29] To give one typical example, when the engine of the auxiliary schooner *Surprise* failed on a lee shore at Koloa, the officers and the ten Japanese crew did not have enough experience to bring her clear under sail and she was totally lost.[30]

IMPACT OF TECHNICAL CHANGE

The decline in sail and the use of steam became widespread in the Pacific at the turn of the century. Sailing vessels that continued in island work were generally retrofitted with auxiliary engines along with power-driven winches and windlasses. These were laborsaving and safety developments that reduced deck crew size. On the big steamships changes in social structure and divisions of labor were considerable. Not only were there fewer sailors on deck, but an engine room component was also added with a crew of about twenty, including a chief engineer and four engineer officers. The technology involved was beyond the everyday experiences of most Pacific islanders. They were still employed in the skilled and dangerous tasks of working cargo and handling boats at landings, but increasingly they were hired locally and cheaply on a part-time basis. The permanent white crews of the trunk line ships were recruited in Australasia and on the Pacific coast of America. A manager of Burns Philp noted in 1913: "A number of natives do nearly all the work on board in the islands, boating and landing copra etc, and the white crew usually have a very easy time."[31] The impact of steam and mechanical deck power was similar in whaling employment. The introduction of mechanized whale catchers and the gun harpoon in 1865, the reductions in the demand for sperm oil against mineral and vegetable products, and shifts of much of the whaling out of the Central Pacific all reduced the demand for Pacific island crews on whaleships.

THE "YELLOW PERIL" EFFECT

The reference by Burns Philp to "native" and "white" crews touched on a topical issue that negatively affected the employment of Pacific island seafarers on the ships of some countries. The white working classes in Australasia and California were increasingly agitated by influxes of Asians as cheap labor. This became a major political issue and a focus of the emerging trade union movement. By this time the populations of Australia and New Zealand included descendants of transported convicts, along with free workers, mainly from the British Isles, who had left Britain in search of a better life. A culture of militancy among them was fuelled by oral traditions, including stories of the Scottish martyrs of 1793, transported Irish dissidents in the 1800s, the arrival of the first British trade union (Tolpuddle Martyrs) in 1834, and the Eureka rebels in the Australian goldfields during 1854. The nineteenth-century Australian proletariat was wary of any threats that cheap labor posed to newly won advances in working conditions.

Much of the Californian working class had similar backgrounds of European radicalism. There were disillusioned gold miners, many of whom were ex-sailors who had jumped ship in 1848 and were now seeking work. The European working population as a whole saw as a threat—termed the "yellow peril"—the Chinese who were brought in for railway construction and ended up in the West Coast. There were seamen strikes in the 1850s over wages and conditions, and attempts to build unions, but these were defeated because of a plentiful supply of labor willing to man the ships. The traditional negotiating procedures of individual crews trying to fix wages and conditions with masters and agents continued to prevail at this time, and strikes were usually ship-specific incidents.

In the late nineteenth century there were amalgamations into bigger companies owning many vessels. These operated scheduled services and had crews that now contained European engine room ratings of working-class origins, all of which facilitated the establishment of seafaring unions as unified negotiating bodies. The Federated Seamen's Union of Australia was founded in 1878, and the Federated Seamen's Union of New Zealand in 1880.[32] In America the Coast Seamen's Union was formed in 1885 by a Norwegian and a Swede (members of the Industrial Workers of the World, or IWW) and became the Sailors' Union of the Pacific in 1889. These and other unions of industrialized maritime countries were linked internationally, ultimately through the International Transport Workers' Federation (ITF) in 1898.[33] At this time ships in the Pacific trade normally had island sailors and European officers (see figure 8.2).

Some maritime unions in the Pacific Rim had already become more exclusive nationally and racially in response to non-European immigrants and the threats of cheap crewing. When the Australasian Steam Navigation Company introduced a low-wage Chinese crew on one of its ships in 1878, the new union brought Australian seamen out on strike and the Chinese were discharged.[34] A few union officials were blatantly racist; others evoked more egalitarian principles, advocating "equal pay for equal work."[35] In 1901 the Australian government, responding to wider political pressures in the country, legitimized racial discrimination under the White Australia Policy.[36] This policy became applicable to Pacific seafarers as government subsidies were awarded only to companies that included the contract clause "No coloured labour shall be employed on board [named ship] except that coloured labour may be employed in and around the islands, but solely in connection with boating and the landing, handling and discharge of cargo."[37] Similarly in New Zealand in 1906 a court ruling "effectively prohibited New Zealand shipowners—notably the Union Company—from employing 'foreign seamen' on their overseas routes."[38]

In America there was a series of seamen strikes, some of which involved the "coolie issue." The unions were eventually successful in achieving major improvements in wages and conditions under the articles of the 1915 Seamen's Act. Part of their objective of "US jobs for US sailors" was also met by the introduction of a language test and the setting of crew qualifications for foreign seamen. According to Andrew Gibson and Arthur Donovan, this was "an indirect way of outlawing the hiring of Chinese crews, such as those that had served very effectively on many American ships sailing in the Pacific."[39] The law also caught some Pacific sailors in its net.

In effect, and sometimes by default, discriminatory actions and legislation from the 1880s up to the First World War that were directed mainly at Asians contributed to the loss of employment among Pacific island seafarers. Conrad Bollinger, who wrote the official history of the New Zealand Seamen's Union, remarks that "the Union's name was put to some very dubious policies in the perfectly legitimate defence of members' jobs and conditions."[40]

Clearly, the political partitioning of the Pacific, new laws, company strength, and the advancement and protection of European employment at sea greatly curtailed the free mobility and choices of Pacific people, and much of their cultural relationships with the sea. As massive as these events were, they were not altogether overwhelming. Traditional voyages persisted in several places, and there were protests and many attempts by Pacific island societies to compete in maritime commercial enterprises.

CHAPTER NINE

Island Protests and Enterprises

THE FIRST WORLD WAR saw the removal of German colonial power. The Japanese, under a League of Nations mandate, eventually occupied all the islands of Micronesia except Guam (US) and the Gilberts (Britain). Britain acquired responsibility for Nauru, Australia took over German territory in New Guinea, and New Zealand acquired Western Samoa. The opening of the Panama Canal in 1914 gave added impetus to French commerce in Polynesia through more direct links with metropolitan France. There was rising resentment over the almost total control of commercial trade and transport by foreigners, and the wealth apparently derived from this.

By the time the postwar depressions affected the Pacific region, power-driven ships owned by foreign companies had taken over from sail in most commercial routes. It was then that the higher costs of steam and diesel propulsion further affected the well-being of the remoter and poorer islands, who had been used to the more economical sailing ships. Many islands in the Tokelaus, Ellice, and Cooks were bypassed at times of low financial returns on copra, and they suffered from loss of basic imports. Crews on these vessels also suffered as the companies in turn experienced cash flow problems with power-driven ships under low freight rates, due to high fixed capital costs of repayments and the operational costs of fuel and crew. This situation may be appreciated from the 1931–1935 log abstracts of the Gilbert Island–based SS *Macquarie*, which belonged to On Chong:[1]

> 9th March to 9th June 1931
>   Coal supply finished, also crews rations, two hands sent to cut wood fuel for galley and three hands fishing five days each week.
> 21st July 1933 (At Sea)
>   Acute shortage of coal. Raised boat sails and awnings as sails. Burnt 3 bags of copra, 2 hatches etc.

27th July 1934
   No coal and short of stores.
15th January 1935
   At Butaritari, no coal and short of stores.

Even at the best of times there were dissatisfactions in many of the outer islands with uncertain shipping services, the low prices received for products, and the high costs of consumer goods. People were not passive when they believed they were being cheated. Already there had been armed resistance to land alienation and loss of rights in New Zealand, New Caledonia, and elsewhere.[2] The most frequent protests were against apparent commercial exploitation. These took the forms of boycotts and strikes, the formation of island-owned trading companies, and attempts at the revival of island-owned shipping. There were numerous difficulties to overcome with these enterprises, not least the opposition from established companies and often from the colonial authorities allied to them, as well as some cultural factors.

Boycotts and Strikes (Taboos)

The boycotts of exploitative traders started early and were widespread. During 1864 it was officially reported that "coconut oil machinery in Fiji was frequently brought to a standstill when Fijians refused to supply coconuts."[3] The Godeffroy company was boycotted in Tonga in 1872, and in Samoa in 1882, when it reduced the prices paid for copra and the people sold their copra to the mission instead, and although it reached the Godeffroy company through that channel, it was a protest.[4] During 1883 a Scots trader on the island of Arorae in the Gilberts complained when the Kaupule (assembly of elders) raised the price of copra and forbid any sales to traders at a lower price.[5] Similar actions were taken by the *hua* (local chiefs) in the Cook Islands,[6] and during 1901 there was destruction of property on Onatoa in a dispute over prices.[7]

The resident traders in the islands maintained they had no control over buying and selling prices, which they said were dictated by the companies. The trader Ernest Osborne observed in his semifictional book set in the 1900s: "The natives are awakening to a desire for a higher price for their produce, which they know is scandalously undervalued. Traders may be willing enough to increase the copra price, but without a corresponding increase in the price paid them by the trading companies, they can't afford to. And the companies secure in their financial power and trading monopolies refuse to an increase."[8]

The companies for their part complained to consuls and visiting warships about unjustified and illegal boycotts. Captain W. H. Maxwell of HMS *Emerald,* on a cruise through the Ellice group, noted judiciously, "The Taboo is their only defence against any dishonest trader, and their only means of enforcing good behaviour upon people towards whom they are not permitted to use force. Still there is no doubt that it may be, and sometimes is, arbitrarily and vexaciously applied."[9]

Protests also took the form of stopping the production of copra. The price-fixing agreements on copra purchases made between Burns Philp, On Chong, and the Jaluit Gesellschaft in 1906–1907 were so deeply resented by people in the Marshalls, Gilberts, and Ellice that a strike on production quickly spread among islands. This meant that the people reverted to subsistence agriculture and fishing, which could be disastrous for trading companies, but in the longer term it would be equally difficult for communities now well accustomed to imported goods, including metal tools and fishhooks. These strikes were periodic but short-lived.

In the Gilbert Islands a strike during 1909 was partly defeated by the intervention of Arthur Mahaffy, the acting resident commissioner. Burns Philp recorded, "This gentleman toured the group in our steamer *Muniara,* the first trip in the new year, and ordered the natives to cease the strike, going so far as to threaten the natives of Tamana that if they did not immediately cut out their copra he would bring natives from other islands to do so."[10] BP also carried the Roman Catholic archbishop to several other islands and asked him to use his influence to break the strike, pointing out that "it was a sinful waste of providence's gifts to the natives to allow the coconuts to rot on the ground because of the stubbornness of the people."[11]

At other islands, people tried to defend traditional rights and marine conservation methods against predatory colonial practices. In the Tuamotus, chiefs protested to the authorities in 1859 against foreign ships bringing divers and diving machines, which were exhausting the oyster stocks of the lagoons by massive extractions of shells and pearls. In the absence of French action over several years, the deposed King Pomare V sent a party from Tahiti to Hikueru Island in 1880 to support the people of this last productive lagoon, who had, they said, "seized the diving machines, those engines which endangered the lagoons." The colonial authorities dispatched a naval vessel and arrested the Pomare party.[12] French government control over lagoon resources was thereby asserted above the customary rights of local communities, chiefs, and the Pomare royal family.

Formation of Indigenous Trading Companies

For many islands it was customary, especially among women, to come together as groups to produce mats, tapa, baskets, and suchlike for presentation, exchange, trade, or sale to meet some social objective. Mainly these were periodic enterprises, such as the *kuataha* of tapa makers in Tonga, the Sogosogo Vakamarama (women's associations) in Fiji, and the *mronron* (round wheels) as forms of proto-cooperatives with trade goods in the Gilbert Islands. It was often more difficult for an individual or small group to set up a permanent trade store. These frequently failed financially as a result of social pressures for sharing stock at the request of relatives, reluctance to ask for receipts when giving goods on credit, and payback in fish and fowls instead of cash.

Such problems were overcome to some extent when a formal trading company was established on an island or on a village-wide basis. It also appeared helpful for success in the cash economy if foreigners not subject to kinship pressures were initially involved, particularly if they had commercial experience. But success did not always follow, and the majority of ventures had to contend with government and company opposition.

Most of the island commercial enterprises that emerged had the primary aims of bypassing foreign traders and running their own ships. A disgruntled European and former employee of a merchant company sometimes took part, or some mixed-raced progeny of sailors, traders, or planters acted as managers. One of the earliest ventures on a significant scale was the Vaitupu Company in the Ellice Islands. The business was initiated in 1870 by Thomas William Williams, who worked for Ruge and Hedemann and Company. He had a somewhat different agenda from that of the one hundred Vaitupuan shareholders. Williams provided the initial stock of trade goods on credit from his former employers. He later obtained further loans to buy the schooner *Vaitupulemele* (named after a historic double canoe). Williams assumed that most of the trade of other Ellice Islands would be diverted to the Vaitupu Company. This did not happen, and when the ship was lost in a hurricane, Williams withdrew, and the shareholders were left to make good on the debts, including the cost of the ship.

The Vaitupuans, out of pride and ethical obligations as well as possible litigation, took nearly five years of hard work to repay Ruge. Doug and

Teloma Munro, who researched the documentation and oral history of this failed enterprise, wrote that even young mothers, who normally did not engage in manual labor, "took their babies into the bush and hung them from trees in baskets while they worked" and that "people cut copra through the night; being relieved at daybreak when the roosters started to crow."[13] Despite the oral records and songs and stories about the event and the dubious motives of the promoter, the Vaitupu people nevertheless supported the first island cooperative in 1926, successfully introduced by D. G. Kennedy, a schoolmaster on the island.[14]

In Samoa during 1905 there was an attempt to compete in trade with the DHPG and its German government promoters. The project was led by Pullack, who was part Samoan and part German and had been educated in America. He obtained the backing of several Samoan chiefs who made up the Mālō (Council) at Mulinuʻu for the formation of a trading company. The chiefs were to raise the capital from the villages, and the company would purchase copra and sell consumer goods at fair prices. The German governor of Samoa, Dr. William Solf, did not approve of the undermining of the DHPG and did not relish any possible political collaboration between Samoans, part Samoans, and discontented Europeans among the tensely divided rivalries in the colony. He banned the company, several of the Samoan leaders were arrested, and they and Pullack were deported. The ambitions of Samoans to compete with foreign companies was resurrected in 1914 as the Toeaina Club. Members of the club started stores and bought a schooner for freight and passenger services coastwise. The company was short-lived, however; it lacked capital, could not earn enough, and was forced into liquidation by a new government.[15]

A similar attempt by islanders to compete in trade started in Tonga during 1909. This enterprise was initiated in Nukualofa by a Scotsman, Alister D. Cameron, who was a former Burns Philp manager. The group's name was Tonga Maʻa Tonga Kautaha (Association of Tonga for the Tongans). A number of statements regarding its justification and objectives were proclaimed at various meetings, such as this one: "The Papalangi has waxed and grown fat on the profits he has made out of your people.... [C]opra was to be sent to the white man's land and people were to receive the correct value of their produce.... [N]o one shall deal with Messrs Burns Philp and Co. Ltd. up to their deaths."[16] Several thousand Tongans joined and invested in the TMTK during the first year, and it spread through Tongatapu, Haʻapai, and Vaʻvau. Stores were opened that bought copra and sold goods, agents were appointed in Auckland and Sydney, and the schooner *Viakamaile* was purchased, along with a launch. The association appeared successful, and Burns Philp and the DHPG expressed alarm.

In August 1910 the British consul general in Tonga, William Telfer Campbell, wrote to the colonial secretary in Fiji, A. Mahaffy, accusing Cameron of fraud. Mahaffy replied that in his opinion the Kautaha was "a particularly noxious form of swindle," adding that "H. E. Dr. Solf, with whom I have been fortunate enough to discuss the matter, has had much experience of this evil in Samoa." Mahaffy argued that the suppression of the TMTK was justified and that Cameron should be taken to the court of the Western Pacific High Commission. Among many actions taken was the issuance of an ordinance (no. 4, 1911) that "forbade any further association of natives and non natives in Kautaha."[17]

There was considerable discontent at all levels of Tongan society. King Tupou rejected the advice of the British consul to support a court case against Cameron. The king acknowledged that he had to listen to the British consul's advice as imposed in 1905, but he said he was not bound by it and would not be coerced. The British Colonial Office in London judiciously agreed with the king's interpretation. King Tupou went further. He subsequently wrote, "I cannot see that the Tongans have lost anything by having a Kautaha, but it is beyond all question that as a result of closing they have lost many thousands of pounds." He went on to request the removal of the dictatorial Campbell from Tonga.

Alister Cameron was ultimately acquitted by the court, and William Telfer Campbell was withdrawn from the Pacific. The ordinance forbidding people from forming trading companies was rescinded, and the British Colonial Office was diplomatically reconciled with the king. Cameron became manager of a new business, the Tonga Ma'a Tonga Company Ltd., but because of the losses of people's savings in the earlier association, much of the patriotic enthusiasm that had heralded the TMTK was diminished, and there was little subsequent success in this respect.[18]

Sometime in 1912 the government of Fiji began to receive reports about a group of Fijians who were "forming a company on cooperative lines for the export of products and the import of goods."[19] It was apparent by 1913 that this movement—called the Viti Company and led by a thirty-six-year-old commoner, Apolosi Nawai—was growing. In 1914 Apolosi, as director of the Viti Company, wrote to all the *buli* (government chiefs) of Fiji, urging them to support the movement. Many did so, and enthusiastic meetings were held at every level of society in all the provinces of Fiji. The aims included "keeping our lands in our own hands and all the produce therefrom both things found in the water and things that grow on the land.... [T]he Company should have a store in every locality.... [T]here should be no more dealings with Europeans therefrom.... [T]here should be a native shipbuilding yard in each province."

The Viti Company received the support of several Europeans, who were somewhat ineffectual. The opposition from the merchant companies and government establishment was formidable. The first overseas shipment of Viti Company bananas was condemned by the Fiji Department of Agriculture inspectors during the loading of the Union Steamship Company ships *Matua* and *Tafua* in November 1914. In retaliation, Fiji banana growers refused to sell supplies of bananas to European merchants.

The colonial secretary considered the Viti Company to be seditious. Apolosi was deported to Rotuma in 1915 for seven years. He returned and was deported again on two occasions. The company declined in chaos and disillusionment. The chief police magistrate at the time, A. Alexander, later wrote with some candor: "The new company was in difficulties from the beginning. It incurred the hostilities of the white planters and merchants, who strongly resented the appearance of a united body of native rivals in business. The Wesleyan Methodist Mission suffered a huge financial loss, when large numbers of natives transferred the contributions they would have ordinarily given to the Mission to the new company. To the government Apolosi was anathema." [20]

In the Gilbert Islands several of the *mronron* were already temporarily consolidating their copra and buying goods wholesale from the trade rooms of some vessels. These they resold to themselves at trade store prices in order to jointly finance local projects. During 1926 this took on a new dimension with the formation of the Tangitang Mronron, meaning the "cry" or "complaint" round wheels. The movement started on the island of Abaiang and involved sending a small vessel to Tarawa, where better prices for copra and cheaper goods were available. The movement diversified and spread among islands as a protest against the traders. It is mentioned in the log abstracts of the SS *Macquarie* on 27 January 1933 at Marakei.

The management of the consolidated Tangitang Mronron in Abaiang, Tarawa, Marakei, and Maiana in 1938 passed to Willy Schutz, a former supercargo with Burns Philp. The association went on to purchase or charter a 30- to 40-ton vessel. The government response was simply "to keep the Tangitang under observation." It was difficult to find anything wrong with the organization; the only adverse statement recorded by an official of the time was "there were large numbers of M/T beer bottles in the vicinity of Schutz's home," from which the resident commissioner concluded that "Schutz was playing [a game of] ducks and drakes with the Tangitang Mronron."[21] The movement and its vessels precariously survived in the four islands of the Gilberts into the 1960s.

Revival of Island-Owned Shipping

As well as the attempts to compete with the big companies in trade, there were many efforts by chiefs and communities to revive and maintain small-scale island-owned shipping, despite prohibitions by colonial authorities. In the 1880s the king of Tonga owned schooners, and M. E. Jule noted that two traditional double-hulled vessels still plied between the Tongan islands at that time.[22] King Tem Binoka of Abemama also had ships, some of which traded overseas, although he told R. L. Stevenson that they invariably returned from voyages in debt, owing to "the world-enveloping dishonesty of the white man."[23] There were also canoes trading with commercial goods in the Carolines, and schooners owned by chiefs in the Marshalls.[24]

From the 1880s onward there was a marked revival in commercial trade, with schooners and cutters owned by communities in many outer islands where chiefs once again became enthusiastic for their own ships. This was made more necessary by the rationalizing of the steamship services of merchant companies as they sought economies of full loads with their expensive vessels. The company steam- and motor-driven ships began to concentrate on the shortest-distance, highest-producing areas and were operated on schedules from a few main entrepôts linked with overseas shipping. This left smaller, less productive, and remoter islands marginalized in the commercial system. The bypassing of places became even more pronounced during depression periods of low prices for copra and fruit, when many islands also lost impoverished European planters with their cutters, and the local trade stores closed. The necessity for acquiring their own vessels to carry goods and passengers was allied to a natural desire and pride of the people for ships and their abilities to sail them.

In the Cook Islands during the 1880s "native owned and operated schooners traded throughout the group as well as up to Tahiti and down to New Zealand," and these ships "were all owned by tribal groups and operated by the respective chiefs who also organised much of the production and most of the marketing."[25] Many of these vessels were built in New Zealand. Hawkins notes that they included the *Lilian* (80 tons), built in 1878 and traded between Rarotonga and Auckland in 1881, and the *Dolly* (42 tons), built in 1879 and bought by Penrhyn Islanders in

1892 (renamed *Teura*). In the same year, the people of Aitutaki purchased the Tahitian schooner *Papeete* (15 tons). When the New Zealand–owned *Julia Pryce* ran on a reef at Aitutaki, she was sold to the Aitutakans. After repairs, she sailed to Rarotonga with 120 deck passengers and later traded fruit to Auckland.[26] Several of the ships purchased by Cook Island communities were in poor condition. The people of Penrhyn bought a schooner from a Captain Pily and tried to enter trading. The vessel was unseaworthy, and this venture ended in litigation for payments, as did the purchase of the schooner *Norval* by the Hau of Omoka in Penrhyn,[27] along with other claims that cost the people dearly.

In Tonga more schooners owned by chiefs were purchased from money collected around the villages.[28] In Tahiti there was considerable building of small craft of 8 to 15 tons that were sold within the group. Building took place in the Tuamotus, where the vessels were then sailed mainly by the people of the islands on which they were built.[29] In Fiji the *waqi ni tikina* (vessel of the villages and province) was controlled by the *buli* (government official), and numerous small craft increasingly owned and sailed by the *mataqali* (extended family). By European standards this boom in local shipping represented a gross oversupply of vessels beyond the needs of most islands. It appeared as a waste of time, resources, and capital and was considered by officialdom as a process leading to impoverishment, not development:

> Oppression is frequently felt and privations endured by communities providing the price of too large a vessel or too many vessels. The raising of such monies necessitates the people's abstentions from the use of coconuts as food, and deprives them of oil and clothes which under ordinary circumstances would be procured by the sale of copra. Growing food is often sold in order to raise money for this purpose. Much of this unnecessary expenditure is caused by the rivalry of tribes and chiefs as to the size of cutters.[30]

The authorities did occasionally encourage communal ownership and even helped with loans where there were no alternative services. For example, in Fiji the government responded to the people of the village of Bouwaqa: "These people isolated in the island of Vatulele have no vessel and therefore sell to a Chinaman at £7 ton—he is the only trader there. He sends it to Suva at £10 profit per ton besides store profit."[31] On the other hand, there was reluctance to subsidize community shipping at the island of Kadavu, near Suva. In 1902 the Kadavu Provincial Council reported, "There is a large fleet of native owned vessels in Kadavu.... [P]eople propose expending some £700 more on new craft. I do not suppose any of the vessels pay the owners, but that does not seem to trouble them so long as they have vessels to do as they like with—it is the one thing they are willing to work and sacrifice for." In 1901 the people of Rotuma bought a 50-ton schooner for 2,000 pounds to carry copra and passengers to Suva and Sydney. It was lost on a reef at Rotuma within eighteen months.[32]

Officialdom considered that this was a period of "mania for ships." C. Percy Smith describes this in 1919 Samoa, where, "like church buildings[,] it has become the fashion of late to possess these boats."[33] In the New Hebrides and New Caledonia there was not the same mania, mainly because in most places the large numbers of planters already had schooners and ketches that carried goods for trade stores and passengers between islands and main ports. However, Anne Dunbar refers to a native company on Tanna during the 1930s that acquired a two-masted schooner.[34] In Hawai'i, with its more diversified economy, mainland company shipping had become well established.

Paradoxically, in most territories the small islands distant from main ports received little help in shipping from the colonial authorities, but they often received a good deal of criticism when they entered the business. By contrast Euro-Australian-owned vessels trading within island groups were consistently subsidized by territory administrations. The coastal areas with largest populations and most productive estates tended to obtain more regular subsidies. The vessels that qualified for these were usually the bigger, faster ships owned by the merchant companies. In effect, under the government shipping subsidy schemes, the most productive and wealthy of the island estates and businesses received improved services and the more affluent shipowners and merchants obtained financial support to provide these.[35]

The merchant shipping companies had trade stores adjacent to the estate areas. Subsidized vessels were, as a result, carrying goods to be sold by their companies' stores, supplying planters who had accounts with their branches, and in some cases serving their own estates. It was left to a few small freight-earning cutters, often owned partly by Europeans (see below), and to the village boat *(waqa ni koro)* to provide for the outer islands, while many small planters in out-of-the-way places had to rely on their own and neighbors' boats. The marketing arrangements that evolved in this situation effectively prevented the expansion of indigenous small freight-earning shipping companies into the most lucrative trades.

The Fiji Shipping Commission of 1915 did have some misgivings about the pattern of subsidized shipping and trade in Fiji. The commissioners cited the large vessel *Adi Keva,* belonging to the foreign-owned Fiji Shipping Company, as giving undue preference "to certain leading firms in Suva," and they felt that the subsidies stood in the way of "legitimate competition." The commission recommended that subsidies "should not as a rule be granted to firms or companies trading as merchants in the colony."[36] Nevertheless subsidies remained, and the merchant companies continued to be the main beneficiaries. During a Fiji Legislative Council debate on the question in 1917 it was argued "the planters served by the *Arma* are amongst the largest and most prosperous in the colonies.... [I]n other words we are taxing all the copra producers of the colony to provide an excellent steamer service for the wealthiest of the copra planters."[37]

In the Gilbert Islands the ban on the use of canoe traffic for long-distance trips was relaxed in 1930. By then it was too late for a significant revival in that mode of transport for commerce. However, a few large wooden sailing craft were built, using money earned by laborers working in the phosphate mining at Ocean Island to purchase long planks, so scarce in the small coral islands. These vessels were used enthusiastically for people to travel between islands.

The gulf between the foreign-owned commercial company, with its selection of profitable routes and receipt of subsidies, and the community-oriented, somewhat informal indigenous sector was partly economically bridged by ships of other nationals of the islands who were without wider social obligations to the communities served. Table 3 provides an example of trends in interisland ship owning in Fiji between 1906 and 1927.

Table 3. Ownership of the Fiji interisland fleet by race, 1906–1927

Year	European No. of vessels	Tons	Fijian No.	Tons	Chinese No.	Tons	Part-European No.	Tons	Indian No.	Tons	Japanese No.	Tons
1906	49	783	122	796	23	252	11	196	—	—	—	—
1909	55	867	130	968	9	137	16	218	—	—	—	—
1911	87	1,495	136	894	9	139	31	278	3	11	—	—
1912	112	2,603	152	982	10	136	—	—	7	36	—	—
1915	96	1,671	78	606	19	157	—	—	10	48	8	75
1918	76	1,528	95	740	19	138	25	210	5	21	4	56
1927	74	—	40	523	10	107	—	—	5	63	1	8

Sources: Colonial Office Reports, *Fiji, 1906, 1909, 1911, 1912, 1915, 1918,* Cmd. 508–530 (1919); *Pacific Islands Yearbook, 1932* (Sydney: Pacific Publications, 1932), 55.

The Fijian-owned *waqa ni koro* still amounted to a substantial tonnage in this period, but other owners of small cutters were emerging, especially those of mixed European and Fijian parentage.[38] Many of the part-European participants in the trade of the islands were descendants of beachcombers, sailors, government officials, and European planters whose estates were subdivided among large families. This mixed-race sector of population owned and operated trade stores and boatyards and were employed by merchant companies as managers, supercargoes, and ship's officers. The most important entrepreneurial role of the part-European sector was increasingly becoming the ownership of small shipping companies (discussed in chapter 10).

Attempts at Maritime Trade Unions

On all the local commercial vessels the crews were primarily island men working on a casual basis. But attitudinal changes were coming about among port workers and the island sailors. These were influenced by changes in crew composition and attitudes on foreign-owned ships running to the islands. The crews of the latter were by the early twentieth century increasingly homogenous in nationality—either American, French, British, or Australasian. They were also unionized. Crews from these ships and those of local interisland vessels met in the sailor enclaves of island port towns. There they shared the traditional unity of sailors and related port workers. Island seafarers learned of current pay levels, unions, and the efficacy of strike action in improving wages and conditions.

The port workers at Lautoka in Fiji came out on strike in 1916 and attempted to form the Fijian Wharf Labourers Union. The organizers were an Australian and the *turaga ni koro* (village headman) of Nanoli, whose village supplied casual workers.[39] They were put down by government action. A more widespread strike was started by sailors in the interisland shipping sector of New Guinea during 1929. Bill Gammage relates how in 1926 the sailor Bohun from Buka Island was mocked by Afro-American seamen at the port of Kavieng for accepting such low rates of pay. Later, on the ship *Ralum* in Rabaul in 1928, Bohun discussed conditions with Sumsuma, captain of the interisland auxiliary schooner *Edith*, who was already agitating about racial inequalities and had heard of strike action achieving better pay. They both organized their people carefully and secretly. A strike was called on 2 January 1929 and soon became general; "overnight almost the entire workforce of Rabaul had vanished," including large numbers of the police force. After three days they were defeated. The leaders were flogged and jailed, Sumsuma for three years. Later he engaged in other protests, started a cooperative with its own trading schooner, and led several protest and progressive ventures. Gammage writes of the sailor Sumsuma as continuously working for the cause of people and the "restless grandeur of his visions."[40]

News of these and other protest actions and trade unions spread easily between ports. Pacific sailors on the bigger ships, who were divorced from village life and social conventions and lived in port towns when ashore, became increasingly militant. Little actual headway was made in the formation of unions, although successions of spontaneous port industrial actions extended into the French colonies. In 1938 a major strike of port laborers and interisland seafarers took place in Hawai'i to achieve recognition of their union in negotiations. There had already been strikes in 1936 and 1937, and when the interisland ship *Waialeale* arrived at Hilo on 26 May 1938, crewed by eighty-four armed nonunion strikebreakers, it was met by longshoremen and sailors. The police, armed with tommy guns, bayonets, and tear gas, fired on the demonstrators. Some fifty people were wounded in what became known in labor history as the Hilo massacre.[41]

Problems of Transition in a Dual Economy

There were probably more failures than successes in all the attempts to achieve a better share in the growing commerce and shipping of the islands. The failure of several island indigenous communities to develop viable commercial trading and shipping enterprises can be attributed partly to a combination of opposition by the expatriate companies, the traditions of a way of life, and the ambivalence of colonial administrators. The latter in the late nineteenth century often ruled with a mixture of paternalism and suspicion toward the commercial aspirations of indigenous society. They could perceive only the apparent wasteful practices in the persistent development of what they considered to be excessive numbers of small vessels, but they gave little support to indigenous commercial efforts.

The reality that some administrators could not appreciate was that island ships owned by communities had important functions that were beyond the criteria of efficiency as measured by Western economics. They fulfilled a dual role, serving social as well as economic needs. Because the ships were owned by the community, most people felt they had a call on the use of the ships, and the ships sailed only when there was a need, not to any schedules or fixed routes. Vessels on the way to a main trading port would make diversions to a series of other places at the apparent whim of the captain, crew, or passengers. There would be protracted stays for a variety of purposes before moving on. This "irresponsible behaviour" infuriated officials, especially amid requests for subsidies and loans.

The subsequent deficits in the financial accounts of island shipping were partly due to the ship remaining as much a social institution as in the precolonial days. The financial problem was that vessels were no longer built in villages from local materials. Instead, they were purchased from elsewhere and were wholly or partly mechanically powered, and this equipment needed to be maintained, spare parts stored, and fuel bought. Insurance was also required by law, a licensed captain at least had to have a regular salary, and while in ports there were berth charges. In strict commercial accounting terms, financial allowances should also have been made for replacement of the ships. All these items of expenditure had to come from the freight and fare earnings of the vessel. Even with a dedicated concentration on commercial operations, sufficient earnings would have been difficult enough, considering the long distances, seasonality, and low load factors usually involved.

The cash flow imbalances and related indebtedness eventually became chronic problems for most island community-owned shipping enterprises. These were usually overcome for a time by raising more money in the community, and this was a price many island people were apparently willing to pay for the values a ship had for them. Damages and losses from weather and reefs would also lead to the abandonment of a ship and the acquisition of another. The resulting pessimism is reflected in the Fijian proverbs. *"Rekirekilaki waqa vou"* (literally, "rejoicing over new boats") is used generally when showing enthusiasm over something that is later neglected; and, *"e dua na nomu waqa levu, e dua na nomu vusi levu"* literally means "you have a large boat, you have a large cat" (on your back as a burden).

When sailors who were engaged in the commercial sector of island shipping tried to improve their conditions and safety, they also encountered problems. Only in New Zealand and Hawai'i did indigenous seafarers achieve a corporate voice, when they were assimilated into the Federated Seamen's Union of New Zealand and the Coast Seamen's Union of Hawai'i. They then served mainly as ratings on both foreign-going and coastal vessels. In the rest of the Pacific Islands, local sailors were engaged only in interinsular shipping. They worked on foreign-going vessels as part-time boat handlers during periodic calls in outer areas. The bigger interinsular steamships and motor ships operating around main islands and plantations were all owned by foreign companies. On these the sailors were under company regulations regarding wages and hiring and firing, and trade unions were discouraged. The situations outlined remained very similar in most places until well into the twentieth century, when there were major changes, discussed in chapters 10 and 11.

CHAPTER TEN

Contemporary Local and Regional Shipping

THIS CHAPTER PROVIDES an account of local and regional shipping from the 1960s onward. Many political, technological, and significant social changes in the maritime sector of the islands have taken place within this period.

The first part of the chapter deals with local shipping, which is the lifeblood of islands where some communities have depended on inordinately small quantities of cargo being delivered to their beaches (figure 10.1). It would be impossible to examine the changes that have, and still are, taking place within this and other practices over several island territories. On the other hand, generalizations for the Pacific as a whole would result in distorted pictures of specific places. For these reasons, Fiji has been selected for a case study, taking two comparative cross sections in time from the period 1960 to 2007. Fiji does in fact embody many of the interisland seafaring activities found in several archipelagos. It also shows the beginning of a social revolution in shipboard relations that will spread to other island territories.

The second related topic in this chapter is regional shipping. Since World War II there has been a greater awareness of Oceania as a geographic region. Despite ethnic and cultural differences, Pacific people express recognition of common components in their maritime heritage, experiences of colonization, types of resources, and the unity of the ocean. From his point of view as a Pacific islander, Epeli Hau'ofa emphasizes that "it may be time that we think much less about geographic and cultural divisions, and much more about our region as comprising places where we can feel at home because of our greater networks of human connections."[1] No doubt, it was thinking along the lines of renewing links across a common ocean space that brought about consensus at the Pacific Forum toward approving the concept of a jointly owned regional shipping line.

FIGURE 10.1 Very small quantities of cargo were landed at places with few road connections. Here, sailors from New Ireland unload the punt of the *Ninsa II* on the east coast of Bougainville. The consignment includes a bundle of old newspapers to be used for smoking local tobacco. (Photograph by the author, 1973)

Local Shipping in Fiji, 1960–1980

As elsewhere in the Pacific, the islands of the Fiji Archipelago in the post–Second World War period experienced the gradual withdrawal of stores related to merchant companies. Small villages then depended on ageing Chinese shopkeepers, a few Indo-Fijian shops, and local cooperatives. These were served by cutters owned mainly by part-Europeans and other nonindigenous citizens of the towns, plus a few provincial vessels and numerous smaller Fijian-owned craft. Ownership of vessels by race is shown in table 4 for 1965.

The six European-owned ships—of the well-known companies Burns Philp, Morris Hedstrom, and W. R. Carpenter—usually had part-European captains, chief engineers, and supercargoes and Fijian sailors. The vessels were steel hulled and diesel powered, including the *Ratanui* (250 gross tons, or GT) and *Altair* (137 GT), and all were around twenty years old in 1965. The part-European sector comprised wooden cutters owned mainly by four firms in Suva. At this time they had their business premises in the corners of warehouses. One of the largest of their ships was the forty-eight-year-old *Melanesia* (30 GT). Indian and Chinese craft were similar and usually linked with small trade stores. The eight wooden auxiliary cutters and schooners under ethnic Fijian ownership ranged from about 5 to 40 tons; the largest and youngest was the two-year-old *Yatu Lau* (40 GT), owned by the province of Lau. There were also numerous unregistered craft, especially those owned by individual Fijians and village communities in the Yasawa Islands on the west of Fiji. These were crewed informally, and passengers were expected to lend a hand during the seven- to twenty-four-hour runs to and from the port of Lautoka.

On all ships the cargoes from port towns included bags of flour, rice, and sugar and cases of tinned meat, fish, milk, beer, biscuits, tea, cigarettes, and tobacco, as well as bulky consignments of clothing, household goods, hardware, items of furniture, and on-deck drums of kerosene. Inward cargo comprised mainly copra. In addition, according to climatic and soil conditions, as well as time and distance, crates of pigs and fowls, fresh fruit and vegetables, dried fish, yaqona plants (*Piper methysticum*, or kava), *voi voi* (for mat making), and tapa (bark cloth) for town market sales. On the bigger ships, cattle would be carried on deck.

Patterns of local trade differed little in the 1960s from those of the more distant past. There were wharfs at Suva, Lautoka, Levuka, Labasa, and Savusavu, at which vessels could lie alongside. In the other three hundred or so local trading places in Fiji, cargo was worked from anchorages or by standing off and on using a ship's boats and the crew as stevedores. On the bigger vessels, livestock was loaded by swimming cattle out for a mile or more and lifting them on board by slings. Passage times were long per ton of cargo. Typically one of the larger ships made sixteen offshore stops

TABLE 4. Ownership of the interisland fleet of Fiji (above 5 GT) by race, 1965

	No. of vessels	Tonnage
European	6	889
Part-European	16	369
Indian	10	141
Fijian	6	163
Provinces	2	40
Chinese	2	30
Total	42	1,632

Source: Records of the Fiji Marine Board, Office of the Harbour Master, Suva.

over four days along the thirty-mile coast of Taveuni Island, unloading 50 tons of general cargo and loading 150 tons of copra by boats, mainly to and from estates. A small cutter spent five days around villages on Koro Island, unloading ten tons and loading thirty tons. Because of reefs, the movements between places were confined to daylight hours.

Time on a voyage could be extended even more due to socializing by crews in villages where they had kinship ties. I wrote elsewhere of this period: "Crews are sometimes composed of men who are all related to one another: the captain may be in command *de jure* but the *de facto* authority may belong to the group as a whole."[2] This was one of the reasons why the company-owned bigger vessels employed nonindigenous captains who were able to exercise authority in trying to keep to schedules.

As well as cargo, all types and sizes of vessels carried passengers. This service was vital for people in the outer islands, and it represented a significant source of earnings for the ships. Fourteen thousand passengers were recorded as arriving at the port of Suva in 1964, and a good deal more went unrecorded on small craft. Passengers usually boarded a few hours to a few minutes before sailing. They brought food for the trip, water and drinking nuts, sometimes live animals, and always assorted bundles of household items. These were stowed where space could be found, and passengers spread their mats on deck and on tops of hatches and housing. Mrs. R. L. Stevenson describes the scene in the 1890s: "The getting on board of people was a wild affair of noise and confusion. Boat after boat was unladen, and piles of the most extraordinary household goods blocked up every space that should have been kept clear."[3] There was little change in the 1960s.

Usually, more than half the passengers were women; they would attend to children, talk, eat, and sleep where they settled. Men played card games and drank kava and beer, and some strummed guitars. The setting was always unsanitary, and in bad weather wet. When approaching an anchorage, the women would revive, roll up mats, comb and oil their hair, and retrieve belongings, while the crew opened hatches and prepared the boat for working cargo. For passengers this was a cheap way to travel that allowed many hundreds to move between places.

The combination of heavily loaded vessels, most of them old and poorly maintained, and navigational hazards rendered interisland voyages risky in bad weather. Captains were frequently under social pressures to take more passengers than was safe, especially in areas where ship arrivals were few and uncertain. Many of the vessels bought secondhand from overseas were modified from their original designs to facilitate deck passengers, often with additional high water tanks and more top burden of awnings and deck housing. All of this would reduce stability. The stability problem was not confined to small interisland craft in Fiji. Table 5 gives an indication of loss of life due to the capsizing of bigger ships at this time in various areas of the Pacific, and table 6 gives the occurrences of major causes of accidents to local vessels in Fiji waters over eight years.

The frequency of loss and damage to ships was a disincentive for owners to invest further capital on the maintenance of their vessels. This neglect in turn contributed to losses due to the deteriorating condition of the ships and added to the difficulties in keeping good crews, creating a dangerous vicious circle for sailors and passengers alike.

Crews in Fiji were drawn from Lau and Kadavu to a significant extent, although many resided in Suva. Employment was casual; there were experienced seamen who came and went as it suited them, and also young boys doing only a single trip. Wages were a matter of agreement with the captain, who was usually the only person with a local certificate. Living conditions on board were cramped, although the captain would normally have a single berth behind a partition abaft the wheel. The food supplied

TABLE 5. Pacific vessels lost due to capsizing (other than Fijian vessels)

Year	Name	Tons	Region	Loss of life	Source
1953	*Monique*	240	New Caledonia	120 (no survivors)	PIM, September 1953, 141
1955	*Elsie B*	280	Papua New Guinea	No survivors	PIM, August 1959, 103
1958	*Melanesia*	241	Solomon Islands	45 (no survivors)	PIM, August 1958, 65–66, 101
1963	*Muniara*	300	PNG	No survivors	PIM, August 1959, 103
1964	*Polurrian*	339	PNG	82 (29 survivors)	PNG Marine Board, Administrative Press Statement no. 47 (1964)
1964	*Kavieng Trader*	100	PNG	No loss of life	PIM, March 1964, 10

Note: PIM = Pacific Islands Monthly.

TABLE 6. Causes of major ship accidents in Fiji, 1956–1964

Cause	Occurrences
Moving along the coast during darkness	6
Careless navigation	6
Master asleep on watch	3
Incompetent master/officer, or captain too old	4
Wrong course steered	3
Bad anchoring	3
Engine breakdown followed by stranding	2
Other strandings and accidents due to collision, stress of weather, overloading, and the poor condition of vessels	25
Total	52

Source: Records of the Fiji Marine Board, Office of the Harbour Master, Suva.

was usually rice, tins of meat and fish, tea, and root vegetables such as *dalo* (taro). Cooking was often done over a Primus stove on deck. Loaves of bread were bought before sailing, and often food was obtained in villages, supplemented occasionally by fishing.

With the exception of the part-European officers on the bigger company ships, crews were usually entirely indigenous Fijians and all male. This composition was partly determined by the need for tolerance in such confined spaces. Ethnic homogeneity was also almost inevitable, since few of the Indo-Fijian population, which had its origins in indentured land laborers from 1879 to 1916, showed any interest in a life at sea during the 1960s, other than in their own boats. This exclusiveness in crewing was further reinforced with the founding of the seamen's trade union in 1946, the rules of which excluded all but Fijians from membership.[4] Stevedoring labor was likewise composed of ethnic Fijians, based on casual employment with high and low demands for labor with ship arrivals. Sailors ashore would be engaged for cargo handling, and in the sugar ports firms would pay the *turaga ni koro* of nearby villages to supply labor.

In practice the crews of interisland vessels were not strongly unionized. They tolerated low pay, poor food, hard work, and physical danger. The excitement and freedom of going to sea when it suited them compensated for the harsh conditions. The men also valued opportunities to socialize in villages and sometimes to carry out informal trading. Sailors would make gifts or barter tobacco and other items for yaqona, *voi voi,* and tapa, which they would sell to middlemen and market stall holders in Suva.

The small-scale trading by sailors was paralleled also by many passengers who carried an array of goods between port towns and islands as gifts and barter and for ceremonial purposes. These informal functions of the interisland vessels were of minor economic importance but very valuable socially. The noncommercial components of such island linkages became more visible when vessels were chartered for the purpose. Some traditional exchanges and other maritime customs that persisted into the 1960s are summarized below from field notes.

Persistence of Maritime Traditions in the 1960s

The first example of traditional exchanges described below appears simply to be barter, although a few border on the major *solevu* so important in the traditional interisland relationships of the distant past. The persistence of the *solevu* belies the prediction by Basil Thomson in 1908 that this would soon disappear: "With the arrival of the trader who, all unconsciously, was set to teach the natives an entirely new system of trade based on commerce, all need for the *solevu* vanished, and each product immediately acquired a recognized place in the scale of values, either in money or calico."[5]

Author's Field Notes and Port Records

10 March 1964: 24 people left Lautoka for Yaqeta Island on the 23ft cutter *Qoroi*. They carried 24 five-gallon drums of kerosene and 18 baskets of salt (locally produced) to exchange for mats and foodstuffs.

18 March 1964: The people of Naidi village near Savusavu and the people of Nabuna village on Koro Island chartered the cutter *Tui Vunalagi* (33 tons) for an exchange. The goods carried included dinner services, large basins, and household implements. They returned with bundles of *voi voi* and bales of tapa.

15 August 1964: A Sogosogo Vakamarama (women's association) from Lautoka arrived at Koro on the *Gau Princess* (14 tons) for a *solevu*. This had been under preparation for about 10 months. They brought 40 tins biscuits, 16 bags flour, 16 bags sugar, 45 gallon drums of kerosene, and 20 yards of material. They received 120 mats, 120 tanoas, several lengths of tapa, and a *tabua* (whale's tooth).

8 September 1964: Women of Nacamaki village on Koro received 10 women from Suva who were wives of policemen. They arrived on the cutter *Adi Maopa* (43 tons) and brought dressing tables, chairs, crockery, and bags of rice. The party spent 2 weeks at Nacamaki and returned to Suva with mats, *voi voi*, coconut oil, dalo, and pigs.

12 October 1964: Women boarded the MV *Altair* at Suva on their way to a Vakabodidrua (100th night end of formal mourning) at the island of Kanacea. They carried soap, yaqona, and kerosene and returned on 22 November with mats and *masi* [bark cloth].

15 October 1964: 48 people sailed from Suva on the *Yatu Lau* for Lakeba. They were returning home after visiting relatives at the Vatukoula gold mines in northern Viti Levu. There they presented mats, masi, taro, yams, and coconut oil. They received money with which they purchased furniture, cloth, and kerosene at Suva.

A MAJOR *SOLEVU* AND MARITIME DISASTER

A large-scale *solevu* took place in March 1964. The following account was put together from participants and from official Fiji police reports about the ensuing disaster at sea. It provides some details of preparations and presentations and also reveals how enthusiasm for the event overrode respect for the sea. This and possibly social pressures on the captain to overload contributed to the loss of the ship. The event was initiated in 1962 through what seems to have been a simple *kerekere* request by women of the village of Waitoga on Nairai Island to a related woman living in Suva, asking for money to repair the church. The recipient Tamalesi of Vatuwaqa contacted other Nairai women in Suva, and at some stage during regular meetings over two years a *solevu* was decided on.

The auxiliary cutter *Kadavulevu* was chartered for the trip. Built in 1920, she was 23 GT, 58 feet in length, and 15 feet in breadth and had recently been surveyed and licensed for the carriage of twenty-two passengers and seven crew (figure 10.2). The vessel carried lifeboats and life rafts to take thirty-one persons, and lifejackets for twenty-nine. The Fijian captain was an experienced seaman, Filimoni Samaki, aged sixty-two. He was qualified for this size of ship and had thirty-five years of sea service locally. The owner was the part-Chinese Samson-Lee, who sailed as engineer; the mate, Peter-Lee, was his brother; and there were four Fijian sailors plus Salesi-Lee, the son of the mate. The arrangements were for a *solevu* party numbering twenty-eight, although some thirty children were soon added. On the afternoon of 26 March members of the party began to board the ship. They stowed their *kaukau* (goods to present) in the hold and elsewhere. These included single and double beds, bales of cloth,

FIGURE 10.2. The Fiji cutter *Kadavulevu* (23 tons) berthed at Levuka. The boat sank in the Koro Sea on 29 March 1964, with the loss of about ninety people. (Photograph courtesy of the Fiji Marine Board, 1962)

mats, and on-deck pens of fowls and drums of kerosene. They also carried food and drink for the trip and AU$800 collected for the church.

People continued to arrive at the berth by taxis up until after 2200. By the time the boat left Suva at 2240 there were some ninety persons on board. Fortunately the weather was favorable for the sixty-five-mile passage. The boat anchored off Waitoga village before midday on Good Friday, 27 March. Everyone disembarked by boats, and the goods were unloaded. After being housed and fed, the visitors presented their *solevu* and money at the *rara* (ceremonial grounds). There were speeches, and quantities of yaqona were consumed, followed by a *magiti* (feast) and *meke* (women's sitting dances) and later a *tralala* (joint circle dance, one behind the other).

On Saturday the Waitoga people arranged their *solevu* in an elaborate display some five feet high. This comprised 250 Nairai thick mats, 3 tons of yams, 4 tons of dalo, 800 coconuts, 3 sacks of tapioca, 8 bundles of bananas, 6 bundles of *voi voi*, 150 bottles of coconut oil, 8 live pigs, and 4 live chickens. A *magiti*, dancing, and drinking went on until midnight and, for some men, throughout the night.

On Easter Sunday all but three of the original passengers boarded along with four additional from Nairai. All the goods were stowed along with personal gifts. The ship sailed at 1530 for Suva. At 1900 they passed the island of Gau. The sea was then rough, and the boat was rolling heavily. After some debate it was decided to press on to Suva rather than shelter at Gau. At about 2300 the *Kadavulevu* capsized within sight of the lights of Viti Levu. There were only three survivors. They were able to relate what happened. One woman (Nina, aged forty-nine), who was supported by mats during the night, came across a raft at daybreak. She climbed on board, as did about ten other people, including two sailors and a boy aged fourteen. On Monday morning there was only debris to be seen in the rough sea. The sailors managed to retrieve green coconuts and peel them with their teeth for the survivors. By Thursday only one woman and the boy remained there to be rescued. All others on the raft had disappeared into the sea. The sailors may have tried to swim ashore for help but never made it. The other woman survivor (Saine, aged forty-three) also left the raft to swim ashore. She supported herself with timber and was washed up on a reef on Thursday morning. From there she swam ashore and gave details of the tragedy to the marine rescue parties already searching. By then about ninety people had drowned.[6]

This tragedy led to more stringent regulations in Fiji regarding the safety of life at sea. Captains were now required to deposit lists of passengers at the office of the harbormaster before sailing, and spot checks would be made to ensure that the number of passengers was within permitted levels. Compliance with these regulations could in practice be monitored only at main ports, however.

These few examples of continuation of traditional maritime customs have a number of common characteristics. Every stage of the exchange system, for example, was initiated by women, who also predominated in the parties who travelled—it was suggested by Fijian men that these exchanges arranged by women were merely excuses for long holidays. In any event they revealed mutual support between related communities. One of the survivors of the *Kadavulevu* could name forty people on board that she knew well. Another feature was the consistent flow of "European" goods from the urban areas against "Fijian" goods from the islands, which presumably brought cultural as well as economic satisfaction to the participants, and emphasized the heritage value of local shipping.

FIJI, 1980–2007

Many structural and social changes took place in maritime activities by the 1980s and onward, although there were still navigational hazards and casualties. Alan Howard again cites the experiences of Rotuman people who purchased the interisland vessel *Wain Rua* in 1992 at a price of F$250,000: "It went aground on a reef at Kadavu in August 1993 and was judged unsalvageable."[7] Nevertheless increased investments were made in infrastructure, including some new types of vessels. This coincided with the withdrawal of foreign merchants from local shipping as their conventional ships went out of class with age.

New port developments, including ramps and other landing facilities, were established at selected central places in several islands at which Ro-Ro vessels, ferries, and barges could berth (figure 10.3).[8] The fast-turnaround Ro-Ro *Princess Ashika* (677 GT) was purchased from Japan. She entered the run between Suva and Kadavu, capable of carrying cargo, four hundred or so passengers, and fifty motor vehicles, thereby replacing the capacity of more than twenty cutters. Other big ships included the *Bulou ni Ceva* (338 GT) and *Queen Salamasina* (647 GT). The latter vessel, as with others, was bought secondhand. She was ex-Japanese and had already operated for twenty-two years between Apia and Pago Pago for a Samoan company.[9] Large numbers of passengers and baggage rooms on these vessels obscured any traditional exchange activities.

With the withdrawal of shipping by expatriate merchant companies, shipping finance now came from equity investments of the business community in Fiji, as well as bank loans and government allocations of overseas aid. The shipping entrepreneurs included the Indo-Fijian Khan shipping group and the rising ship-owning Patterson family of Suva. There were also substantial investments by overseas hotel and cruise enterprises such as the Captain Cook, Beachcomber, and Blue Lagoon companies. By the year 2000, out of 166 vessels registered, 115 were tourist related. There were in addition many very small craft in island trading.

FIGURE 10.3. Modern Ro-Ro berth at Kadavu Island, Fiji, and adjacent platform for landing craft and barges. (Photograph by the author, 1986)

MODERN SAILORS IN FIJI

The more sophisticated vessels required better-trained and better-qualified seafarers. Achieving this has been promoted and coordinated in all states through the Maritime Advisory Services of the Secretariat of the Pacific Community (SPC). A South Pacific Maritime Code, first introduced in the 1980s, laid down regulations based on International Maritime Organization (IMO) conventions but customized for interisland trading.[10] The aim of the most recent IMO convention of 1995 is to ensure that each officer and rating is trained and examined for competence in the functions he or she is to perform on board. Of particular importance are training in safety standards, especially as relating to crowd control, stability, and emergencies on Ro-Ro vessels, as the greatest recent loss of life occurred from eight Ro-Ro craft sinking in similar interisland operations in the Philippines between 1980 and 1988, with a total loss of 6,092 people.[11] The information that follows on training, individual sailors, and present-day human relations in Fiji is derived primarily from observations, interviews, and personal communications.

In Fiji, training is carried out at the Fiji Institute of Technology, School of Maritime Studies (SMS) in Suva and in the Western District. Courses include ratings up to AB and motorman, cadets, and deck and engineering officers from Class 6 (small craft and restricted distance) to Class 1 (master mariner and chief engineer foreign-going). The intermediate grades 2 to 5 qualify candidates for varying distances and ship tonnages. The school enrolls male and a few female students from Fiji and elsewhere and is multiracial.

Deck and engineering ratings have been consistently male. This is based on past seafaring traditions, the beliefs of employers that females are not capable of the hard physical work on deck and in engine rooms and may cause problems on board, and the additional costs of supplying separate facilities on small vessels. As a result, most Pacific island women have until recently been confined to hotelling and catering work on bigger ferries and cruise ships.

The profile of the average AB on a local ship is male, about age twenty-eight, who has left school early in his secondary education, engaged in other work, had some maritime family contacts or met seafarers in urban areas, and decided to enter local shipping and train as a junior rating. At one time he would probably have come from the outer islands. Nowadays recruitment is more diverse—from towns, islands, and even highland rural villages.

The profile is different for potential officers. Apprentice officers after secondary school may start on bigger local ships and progress as cadets on foreign-going vessels while following courses at the SMS at specified periods. The progress in the officer corps from cadet to Class 1 certificate may best be illustrated by summarizing the career of a modern Fijian sailor with typical ambitions and ambivalences to life at sea.

Tomasi Cama Kete was born in 1963 of parents who were originally from Lau. He reached sixth form at school and was eventually attracted to shipping. He attended SMS, served as a cadet on Marine Department vessels, then on the foreign-going ships of the Sofrana line. He followed certificate courses at the SMS and the Australian Maritime College. When qualified as an officer, he sailed with Samoa Shipping Services, Zapata USA, Blue Lagoon Cruises, Botany Bay Shipping, and other companies at all levels, including relieving master. There are high demands for such sea experience and qualifications ashore in education, government, ports, and commerce, as well as shortages at sea. Kete was sought after, and he taught for a time at the school. He says:

> I quit being a permanent seafarer in November 1995 due to family commitments, but I still go out to sea at school breaks when time permits. I finally attained my Ship Master Class 1 [in Australia] in October 2003,

which I think is the peak of my seafaring career—even though I have not commanded a huge ship, which was one of my dreams when I started as a cadet. But I loved my time at sea, especially travelling around the world, with all its fun and available finances that go with it. My family is my main priority, and my main investment is my kids back home, as my presence alone with them will make a lot of difference to their future. I feel that I still need to go out to sea, but at a shorter period, to ensure that my Ship Master Certificate of Competency is valid at all times. It was through my seafaring career that I was acknowledged back home by my family and also motivated other youngsters back home to acquire an opportunity in the seafaring industry. My village alone has bred two Master Class One certificate holders.

In 2007 Captain Kete received a scholarship for a master of science degree at the United Nations World Maritime University, Malmö, Sweden.

As well as improvements in maritime education and training under IMO regulations, there has also been a veritable social revolution in Fiji. The young generation of Pacific sailors no longer seriously ascribes to the old tradition that females bring "bad luck" to a ship. Pacific women have shown considerable strength of character, as well as new professionalism, in taking charge of crews and in coping with family. A few summarized profiles will convey something of this new gender phenomenon in Pacific sea life:

Asenaca, age 25: In 2002–2006 qualified for a diploma in nautical science at SMS. Sea time as a cadet, was on the cruise ships *Spirit of the Pacific* and *Reef Escape*. She married a fellow seafarer in 2006, and in 2007 she was bosun of the cruise ship *Ra Marama*. She had a baby girl in 2007 and was studying for a Master Class 3, with the aim of a shore job.

Ofa, age 33: From 1996 to 2000 was cadet on cruise and Ro-Ro ships. She had a baby in 2000, which delayed her seagoing career for eleven months. During 2001 she flew to Honolulu and joined a long-liner fishing vessel. In 2002, while looking after her son, she passed certificate exams for Master Class 4. In 2003–2004 she served as chief officer on the local tourist ship *Tui Tai* and as second officer on the *Spirit of Fiji Islands* and the Ro-Ro passenger vessel *Sullivan*. In 2005 Ofa married an engineering officer, and in 2006 her second son was born. In July 2007 she was ashore with prospects as an operations manager of a shipping company and studying for Master Class 3.

Rebekah, age 29: She went to sea before her eighteenth birthday on inter-island general cargo and Ro-Ro passenger ships. Then in 1996 she sailed as a cadet on gas tankers throughout the Pacific. In 1998 she married a fellow seafarer ("No, we did not meet on the same ship"). Rebekah joined an American-owned jig boat as fishing master/chief officer, catching albacore in the North Pacific and discharging in Ilwaco and Honolulu. She sailed out of Honolulu for another six months on long-liners, returning in 2002 to SMS to study for a Class 3 certificate. She taught safety courses at SMS, then sailed as third officer on *Boral Gas* until the start of 2005, "when pregnancy to my fellow seafaring husband beckoned me home." From 2005 to 2007, she was studying, via distance learning, the Advanced Diploma Maritime Business and Logistics Management course at the Australian Maritime College in Tasmania, as well as taking care of her son. She was also actively involved in the Pacific Women in Maritime Association (PacWIMA).

Susana, age 30: Joined as a cadet in 1997. She served on local vessels, cruise ships, and *Pertiwi 9*, a foreign-going ocean tug. She qualified at SMS to Master Class 4. Her seagoing career includes chief officer of the ocean tug *Pertiwi 9*, chief officer of supply vessels MV *Celeste* and *Pacific Hawk*, and master of MV *Celeste*, engaged in voyages to Singapore and other Asian ports, Australia, New Zealand, and the Pacific Islands. In 2007 she was preparing for Master Class 3.

The other change in human relations in Fiji has been an amelioration within the maritime sector of the sensitive issue of race relations. The exclusion of all but indigenous Fijians from the Waterside Workers and Seamen's Union, which was registered in 1946 with a specific racial limitation clause, continued until a rival unsegregated seamen's union emerged in 1992. The reasons for the initial segregation are deeply embedded in colonial history. However, with the increase of Fijians as wage earners in ports and shipping, trade union exclusiveness seemed as much a matter of class as race. Ports and shipping had Fijian laborers and ratings, while Europeans and part-Europeans were officials and officers. Capital in turn came from the United Kingdom and Australasia and locally from Indo-Fijian commercial sources. The more class-conscious union organizers saw the Fijians as "workers" and the others as "bosses" who were not eligible for union membership.

The mobility of a few Fijian ratings with sufficient education to junior officer levels and the increase of indigenous Fijians serving as cadets and officers on local vessels have reduced the basis for class resentment. There are still racial problems, but younger Fijian sailors recognize the merits of Indo-Fijians as mariners. For example, the Khan family on the island of Nairai have long been regarded as good sailors, running their own cutters, and Captain Khan is a highly respected master in command of a Ro-Ro with Fijian officers and crew.

By way of emphasizing both of these social changes, there is the experience of Carol Dunlop. She is ethnically a European of English origin who became a citizen of Fiji. She was an experienced yachtswoman, but when she applied to the SMS to study for Master Class 4, she was rejected on the grounds of race, gender, and mistaken nationality by a Fijian maritime official of the old school. Later a more enlightened professional welcomed her. She was successful in the examination, although when seeking a sea appointment, she "contacted every single shipping company" and got the same sort of replies: "We don't employ women," "No accommodation," "A woman will cause trouble on the ship." In a changing social environment, she became chief officer with a Fijian crew, and master of the *Surprise*—one of the most modern cruise vessels in the region—with officers and sailors from Fiji.[12]

The other partial force for change is the trade union movement. This movement has a checkered history in the maritime sector. Sailors, while intensely loyal to shipmates, are difficult to organize nationally, due to their mobility and a certain independence from shore authorities. The formation of unions was never favored in colonial times, and the national governments after independence used inherited penal measures against them. This approach saw several of the leaders of the Fiji Waterside Workers and Seamen's Union jailed for strike action in 1977. Successive attempts at new trade union organization failed due to bad management and financial problems, including the multiracial Seamen's Union founded in 1992. During 2006 another nonracial union was under formation, led by young, well-educated seafarers in Suva. One of the many issues in their agenda was the low levels of wages and their disparity between ships and companies. The rates for ABs on local ships in 2006, for example, ranged from US$260 to US$460 per month, with little in the way of collective bargaining, which was a union aspiration.

A Pacific Regionally Owned Shipping Line

The attempts in the nineteenth and early twentieth centuries by island trading and shipping enterprises to bypass foreign shipping were revived in the mid-twentieth century. This was a time of rising ocean freight rates and a greater awareness that the rates for the carriage of manufactured goods were generally passed on to island consumers as higher prices, while the freight rates in the export of raw materials were deducted from the payments made to island producers. This, allied to the innate desire of islanders to run their own ocean transport, gave rise to renewed attempts at obtaining national shipping capacity.

In 1959 the government of Tonga purchased the MV *Aoniu* to carry overseas cargoes consigned to Tonga, which were discharged at Suva. By this means at least most of the transshipment freight would accrue to a Tongan vessel. The *Aoniu* also conducted interisland trading and passenger carriage in Tonga along with local barge transport. Keeping schedules was difficult and sometimes was made more so by the ship being used to carry the royal family on state visits to Samoa. In 1963 Tonga purchased an additional cargo passenger vessel, the *Nuivakai*, which was put on the Australia-Fiji-Tonga regional service in competition with the Union Steamship Company of New Zealand. The ship at that time employed European captains and officers and Tongan sailors.

During this period the United Nations Conference on Trade and Development (UNCTAD) was encouraging national shipping in developing countries to help regional integration and present countervailing power in the setting of liner freight rates.[13] Over the years 1960–1971 the phosphate-rich government of Nauru started a national line with the MV *Eigamoya, Rosie D,* and *Enna G*. These ships had European captains and officers and Tongan sailors. In 1970 the Cook Islands government founded a national shipping company, chartering the *Thallo* and *Lorene* for the fruit trade to New Zealand. British and New Zealand masters and officers were employed, with Cook Island ratings. This was the start of a controversy over national crewing entitlements, since the Cook Island vessels received financial support from the New Zealand government.

These national endeavors in shipping gave rise to discussions at the Pacific Forum. The forum, comprising sixteen Pacific countries, approved a concept of a jointly owned regional shipping line, the Pacific Forum Line, or PFL. All member states became eligible as shareholders, either by allocating ships or by making financial investments. Those that joined were the Cooks, Fiji, Kiribati, the Marshalls, Nauru, New Zealand, Niue, Papua New Guinea (which had started a national line in 1976), Samoa, the Solomons, Tonga, and Tuvalu, while Australia offered some financial support.

The new regional line, which had social as well as economic functions, faced many problems, including trading between islands, many of which were virtually monocultural in copra production; providing viable services to distant islands with low volumes of trade; and competing with already established shipping lines on high-volume routes, several of which were overtonnaged. At the same time, charter rates for foreign ships were often high and currency fluctuations unfavorable. Then there was the issue of chartering ships from the national lines of members, which in the case of New Zealand also meant higher charter rates due to the better wages and conditions of New Zealand seafarers.

The issue of the wages of seafarers on routes from Australia and New Zealand to the Pacific Islands was of long standing and emerged again just before the PFL started operations. New Zealand seafarers were already losing employment. The workforce was reduced by almost a quarter during the early 1970s as a result of the replacement of conventional vessels by container ships, and reduced manning on all vessels with the introduction of general-purpose crews and labor-saving equipment. The Union Steamship Company of New Zealand (USS Co.) in turn was losing profitable passenger traffic to air transport and, as a result, was withdrawing the New Zealand–crewed passenger-cargo liner *Tofua* from the New Zealand–Fiji–Tonga–Samoa service. The Nauru Pacific Line seized the opportunity to send the *Enna G* with a Fijian crew to enter the New Zealand–based route vacated by the *Tofua*.

Under the circumstances it was no surprise when the maritime unions in New Zealand declared the low-wage *Enna G* "black." The New Zealand Seamen's Union agreed in principle to the rights of vessels flying the flags of Pacific states that were entering trade between New Zealand and their Pacific home state, providing the crews were paid at ITF rates and were union members. Nauru challenged this as discrimination. The Fijian crew ultimately expressed agreement with the New Zealand seamen on rights to equal pay with New Zealand crews and were discharged by the company. The *Enna G* was held in Wellington from May to September 1973. The ship then left to trade elsewhere with some reinstated Fijian seafarers on island rates.

When the PFL finally started in 1978, it had to avoid the prospect of another *Enna G* type of issue over crewing and wages. The National Shipping Corporation of New Zealand chartered the *New Zealand II* to the PFL. The vessel had a New Zealand crew, but the extra costs of this was borne by the New Zealand government. The early patterns of PFL services were on circular routes from Australia and New Zealand to the islands, and between islands.

The long-distance, low-volume route from Auckland through Suva, Funafuti, and Tarawa to Majuro in the Marshalls proved uneconomic. A feeder service was substituted, starting from Suva with transshipments to Tarawa. Even with the reduced trading distance, this service could survive only with subsidies from Australia and New Zealand. In the early 1980s two new ships specifically designed for the Pacific island trades were chartered. These were built with aid from West Germany—one to Tonga, the *Fua Kavenga* (meaning "the bearer of heavy responsibility"); and the other, the *Forum Samoa*, to Samoa. They were replaced in 2002 by the very modern *Forum Samoa II* (figure 10.4) and *Captain Tasman (Fua Kavenga II)*.

FIGURE 10.4. The Pacific Forum Line's *Forum Samoa II* (2002)—like her sister ship, *Captain Tasman*—carries 310 containers and has refrigerated and bulk liquid space, a twenty-six-ton gantry crane, a Ro-Ro ramp, and a speed of 15 knots. She has a crew of thirty, which includes a large number of trainees. (Courtesy of the Pacific Forum Line)

TABLE 7. Crew composition on the *Forum Samoa*, 18 August 1999

Officers and petty officers			Ratings		
Rank	Nationality	Age	Rank	Nationality	Age
Master	Filipino	48	AB	Dominican	31
Chief officer	Filipino	48	AB	Filipino	35
Second officer	Fijian	35	AB	Samoan	35
Chief engineer	Fijian	52	OS	Samoan	26
Second engineer	Filipino	38	OS	Samoan	27
Electrical engineer	Honduran	40	Engineer trainee	Samoan	26
Oiler	Samoan	26	Engineer trainee	Samoan	22
Engineer cadet	Samoan	24	Cook	Samoan	31

Source: Crew lists.

TABLE 8. Crew composition on the *Captain Tasman*, 10 August 2007

Officers and petty officers			Ratings		
Rank	Nationality	Age	Rank	Nationality	Age
Master	Fijian	35	AB	Tongan	23
Chief officer	Fijian	41	AB	Tongan	26
Second officer	Tongan	42	OS	Tongan	20
Third officer	Tongan	26	Cook	Tongan	24
Chief engineer	Polish	44	Trainee steward	Tongan	24
Second engineer	Tongan	30	Assistant deck mechanic trainee	Filipino	45
Third engineer	Tongan	34	Deck trainee	Tongan	22
Electrician	Filipino	48	Deck trainee	Tongan	21
Chief steward	Tongan	54	Deck trainee	Tongan	39
Fitter	Tongan	33	Deck trainee	Tongan	25
Oiler	Tongan	26	Engineer trainee	Tongan	22
Bosun	Tongan	24	Engineer trainee	Tongan	21
			Engineer trainee	Tongan	20
			Engineer trainee	Tongan	28

Source: Pacific Forum Line.

The four or so PFL ships continue to be time-chartered from the Pacific and overseas companies that own them. Consequently the owners provide the crews. The PFL encourages them to employ Pacific island officers and sailors, but only on ships owned by Pacific Forum states is it possible to have a majority of the crew from the Pacific. Table 7 lists the nationalities of the crew of the older *Forum Samoa* by ranks and ages on 18 August 1999 and shows only two Pacific islanders as officers. By way of comparison over time, the crew list of the *Captain Tasman*, in which the PFL has an investment, is given in Table 8 for 10 August 2007. On this list the captain is a thirty-five-year-old Fijian, and most of the officers are from the Pacific; only the chief engineer and the electrician are non-Pacific. Another Pacific crewing feature is the extra numbers of deck and engine trainees carried. This demonstrates the PFL's ongoing commitment to the future seagoing community in the Pacific.[14]

There were undoubtedly occasions when the Pacific Forum Line appeared as if it would collapse in much the same way as earlier island-owned ventures. That it did not was due to the loyalty of the shareholder states. Part of this resilience was the pride of the Pacific community in seeing island ships sailing again on Pacific ocean routes. Fiji Prime Minister Ratu Mara expressed it very simply: "When you see this boat floating around with the Forum symbol—it is a great thing."[15]

CHAPTER ELEVEN

The Global Pacific Seafarer

THE ECONOMIC CRISIS after 1973 brought a fall in ocean freight rates and fierce competition within an overtonnaged world merchant fleet. This was followed by increased shifts in the recruitment of seafarers from western Europe and North America to the lower-labor-cost countries of Asia and the Pacific and, more recently, to Russia and eastern Europe. Of the one and a quarter million merchant seafarers supplied to international shipping in the year 2005, more than half a million came from the Philippines, Indonesia, China, Turkey, and India. The Pacific Islands supplied only about 7,300 officers and ratings (table 9). However, this number is of great economic significance for many small islands, and the regular rotation mainly of young men between sea and land has profoundly affected island social and cultural life.

The overseas merchant ships on which Pacific islanders serve belong predominantly to German, French, British, and American companies. Many operate under the flags of convenience (FOCs) of Liberia, Cyprus, Antigua, and Panama.[1] FOCs enable owners to recruit from anywhere in the world at reduced labor costs and avoid home-state corporation taxation and social legislation. The less scrupulous FOC shipowners can also disregard the rights of seafarers with impunity; they can conceal their own identities and safely assume that the states whose flags they use have neither the will nor the capability to enforce international safety conventions on their vessels.[2]

Hiring out their sovereignty as FOCs is a source of revenue for many developing countries, including some in the Pacific. The Marshall Islands by 2006 had moved to fourth-highest place in the world shipping league, with 953 ships, totaling nearly 33 million GT, under its flag. Vanuatu had 419 ships, aggregating 2 million GT; Tonga, possibly nearly 0.5 million GT; and Tuvalu, 60 vessels.[3] These Pacific-registered ships trade internationally, have no genuine ownership links with the flags they fly, and, considering the hundreds of ships involved, employ only a few Pacific island sailors. The island governments benefit mainly from ship registration fees.

In addition to the FOC system, Germany, France, and Britain register vessels under a second register.[4] These ships fly nationally related flags that have to comply with several national laws, but the shipowners enjoy tax-haven allowances and the same freedom to recruit anywhere in the world ("crews of convenience"). Most of the vessels sailing under FOCs and sec-

TABLE 9. Supply of seafarers to international shipping from the Pacific Islands, 2005

	Officers	Ratings	Total
Cook Islands	58	72	130
Federated States of Micronesia	91	122	213
Fiji	597	208	805
French Polynesia	318	497	815
Guam	8	12	20
Kiribati	30	1,970	2,000
Marshall Islands	15	25	40
New Caledonia	77	121	198
Northern Mariana Islands	10	20	30
Papua New Guinea	434	553	987
Samoa	NA	NA	NA
Solomon Islands	134	207	341
Tonga	54	121	175
Tuvalu	33	650	683
Vanuatu	266	520*	786
Wallis and Futuna	41	73	114
Total	2,166	5,171	7,337

Source: BIMCO ISF *Manpower Update—The World Demand for and Supply of Seafarers* (Coventry: Warwick Institute for Employment Research, 2005).

*In 2007 there were 180 ni-Vanuatu "catering attendants" (including 50 women) sailing on Carnival Cruise ships out of Australia and about 30 ni-Vanuatu seafarers on other foreign flag ships. None were on any Vanuatu flag-of-convenience vessels, according to SPC Regional Maritime Programme data. Some of the returns in the BIMCO ISF survey on the supply of seafarers in this table must include crews of bigger interisland ships as well as international vessels. There is validity in this, since sailors move from one sector to the other.

ond registries have multinational crews. The global hierarchical structure is broadly 40 percent officers from countries in the OECD (Organisation for Economic Co-operation and Development), plus Russia, Poland, and some of the eastern European states, and most of the ratings from eastern Europe and developing countries, including some Pacific islands.

Increasingly, young men and a few women from the Pacific are moving to officer ranks on foreign-flag ships, as there is a dire shortage of officers in the developed ship-owning states. The shortage is due to both declining interest in careers at sea and the losses of trained personnel arising from demands ashore in business, technology, and administration for well-qualified mariners. One of the several advantages to Germany, for example, of recruiting lower-cost sailors in Kiribati and training some of them to officer levels is the lack of well-paid employment in islands for their skills, which would attract officers ashore. Thus there is a minimizing of wastage from manpower training investments.[5] There are twelve maritime training institutions in the Pacific Islands. Only Fiji and Papua New Guinea provide the full range of education and training from pre-sea, rating, and officer courses to Class 1 foreign-going masters and chief engineers. Several other places offer training of ratings and/or junior officers. There is mobility in training, with concentrations for special courses under the coordination of the SPC Regional Maritime Programme.

The example chosen for a case study in global seafaring is Kiribati, for several reasons. Kiribati in 1959 (as part of the Gilbert and Ellice Islands crown colony, GEIC) was already supplying seafarers to the China Navigation Company of Britain. There were also crews and a few I-Kiribati nationals serving as officers, usually with European captains, on colony ships sailing on long-distance interisland routes. In terms of distance, Kiribati shipping was virtually foreign-going. There were the requirements to service 1,000 miles of small islands of the Gilbert and Ellice, and round-trips of 3,600 miles to Christmas Island. The *Moana Raoi* (250 tons) was one of two vessels making these trips and also connecting with Fiji. Voyages to distant islands were made carrying small quantities of cargo and many deck passengers (figure 11.1). In 1964 the last of the Tangitang vessels, the *Aratoba,* was finally abandoned, and the crews were seeking work. During 1966 a vessel of the Hamburg Süd line of Germany called at Tarawa, where the captain was impressed by these developments and by the sturdy, amiable young men clearly keen and available to work as sailors. The company followed this up, and as is evident from table 9, Kiribati is now the principal country in the Pacific island region for supplying seafarers.

FIGURE 11.1. The MV *Moana Raoi* (250 GT) was one of two interisland/foreign-going vessels of the Gilbert and Ellice Islands. The ship was on a passage from Tarawa to Suva, calling at all islands on the way and working cargo and carrying passengers between them when this photograph was taken. Ship boats are shown landing deck passengers at Funafuti, Tuvalu. (Photograph by the author, 1964)

Selection, Training, and Crewing in Kiribati

In 1967 Hamburg Süd, with assistance of the British and German governments and the UN, established what became the Marine Training Centre (MTC) at Betio, Tarawa, under the agency of the South Pacific Marine Services (SPMS). It ultimately developed as the leading center for the training and supply of I-Kiribati seafarers to nine German-owned shipping companies. Recruitment is carried out in conjunction with the government of Kiribati, based on a quota determined by the size of population on each island. Selection includes written tests in the English language, and basic mathematics, physics, and geography, together with an interview and a physical examination. These are relatively high requirements for positions as ratings, and they form the possible basis for junior officer courses that are conducted in Fiji. Later in their careers they may take senior courses (master mariner and first class marine engineer) available in Fiji, Papua New Guinea, New Zealand, Australia, and the UK financed by foreign scholarships and interest-free loans from German companies. This makes a career at sea highly attractive, and applications for the hundred places available at MTC are received each year from more than one thousand young men. No females had been accepted as of 2007.

While at MTC, students are generally at ages eighteen to twenty-four but are accepted to age thirty. They obtain their keep and receive a small spending allowance of AU$10 per week. There is rigorous pre-sea training, which lasts for fifteen months and includes voyages on a local trading ship fitted with training facilities. Successful students are then allocated to German-owned vessels as general-purpose ratings. Later, as ordinary seamen (OS), they are divided into either deck or engine room duties, according to aptitude and preferences. Voyage contracts are for twelve months. After prescribed sea time, further training courses are conducted at MTC for upgrading to AB and motorman (MM). A similar center, established at Funafuti in Tuvalu after the partition of the GEIC in 1979, also supplies sailors for German-owned shipping, partly through SPMS.[6]

Analysis of Crew Lists

As in the past, there is considerable mobility of multinational ships' crews and therefore difficulties in obtaining accurate data. For this reason, determining details of crewing depends on acquiring the crew lists of specific ships at a single port on one day of a voyage. In 2001 there were 874 I-Kiribati ratings on German-owned ships, primarily under the Liberian and Cypriot flags, and 326 under German second register. Other seafarers were on leave. Analysis of one hundred crew lists of ships with Pacific sailors for 1998–1999 indicate that I-Kiribati ratings made up full deck crews on most ships on which they served; on others, there were additions mainly from Tuvalu and Sri Lanka, and especially in the engine rooms there were several Fijians, Filipinos, and Ukrainians. On deck there were also two young Germans as trainees under I-Kiribati supervision. The officer composition on all vessels is more diversified than that of ratings, as indicated by a crew list for the MV *Buenos Aires,* for example (table 10). A crew list for the MV *Columbus Canada* shows the wide spread of islands in Kiribati from which ratings were drawn and the positions of I-Kiribati officers (table 11).

The one hundred crew lists include twelve vessels with I-Kiribati officers. Table 12 presents positions and average ages of the I-Kiribati and German officers and indicates the potential for the nineteen I-Kiribati junior officers to move upward in rank. The absence of I-Kiribati as engineer officers is also apparent in the table and is probably due to low levels

TABLE 10. Crew composition on the *Buenos Aires*, 1999

Rank	Nationality
Captain	Bulgarian
Chief officer	Sri Lankan
Second officer	Croat
Third officer	Russian
Chief engineer	Polish
Second engineer	Sri Lankan
Third engineer	Polish
Electrician	Polish
Bosun	I-Kiribati
Ratings (11)	I-Kiribati

Source: Crew lists.

TABLE 11. Crew composition on the *Columbus Canada*, 1998

Officers and petty officers		Ratings	
Rank	Nationality	Rank / island	Rank / island
Captain	German	AB / Aranuka	Fitter / Makin
Chief officer	Polish	AB / Aranuka	MM / Makin
Third officer	I-Kiribati (Tarawa)	AB / Marakei	MM / Tabiteuea
Third officer	I-Kiribati (Abaiang)	AB / Nanouti	MM / Tarawa
Chief engineer	Polish	AB / Tarawa	Cook / Abemama
Second engineer	Polish	OS / Tamana	Steward / Butaritari
Third engineer	Polish	OS / Tabiteuea	Laundryman / Beru
Electrician	Austrian	OS / Tabiteuea	
Storeman (PO)	German	OS / Onatoa	
Bosun (PO)	I-Kiribati (Butaritari)		

Source: Crew lists.

TABLE 12. Officer composition on twelve ships that included I-Kiribati officers, 1998–1999

Rank	Number (and average age) German	Number (and average age) I-Kiribati	Other officers (engine and deck)
Captain	12 (54)	—	Filipino (engineer)
Chief officer	10 (38)	—	Polish (engineer)
Second officer	4 (30)	8 (27)	Swedish (engineer)
Third officer	3 (29)	11 (26)	Austrian (engineer)
Chief engineer	12 (51)	—	Tongan (second mate)
Second engineer	12 (40)	—	Tuvaluan (third mate)
Third engineer	13 (32)	—	
Other engineer	2	—	

Source: Crew lists.

of technological experience in the Kiribati islands. This contrasts with a more mechanized Fiji, as indicated earlier in the discussion of the crew composition on Pacific Forum Line ships (see chapter 10).

Fijian sailors are in fact more widely distributed over the global fleet than those of Kiribati, as for instance in a crew list of the French tanker MT *Henry Martin*. This French ship would be expected to employ a preponderance of sailors from French Polynesia. Instead the captain and chief engineer are French, the chief officer Panamanian, other officers Filipino, all the deck and engine ratings Fijian, and the catering staff Vanuatuan. It reflects also the shortages of officers from French Polynesia. Equally counterintuitive is a Vanuatuan-flag ship with a British captain, all Fijian deck and engineering officers (except the Filipino second engineer), and Fijian ratings, with only the bosun, steward, and cook Vanuatuan.

Most of the vessels on which Pacific islanders served are container and Ro-Ro ships trading to every part of the world. The crew list sample also shows them on quite small craft operating permanently in the coastal and short sea trades of northern Europe. The MV *Marman* (1,782 GT), under the Antiguan flag in 1999, was running from Duisburg on the Rhine to Cardiff in Wales. The crew consisted of a German captain and a Polish mate, while the only others on board were from Kiribati—one MM, two ABs, and one OS. As a small crew, they would have experienced exhausting work and frequently alien, dark, cold, and stormy conditions during the winter. I-Kiribati ratings normally sail as groups on SPMS ships, but a few are shown as spread individually on ships under British, Singapore, and Hong Kong flags.

Life at Sea

The life of an I-Kiribati sailor is similar to that of most other Pacific islanders in the global maritime labor market. By virtue of a national recruiting agency, and contracts that are negotiated and monitored by trade unions, most I-Kiribati sailors are spared the worst abuses that some other sailors under FOC endure, including abandonment in foreign ports and deprivation of wages.[7] The I-Kiribati sailors face only the generally accepted hazards that all sailors experience from bad weather, ship losses, accidents, attacks at sea from modern-day pirates, infectious diseases, and isolation. This account of life at sea is based on interviews with seafarers, managers, and trade union officials, as well as on personal observations ashore and afloat.

It is generally agreed by managers and officers that I-Kiribati sailors adapt well enough to life on a multinational ship. Nevertheless, some I-Kiribati ways need to be taken into account. The following is a generalized national profile, with all the defects that a generalization involves. The I-Kiribati sailor is considered polite and expects to be treated in a like manner. He has a spirit of competitiveness in trying to be the best on board—which is a tradition markedly displayed by I-Kiribati fishermen in home islands. He expects others to pull their weight in the crew and can be humorously dismissive of less sturdy shipmates from elsewhere. The tough environment of many Kiribati islands has also bred a resilience to hardship; thus, he usually endures strenuous work without complaint. As a sailor, he is willing to take risks, being accustomed to the treacherous sea conditions of the islands, but he does so with care, being conscious of family responsibilities. On the other hand, heavy drinking can release invective and aggression from stored-up feelings of mistreatment—he is more likely to forget a punch than an insult.

In practice, I-Kiribati crews are, like most sailors, quite culturally adaptive and can live and work with others of different national, religious, and ethnic backgrounds. They are not themselves totally homogenous. Those from the northern islands are usually Catholic, and some are accustomed to the hierarchically based governance of the *uea* (chiefs). Those from the south are generally Protestants and have a more democratic community governance system based on *maneaba* discussions led by the *unimane*

FIGURE 11.2. Modern Kiribati sailors on the German-owned container vessel *Cap Polonio* enjoy clean, air-conditioned accommodations. Their messroom is important for communal eating and socializing. (Photograph courtesy of the Hamburg Süd line, 2004)

(old men). When they come together on board, they follow the company-approved maritime union rules in electing a spokesman. This would not necessarily be the eldest, nor would a competent youngish bosun from elsewhere necessarily be resented as spokesman. This again shows something of the relative strengths of crew cultural identity, which can override differences in crew compositions.

There are always adaptations that have to be made by most Pacific sailors on foreign ships. Accommodation is good on the German vessels, although food is a problem for those who cannot tolerate for too long soups, stews, sausages, rye bread, cheese, or even potatoes and apples. This diet, while nutritionally beneficial, is a source of complaint, and I-Kiribati make requests for rice and fish. By contrast there is a considerable liking for German and other beers. These are normally for sale at sea, although spirits are banned. In the messroom, beer is the accompaniment to talking, smoking, and watching videos, including blue movies obtained in European ports. These limited forms of recreation on longer, boring passages are interspersed with escapist sleep and, very occasionally when at sea, a fight, usually induced by drink and an injudicious joke or remark. Fighting can result in a reprimand entry in the official logbook. For those involved, repetitions can mean dismissal and being sent home, with travel costs deducted from earnings. For this reason, fights rarely happen at sea; when they occur, they are usually in port.

Occupational Safety and Health

A modern ship can still be a dangerous place. Most deaths at sea are from marine disasters, but falls on slippery wet decks and injuries during mooring and in proximity to moving cargo gear are common nonfatal occurrences. Deaths and injuries in port can result from encounters with port equipment and falls from gangways between ships and quay, both of which can occur when returning on board inebriated. Drinking ashore is in fact a major hazard. Attacks take place when sailors are returning to the ship, and the crew try to keep together for mutual support in certain ports. This can equally well lead to trouble—one company manager described how a provoked I-Kiribati crew managed to "turn a bar from north to south." Of more concern to some sailors these days is the vague recollection of unprotected sex when drinking ashore.

Overall the health of Pacific sailors is probably better than that of home island populations. This may not appear so from statistics, as they often reflect the more frequent medical examinations of seafarers relative to other people. In Kiribati there is measurably less tuberculosis among seafarers. This applies also to hepatitis A, another common ailment in Kiribati. On the other hand, seafarers are exposed to malaria, typhoid, and cholera in tropical ports, influenza and chest complaints in high-latitude winter conditions, and sexually transmitted infections anywhere.

Common injuries at sea include back problems from lifting against ship motions, and general fatigue from poor-quality sleep in bad weather contributes to accidents. Common causes of death from illness among present-day sailors of all nationalities are cardiovascular disease, followed by malignant neoplasms and to a lesser extent cirrhosis of the liver. These are related to lifestyles with addictions to smoking and drinking and, in some cases, to obesity and lack of exercise. The number of deaths from these causes are increased at sea due to the lack of direct medical attention on most ships. Only when the ship is in or near port is there professional assistance or, if death occurs, a proper autopsy. A contrast in medical records is also seen. For example, the entry for a Fijian AB, aged forty-three, who died in port read: "Found dead in cabin—cause myocardial infraction, coronary thrombosis." But when sudden death occurs at sea, the reports may state merely "due to natural causes" or, as in the case of a Tuvalu sailor, "cause unknown, probably heart attack."[8] As in the past, deaths and injuries of seafarers are difficult to quantify internationally and are always underreported. Even less is known about the specific physical and mental problems of women at sea and how to deal with these in mixed-gender crews without medical staff.

Table 13 is an extract of I-Kiribati deaths on ships of British, Singapore, and Hong Kong registers over a period of twelve years. Since it is not known how many I-Kiribati sailors were serving on these ships, the table illustrates only the types of fatal occurrences and the forms of reports, not a statistical measure of mortality.

When an entry is "missing at sea," suicide is presumed, but usually this cannot be proven, as sailors very occasionally fall overboard accidentally. It is more likely that a depressed or otherwise stressed sailor decided to "go over the wall" rather than use other methods of killing himself. This may protect compensation payments to dependents, since his contract states that compensation is excluded from "death by willful acts." There are in fact few but regular cases of suicide on board ship. Reasons recorded, mainly from unsuccessful attempts, include loneliness, being shamed or ridiculed, news of a death or crisis at home, belief in the adultery of a partner, or an irrevocable belief in having a sexual disease.

TABLE 13. Causes of mortality in I-Kiribati seafarers on British, Singapore, and Hong Kong ships (1983–1995), from sample of masters' return forms

Rank	Cause of death	Location
MM	Cerebral anoxia	Died in cabin
Steward	Natural causes	Died in cabin
MM	Missing at sea	Last seen in cabin
AB	Missing at sea	Last seen in cabin
Steward	Internal bleeding due to knife wound	Stabbed in alleyway by AB in crew when drinking and arguing—ship at anchor

Source: UK Confidential Return Forms for Deaths of Merchant Seamen.

Statements by shipmates often indicate morose behavior and heavy drinking prior to suicide. The social defect in the community of most ships is the lack of opportunity for a stressed sailor to talk to someone in confidence about problems.

The very short and busy time of the modern ship in port has greatly compounded the problems of stress. The chaplains of the various missions to seafarers now have less chance ashore or on board to reach those with social or mental health difficulties. On some French ships, "worker priests" are signed on as sailors, often in catering, where they are in contact with all the members of the crew. A few German chaplains also go to sea from the missions. They, like the French, are primarily listeners and trained to give appropriate advice. They do not preach, unless invited to by seafarers, which makes them more acceptable on multifaith ships, and no doubt this reduces the perceived unluckiness of having a priest on board while at sea. On some vessels a trade union delegate will help, and on Chinese ships the former political commissar has been retained as part of the crew. He has several conflicting roles but can act as a nonjudgmental person who can talk to sailors and promote their welfare needs.[9]

The need for such onboard services, despite recent better access by family to radio telephone and sometimes e-mail communication, is recognized by progressive management. Modern communications can in fact sometimes exacerbate the stress situation, since wives regularly bring up immediate family problems, which are outside the ability of a remote sailor to deal with. Anguish and stress related to mental health problems affect only a relatively small number of seafarers, but proportionately they are considered to exceed those in most shore-based occupations.

These days the major health concerns that reach into the wider Pacific community are those of sexually transmitted infections (STIs), which are frequently attributed to foreign-going sailors. This has continuously been a worry since the time of Cook. The *Pacific Islands Monthly* in 1964 referred to "the rising incidence of VD [venereal disease] cases . . . in Fiji, Tahiti, and the Cook Islands" and went on to say that "most of the blame [is] laid at the door of professional seamen."[10] STIs are still on the increase. In 2000, seventy to eighty cases of gonorrhea were reported under treatment in Tarawa, and hepatitis B was being spread through sex, drug needles, and even tattooing. It is possible that the brief and busy time that the modern ship spends in port is exacerbating the problem, since sailors are more exposed to the lower categories of sex workers outside port gates compared with those in the former "sailor town" establishments.

Sexually transmitted disease has taken on a critical dimension with

HIV/AIDS. Treating this STI is not a matter of simply getting a shot of penicillin on board and medical attention ashore. Rather, death is the likely outcome. The carriage of the infection to small island populations, where medical services are deficient, could clearly be disastrous. The first reported case of HIV in Kiribati was in 1991. There has been a slow spread in the Pacific Islands generally, with 2,345 cases of HIV reported as of 27 May 1999, of which 832 had developed into AIDS. The infection is the most prevalent in Papua New Guinea. Many islands have no reports of the infection, although underreporting is always likely. In Kiribati there were 36 recorded HIV cases in 2001, with a small cluster in the seafaring sector of 18 seamen (11 developed AIDS) and 5 spouses of seamen. This high proportion related to seafarers could be attributed to the frequent routine medical examination of sailors.

The approach to controlling the problem has been to embark on more publicity and education. To focus on this, it was necessary for health workers to consider closely the behavioral characteristics of Pacific seafarers on foreign-going voyages. From December 2004 to July 2005, surveys were conducted under the ministries of health and the SPC in six Pacific island countries, with the assistance of the World Health Organization and other bodies. A summary of the main findings for Kiribati reveals a not unexpected, but very worrying, result for the families of seafarers. The survey was by interview, questionnaire, and some laboratory tests. There were 304 voluntary seafaring subjects, from three sites in Kiribati. This was a very large sample of the total 2,000 serving sailors.

Profile of the seafaring subjects
Age 21 to 54 (mean 37.4 years, st. dev. 8.5 years).
59.3[%] had secondary school education.
3.3[%] had attended university or college.
2/3rds were married and lived with their spouses.
15% of married seafarers reported more than one wife.
96.4% had marine work experience outside of Kiribati.
The average time away from home during last contract was 12.1 months.
The most common job on board was able-bodied seaman followed by motorman and bosun.
52% were current smokers.
75.2% reported drinking alcohol.
12 percent used drugs.
2 (0.7%) had injected drugs in the last 12 months.

Sexual behavior
90.1 percent had sex in the last 12 months.
68 (22.5%) had sex with commercial female partner(s) in the last 12 months.
52 (17.2%) had sex with casual female partner(s) in the last 12 months.
111 (36.8%) had multiple female partners in the last 12 months.
3 (1.0%) had sex with a male partner in their lifetime.
26 (38.2%) of the 68 used condoms with commercial female partners.
17 (32.7%) of the 52 used condoms with casual female partners.
18 (6%) reported having a sexual infection (most frequently gonorrhea) in the last 12 months.
80 (26.5 percent) had correct knowledge of HIV protection.[11]

There have been anti-AIDS activities in Kiribati over several years to induce protection and behavioral change. Churches, trade unions, and the government have been involved. So also in their own ways have some members of the Seafarers' Wives Association (SWA). This group formed in the early 1990s and is modeled on similar organizations in the main maritime labor supply countries, especially the Philippines. These women are aware of HIV/AIDS, but gender relations make discussion of the subject difficult, and there are strong indications of domestic stress and violence.

Although the details given above are specific to Kiribati, they would generally apply in many respects to Pacific seafarers as a whole. Solutions are similarly applicable. Since 1998, and now reinforced by the surveys referred to, major projects have been aimed at the seafaring population under "prevention and capacity development." These include training of trainers in the subject of STIs for staff at the maritime colleges and establishing "seafaring centers" at several key places in the Pacific, providing information and incentives for behavioral change and STI preventative measures. Very important in this has been the inclusion of efforts to empower maritime-related women. The Pacific Women in Maritime Association (PacWIMA), which started in Suva during 2005, is raising many issues of awareness and social responsibility in the maritime community. These medical and social pressures will ultimately change what has been regarded in the past as traditional behavior of "Jack ashore" in foreign ports.

TRADE UNIONS

The maritime trade unions in Kiribati have been more stable and influential than elsewhere in the Pacific Islands, other than French Polynesia (affiliated with the French Confederation of Labor) and Papua New Guinea. Up until World War II, trade unions were not popular with the authorities in the colonial Pacific. In the postwar period there was some encouragement in promoting "responsible unionism."[12] This was to circumvent any formation of pro-communist labor movements in the Pacific during the cold war. In Kiribati there was also an element of paternalism in promoting unions, as in the earlier development of the cooperatives. The first seafarers' union was inaugurated in the Betio *maneaba* on 22 December 1971 as the Gilbert and Ellice Islands International Overseas Seamen's Union (GEIOSU). It was attended by Harry Murphy, the colony commissioner of labor, who promised some minimal financial help from the British government, including the mailing of application forms to seafarers.[13]

The newly formed union began negotiations with the SPMS. It was agreed that union membership was compulsory on German vessels, and the company would deduct subscriptions from salaries on behalf of the union. This and other agreements regarding wages and conditions got the organization off to a good start. However, the union records on 16 June 1972 report with some consternation that "the Australian Waterside Workers Federation was refusing to work on ships carrying GEIC crews." The union resolved to make contact with the AWWF and to write to the International Transport Workers' Federation (ITF) and apply for affiliation. Affiliation was eventually accepted, and the waterside workers ultimately expressed goodwill toward the GEIOSU and its policies on wages and conditions. Independence came to the GEIC in 1979, and the seafarers of Kiribati and Tuvalu were regrouped under the Kiribati International Overseas Seamen's Union (KIOSU) and the Tuvalu Overseas Seamen's Union (TOSU). Both unions continued joint negotiations with SPMS and the ITF on wages and conditions.

The determination of wages for seafarers internationally starts at the Joint Maritime Committee (Unions and Owners) of the International Labour Organization (ILO). On the basis of a forty-eight-hour work week, the minimum wage for an AB is arrived at, which acts as a benchmark for other ranks. The International Shipping Federation (owners) and the International Transport Workers' Federation (ITF) then negotiate the rate upward, taking into account actual working times and other factors. They agreed, for example, on US$851 per month for ABs in 2002. The ITF makes further upward adjustments to the base rate minimum in relation to sailors serving on FOC ships to cover social security and other payments normally made under national flags. The ITF rate becomes part of a wider collective bargaining agreement with FOC companies.[14]

In the case of Kiribati there are further negotiations between SPMS, KIOSU, and ITF. These take into account the extra costs to SPMS of transporting crews from and to Kiribati. The end result for 2002–2003, for example, was monthly minimums of US$881 for an AB and US$1,781 for a second officer. These examples can be compared with shore employment in Kiribati, where in 2002 a middle-ranking government officer received about US$350 and a permanent secretary US$1,300.[15]

When they sign on for a voyage, all seafarers are required to leave a monthly allotment from their salary. This is made to a wife, mother, other relative, or girlfriend or goes entirely into their own account in the bank. The allotment money can be spread quite widely among relatives, meeting the costs of food, school fees, uniforms, church donations, feasts, and special occasions. Most seafarers are supporting at least six other persons from the allotment, and many in practice support a good deal more. The sailor can draw on some of the remainder of his salary during the trip, and the final balance is handed over in cash when paying off.

HOME FROM THE SEA

When they have completed twelve months' service, sailors are repatriated by SPMS to Tarawa. Wives who are resident there usually meet their husbands at the airport with children; others are met by relatives and girlfriends, and often by someone from the union. After sailors have been away from Kiribati for a year, it is a time for refamiliarizing with places and rebonding with kin. Those going to outer islands often stay for a time in South Tarawa, sometimes with resident relatives from their home islands. The sailors are all on paid leave for over two and a half months. They already have money in the bank, ready cash they were paid off with, and gifts. Some of the latter are depleted by *bubuti* requests before they go home, and the payoff and leave money may have been eroded by other diversions.

South Tarawa offers bars, girls, a seamen's hostel, and the company of other mariners. The returned seafarers are regarded there as something of an elite to be admired, resented, envied, and even feared by different sections of the population. A view much publicized is that of Teuea Toatu, referring to 1977, not long after the first generation of seafarers started to return on leave:

> Most of them who were once used to rural life—simplicity, sobriety and good behaviour—are completely transformed. They are heavy drinkers, patronising public bars every day, and of course, they have

lots of money in the bank.... [I]n the public bar they group themselves together in one corner, and if they are tired of speaking Gilbertese, they speak German.... In view of the luxurious life of these local seamen they have emerged as a new elite group in Kiribati. One can easily recognise these seamen with their long hair, long trousers, shoes (for in Kiribati it is rare to see people wearing long trousers or shoes) and brand new motorcycles. This is resented by some people but in most cases it influences the rest of the local population to try and adopt their way of living, irrespective of their limited resources.[16]

Some of the "brand new motorcycles" might have a young nurse riding on the pillion. She too might be away from her home village and earning an independent living working in a hospital, an institution not unlike a ship in its structured regime. The seafarers and other "detribalized" young people in South Tarawa have been regarded as a force for change in I-Kiribati society, for better or worse.

About two-thirds of the returning seafarers are from the outer islands, where their parents generally live, and some of the sailors have waiting wives and children. Many reenter a community where decisions are made by the *uea* in the north and the *unimane* in the south. Their extended family *(kaainga)* will have a sitting place *(boti)* in the *maneaba*, and the eldest male will speak for the *kaainga*. A seafarer unwinding from a worldwide voyage of a year and the regime of the ship is often not ready for the control of elders or chiefs, with their more limited horizons. But he will need to pick up family and communal obligations, and eventually he will talk in the *maneaba* and village, with tact and due deference to elders or chiefs. These days the elders tend to realize their own deficiencies in the ways of the wider world and allow young men to do so, although the women still sit quietly at the back of the *maneaba*.

While he has been away, his parents and, more so, a wife will have missed his labor. The roles of men in offshore fishing, digging pits to grow *babai* (marsh taro), climbing and tapping toddy, making house and boat repairs, and performing other male rights and duties would have been carried out, if at all, by kinsmen. The required tasks of a married woman include looking after the children, pigs, and poultry; harvesting *babai*, gleaning on the reef, washing, and cooking. As the wife of an absent sailor, she would have the additional stress of the family finances, discipline of children, and communal and church obligations, as well as dealing with in-laws. The returned sailor will have to rearrange some displaced domestic matters and repossess traditional tasks and authority.

A sailor will enhance his own and his family's status with money, gifts, and the purchase of expensive items such as a generator, video equipment, a sewing machine, or an outboard motor. This has the effect also of creating a quasi class division in a community with strong redistributive traditions. For the unmarried sailor such affluence also renders him a fitting person for aspiring parents to consider as a husband for a daughter. Previously the main criteria in the matching process would have been the reputation, genealogy, landownership, and reef tenure of the boy's family and possibly the skill of the young man as a boat builder or an offshore fisherman. His regular cash income as a sailor would now take precedence in their choice. The girl's dowry *(buraenriri)* would have included quantities of coconuts in the *okai* (storage hut) as a measure of wealth and insurance. The dowry would now be mainly money, possibly derived from a seafaring relative.

Marriages to seafarers do not always last. The problems seem to stem from a growing gulf over the many months of separation due to differences in the experiences of both parties. Behavioral frictions are also reported, with sailors trying to impose a shipshape regime on the home living area, discipline of children, and disagreements over how and what food is prepared and presented. There are sometimes jealousies, questions of fidelity, his drinking, and her trouble with in-laws. Clearly, most marriages survive, but if a divorce takes place, it is the sailor who usually initiates it and whose parents by custom take custody of the children on his behalf. The former wife returns to her home village or island. Lambert observed on the northern island of Makin: "A wife may consider herself divorced because her husband, an overseas seaman, does not send for her when he returns to Tarawa on leave. . . . There have also been a few cases of marriages broken up by the husband's kinsfolk on Makin or Tarawa because they disapproved of his wife's behavior while he was away."[17]

The social gulf is considered to be minimized if the family moves to Tarawa. They tend to do so, as is common with many seafaring families worldwide who eventually leave distant homes and settle in the more accessible main ports of a country. Life in the urban area of South Tarawa brings its own problems. There are thirty-five thousand people in South Tarawa (7.2 square kilometers); most are on Betio in a very confined area of 1.3 square kilometers. The fragile ecosystem of this part of a coral atoll cannot support such pressures on freshwater supply, sewage disposal, reef resources, and visual and other amenities. There has been the perennial urban drift from outer islands (previously banned by the colonial authorities) and the growth of shanty dwellings, unemployment with accompanying pressures on employed relatives, petty crime, hidden prostitution, and drunkenness, along with lower nutrition.

Many sailors eventually are able to purchase a piece of land on Tarawa or nearby Abaiang Island. They have houses built of concrete, brick, and board, with solid roofs and water tanks. These are more prestigious than the traditional thatched dwellings, although less comfortable in many respects. More important, such houses afford greater privacy and safety for the family during a sailor's absences. The family can, especially in more senior ranks, afford a house girl, their own generator, and many indoor domestic and entertainment units (such as microwave ovens and video equipment). In this change to a near I-Matang (foreign) lifestyle, partners will drink and eat out at some of the few hotels toward the international airport.

If the wives of seafarers adjust to the conditions of South Tarawa, life changes in several ways. There are better educational and medical facilities in the area, and away from the scrutiny of in-laws they have also more control of their money from allotments. Some with secondary schooling become more independent through employment as teachers, nurses, and government officers, and most belong to the Seafarers' Wives Association. The association helps build up social networks across islands of origin. It provides wives with a meeting place to reduce loneliness, the chance of shared problem solving, and other support and welfare functions. The organization has also given a corporate voice to the women in matters of STIs, especially HIV, and on wages and allotments. A public demonstration in Tarawa by the women over allotment payments was something of an embarrassment to the union, the company, and some of the husbands.

The SWA and other activities in Tarawa may be affecting traditional gender attitudes overall. Many young women have higher school qualifications than young men but are excluded from certain opportunities, including training at the MTC, which has been raised as an issue with PacWIMA. Attitudes toward gender equality may also be percolating to outer islands. It was noted in discussions with seafarers that some wives without children were going fishing beyond the reefs with other members of the family. This formerly has been a male preserve, with all its related dangers and masculine secrecy. It now carries less prestige than working at sea on foreign-going ships and may be more readily given up to women.

THE SEAFARING PARADIGM

The natural resources of Kiribati in modern times are very narrowly based in support of more than 100,000 people. Copra production in the outer islands is primarily part-time and employs the equivalent of about 1,000 full-time villagers. This provides fluctuating returns of AU$2 million to AU$3 million per annum. Then there is seaweed and some minor seaweed products, totaling about AU$1.5 million. Such is the sum total of direct productive activities from local resources. The main national income comes from licensing the ocean fishing zone to foreign vessels and from voluntary overseas aid. These together amount to possibly AU$55 million. In addition there is a reserve fund from the interest received on money from previous phosphate mining on Banaba. Of the total population only 11,000 are actual wage earners, of which 7,000 are employed in government services. The only significant other real cash flow into the economy is the AU$12 million or so in allotment remittances, leave money, and goods from I-Kiribati crews on foreign ships.[18] This is vital and is often spread widely over extended families in outer islands.

Like most sailors, the I-Kiribati at some stage ceases to see life at sea as permanent, yet there are few opportunities for his skills and experiences ashore. One choice is that of returning to a life of semisubsistence agriculture and fishing in his home island, supported by regular interest from bank savings. It is quite an attractive prospect for many to contemplate. One interviewed sailor was already embarking on this after fifteen years at sea by settling in remote Kiritimati, ensuring also, he said, a refrigerator for his beer.

Other seafarers are more ambitious and have made investments in local enterprises, sometimes with family members, while continuing temporary employment at sea. Such investments may include a shop, café, or bakery, bus and taxi services, vehicle repairs, electrical maintenance, video rentals, and boat and house building. In the distant past, commercial ventures and services have been provided mainly by Chinese and Europeans who settled in the islands. Kum-Kee is well known from the On Chong days, and his descendants own and run the last of his stores in South Tarawa. Some other descendants of European sailors and traders who made their homes in Kiribati and Fiji can be recognized today in the names of ship's officers, boatbuilders, and owners of domestic shipping companies, including Murdoch, Patterson, Redfern, Schutz, and Whippy. These men made major contributions in establishing commercial enterprises with their technical skills and relative independence from community pressures. The current generation of sailors are likewise capable of bringing new skills and attitudes ashore.

There is a problem of limited potential for large-scale economic developments in Kiribati, where only the national sea area and people are plentiful. Going to sea on international ships is vital in its income reliability and is still capable of considerable advances. The main output of the MTC in Tarawa is ratings. There is, however, a surplus of ratings in the world, estimated at 135,000 in 2005. On the other hand, there was a shortage of 10,000 ship's officers in that year.[19] There is clearly an incentive for the conversion of ratings to officers internationally. In Kiribati the opportunity is certainly there to add value to the local output by more officer training, since the young men and women of Kiribati have good educational and language advantages, as English is the working language at sea.

The other potential for enterprises lies in the sea area under national jurisdiction. Currently this is simply rented out for foreign fishing, with few local people employed (about sixty on Japanese catchers). The maritime skills and knowledge in the seafaring community could change that in many ways. The tourist industry in Kiribati has in turn always tended to be written off in comparison with other Pacific countries, due to the remoteness of the islands. This could well be a main asset in cruising, as could the abilities of I-Kiribati sailors to run adventures under sail and other tourist sea activities, including diving and whale watching. Such marine enterprises are in line with the advocacy of Te'o Ian Fairbairn in the early 1990s regarding the Kiribati economy, but now they have a stronger foundation in modern maritime skills.[20]

Epilogue

SOME CONTEMPORARY RESONANCES

THE DEPENDENCE OF the Pacific Islands on sea trade has continuously increased over time, and multiplicities of social and economic activities are related to the cargoes and the people flowing through island ports. The sailors who are engaged in regional and international shipping are now less visible, as the old "sailor town" enclaves have given way to tourists. Apart from cruise ships, most vessels berth at distant secure terminals, and many sailors travel overseas to and from their ships by air transport. Nevertheless, island people are aware of maritime links and of numerous aspects of maritime history and heritage. Several features of this history and heritage, which have been outlined here, are manifested in the cultural milieu of the contemporary Pacific.

At the level of remembering the great voyages of the ancestors, there have been regional festivals, as well as revivals of oceanic canoe building and long-distance sailing. In the 1960s this was led in Hawai'i by Ben Finney and the Polynesian Voyaging Society. It resulted in the voyages of the double-hulled ocean canoe *Hokule'a* in 1976 and 1985–1986, which included seven archipelagos between Hawai'i and Aotearoa. The sea-kindliness of the craft was tested, and navigation was by traditional methods derived from the knowledge of Mau Piailug of Satawal. He passed this on to the ultimate navigator of the *Hokule'a*, the Hawaiian Nainoa Thompson. David Lewis was likewise engaged in his seminal work on indigenous navigation from 1965 onward and was accompanied by the Micronesian navigators Tevake of Pileni and Hipour of Puluwat. Similarly, in 1999 Mau Piailug navigated the *Makali'i* (Eyes of the Chief) by traditional methods some 2,300 miles between Hawai'i and Majuro and onward.

These vessels and others were crewed by Pacific islanders, including four women on the 1999 passages.[1] They were welcomed with pride by people throughout the Pacific as remembrances of the achievements of their ancestors. Another sort of revival has revolved around overcoming the restrictions of colonial times, which curtailed movements between island groups. This includes the unification of maritime training, mobility in crewing, and the operations of the Pacific Forum Line.

The employment of island seafarers on foreign ships replicates periods in the eighteenth and nineteenth centuries. Pacific sailors are now, as then, recruited to overcome the reluctance of people in the traditional ship-owning countries to follow careers at sea. The Pacific sailors take their places within multinational crews on worldwide services. Because of rapid port turnaround, they spend long periods at sea. This has resonances with the days of sail, but without the compensation of time in port. This disadvantage adds to the loneliness and stresses of modern ships.

As in the past, there is also the transmission of sexual infections to island communities, although now in a more virulent form. Unlike in the nineteenth century, this is being dealt with to a greater extent by Pacific women. Sailors' wives have had to take over several traditional roles of their husbands during long absences. As a result, many are becoming more confident and assertive and are supported in health and behavioral campaigns by new local and regional organizations of women. These differences from the past are also accompanied by successful demands for greater gender equality in seagoing employment.

The maritime history of the Pacific peoples is recognized as part of the shaping of Pacific societies but is also a basis for comparison in making changes for the future. Not least is the possibility of a renaissance of commercial sail under changing economic relationships between distance, rising costs of fuel, environmental concerns, and the always available Pacific wind systems for assistance in ship propulsion.[2]

NOTES

Introduction

1. Karen Wigen, "Oceans of History," *American Historical Review* 3 (2006): 717.
2. Based on R. Gerard Ward, *Widening Worlds, Shrinking Worlds? The Reshaping of Oceania* (Canberra: Australian National University, 1999).
3. Fishing was, and is, vital around all the islands, but this book concentrates on trading and deep-sea whaling activities; it does not directly engage with fishing as a main activity.
4. Pablo E. Pérez-Mallaína, *Spain's Men of the Sea: Daily Life on the Indies Fleet in the 16th Century* (London: Johns Hopkins University Press, 1998).
5. Eric Sager, *Seafaring Labour: The Merchant Marine of Atlantic Canada 1820–1914* (Montreal: McGill-Queens University Press, 1989), 5.
6. Epeli Hauʻofa, "Our Sea of Islands," *Contemporary Pacific* 6 (1994): 148–161.
7. Paul D'Arcy, *The People of the Sea: Environment, Identity and History in Oceania* (Honolulu: University of Hawaiʻi Press, 2006).
8. David A. Chappell, *Double Ghosts: Oceanian Voyagers on Euroamerican Ships* (Armonk, NY: M. E. Sharpe, 1997).
9. Richard Feinberg, ed., *Seafaring in the Contemporary Pacific Islands* (DeKalb: Northern Illinois University Press, 1995).

1. Sailors, Myths, and Traditions

1. Richard Feinberg, "The Island and Its People," in *Polynesian Seafaring and Navigation: Ocean Travel in Anutan Culture and Society*, ed. Richard Feinberg (Kent, OH: Kent State University Press, 1988), 11.
2. I. Futa Helu, "South Pacific Mythology," in *Voyages and Beaches: Pacific Encounters, 1769–1840*, ed. Alex Calder, Jonathan Lamb, and Bridget Orr (Honolulu: University of Hawaiʻi Press, 1999), 45–54.
3. Pat Hohepa, "My Musket, My Missionary, and My Mana," in Calder et al., *Voyages and Beaches*, 180–202.

4. Joel Bonnemaison, "The Tree and the Canoe: Roots and Mobility in Vanuatu Societies," *Pacific Viewpoint* 25, no. 2 (1984): 117–151.

5. Teuira Henry, "Tahitian Astronomy," *Journal of the Polynesian Society* 16 (1907): 101–104.

6. Arthur Grimble, "Gilbertese Astronomy and Astronomical Observations," *Journal of the Polynesian Society* 40 (1931): 197.

7. Lawrence Marshall Carucci, "Symbolic Imagery of Enewetak Sailing Canoes," in Feinberg, *Polynesian Seafaring and Navigation*, 17.

8. Ibid., 26.

9. Joseph Conrad (1906), quoted in Michael Mason, Basil Greenhill, and Robin Craig, *The British Seafarer* (London: Hutchinson/BBC in association with the National Maritime Museum, 1980).

10. Pérez-Mallaína, *Spain's Men of the Sea*, 243.

11. J. M. M. Hill, *The Seafaring Career* (London: Tavistock Institute of Human Affairs, 1972), 60.

12. Nico de Jonge and Toos Van Dijk, *Forgotten Islands of Indonesia* (Leiden: Periplus Editions, 1995), 40–42.

13. Stephen D. Thomas, *The Last Navigator* (New York: Ballantine Books, 1987), 170.

14. Anne Salmond, *Between Worlds: Early Exchange between Maori and Europeans, 1773–1815* (Auckland: Viking Press, 1997), 87.

15. D. G. Kennedy, *Field Notes on the Culture of Vaitupu, Ellice Islands* (New Plymouth, New Zealand: Polynesian Society, 1931), 131.

16. Nathaniel Philbrick, *In the Heart of the Sea* (London: Harper Collins, 2001), 14.

17. British Parliamentary Papers, *First Report of the Royal Commission on Loss of Life at Sea (1885)*. Before this report on British seafarers, there is considerable evidence of the high incidence of mortality aboard merchant ships. The 3,910 seafarer deaths referred to in this report is an underestimate, since it does not take account of seafarers who died onshore after accidents on board, nor subsequent deaths due to infectious diseases contracted during sea service. See also Ronald Hope, *A New History of British Shipping* (Edinburgh: John Murray, 1990), 320–321.

18. Pérez-Mallaína, *Spain's Men of the Sea*, 240.

19. Stan Hugill, in *Sailortown* (London: Routledge and Kegan Paul, 1967), describes the sailor towns of the world as the earthly Fiddler's Green, with their "pubs, dance-halls, groggeries, and brothels." See Ronald Hope, *Poor Jack* (London: Chatham Publishing, 2001), 269, for a description of the sailors' hopes for the mythical Fiddler's Green after death.

20. Solange Petit-Skinner, "Traditional Ownership of the Sea in Oceania," in *Ocean Yearbook*, vol. 4, ed. Elizabeth Mann Borgese and Norton Ginsberg (Chicago: University of Chicago Press, 1983), 312. The frigate bird, according to Louise Becke, was used in the nineteenth century for carrying messages

between traders in the Ellice Islands. See Becke, *Notes from My South Sea Log* (London: Faber and Unwin, 1905), 119–121.

21. Joseph Conrad (1906), quoted in Mason et al., *British Seafarer,* 16.

22. Mifflin Thomas, *Schooner from Windward: Two Centuries of Hawaiian Interisland Shipping* (Honolulu: University of Hawai'i Press, 1983), 11.

23. R. A. Derrick, *A History of Fiji* (Suva: Government Press, 1963), 16.

24. Ibid.

25. A. M. Hocart, *The Lau Islands of Fiji* Bernice Bishop Museum Bulletin 69 (Honolulu, 1929).

26. Owen Rutter, ed., *The Journal of James Morrison, Boatswain's Mate of the Bounty,* (London: Golden Cockerel Press, 1935), 206. For the full context of the W. Solomon Rites, see Nicholas Thomas, *Entangled Objects* (Cambridge, MA: Harvard University Press, 1991), 47.

27. R. M. Lawson, and E. Kwei, *African Enterprise and Economic Growth: A Case Study of the Fishing Industry of Ghana* (Accra: Ghana University Press, 1974), 63.

28. The analogies between launching vessels, childbirth, and the rhythms of the sea range from modern onboard stories of sailors being refused leave to attend the birth of their children on the grounds that "they were required only to lay the keel and were not needed for the launching" to the display in the hospital at Palau of tide tables to predict times of births and the comforting of women in labor by telling them "the tide will turn soon and the baby will come." R. E. Johannes, *Words of the Lagoon: Fishing and Marine Lore in the Palau District of Micronesia* (Berkeley: University of California Press, 1981), 35.

29. Nicholas Thomas, *Oceanic Art* (London: Thames and Hudson, 1995), contains detailed descriptions and interpretations of Pacific island figureheads and other canoe decorative art.

30. Pérez-Mallaína, *Spain's Men of the Sea,* 241.

31. Greg Dening, *Islands and Beaches: Discourse on a Silent Land; Marquesas, 1774–1880* (Honolulu: University of Hawai'i Press, 1980), 57.

32. Alan Howard, "Rotuman Seafaring," in "Historical Perspective," in Feinberg, *Seafaring,* 129.

33. Ed Knipe, *Gamrie: An Exploration in Cultural Ecology* (New York: University Press of America, 1984), 95.

34. Jocelyn Linnekin, "New Political Orders," in *The Cambridge History of the Pacific Islanders,* ed. Donald Denoon (Cambridge: Cambridge University Press, 2004), 200.

35. Knipe, *Gamrie,* 94.

36. S. D. Thomas, *Last Navigator,* 170.

37. Sager, *Seafaring Labour,* 231.

38. Ibid., 130.

39. Hill, *Seafaring Career,* 66.

40. Feinberg, "The Island and Its People," 132.

41. In Samoan society the *fa'a fafine* (like a lady) are boys reared as girls and do women's work. They are not necessarily homosexual. In Tonga they are known as *fakaleiti* and dress and act like women. In Tahiti they are the *mahu*. Over all of Polynesia in fact this form of (male) transvestite appearance and behavior has always been a part of society. Bengt and Marie-Thérèse Danielsson write of Tahiti in 1978: "In sharp contrast to the basically negative attitude towards homosexuals in western society the individuals in Polynesia who follow the traditional Mahu way of life are not only tolerated but meet with general approval and praise" ("Polynesia's Third Sex: The Gay Life Starts in the Kitchen," *Pacific Islands Monthly,* August 1978, 11). See also Deborah MacFarlane, "Transsexual Prostitution in Polynesia: A Tradition Defiled?" *Pacific Islands Monthly,* February 1983, 11–12.

42. Regarding "Ma Gleeson's," Stan Hugill in *Sailortown* refers to the many women known to sailors as "Ma" and "Mother" "throughout the Seven Seas." These women who ran sailors' houses and brothels included Mother Hall in Newcastle, New South Wales; Ma Grant in Astoria, Oregon; Ma Egerton in Liverpool, England; and Ma Jackson in Rio de Janeiro.

43. Herman Melville, *Moby Dick* (London: Penguin Books, 1994), 33.

44. Howard, "Rotuman Seafaring," 130.

45. R. L. Stevenson, *Treasure Island* (1881; London: Penguin Classics, 1999), 41.

46. Hugill, *Sailortown,* 78.

47. Teuea Toatu, "Seamen and Cultural Change in Kiribati," *Pacific Perspective* 8, no. 2 (1975): 31–32.

48. Francoise Péron, "Seamen of the Island and the Faith: The Example of Quessant," *INSULA: International Journal of Island Affairs* (Paris)1, no. 1 (1992): 38.

2. The First Pacific Seafarers

1. Peter Bellwood, "Footsteps from Asia: The Peopling of the Pacific," in *The Pacific Islands: An Encyclopedia,* ed. Brij V. Lal and Kate Fortune (Honolulu: University of Hawai'i Press, 2000), 53–58.

2. Geoffrey Irwin, *The Prehistoric Exploration and Colonisation of the Pacific* (Cambridge: Cambridge University Press, 1996), 19–30.

3. Ibid., 23.

4. Patrick Vinton Kirch, *On the Road of the Winds* (Berkeley: University of California Press, 2002).

5. Ben R. Finney, *Voyages of Rediscovery* (Berkeley: University of California Press, 1994), 182. About two-thirds of the way on the voyage from Rarotonga to Aotearoa, he sighted the high Kermadec Islands, where there is evidence of early Polynesian occupation.

6. Kirch, *On the Road of the Winds*, 207, puts the date of colonization as AD 1000 to 1200.

7. Finney, *Voyages of Rediscovery*, 287.

8. Robert Langdon, "The Bamboo Raft as a Key to the Introduction of the Sweet Potato in Prehistoric Polynesia," *Journal of Pacific History* 36 (2001): 32–58. See also Thor Heyerdahl, *The Kon-Tiki Expedition* (London: George Allen and Unwin, 1951). For Micronesia, see Kirch, *On the Road of the Winds*, 165–178.

9. S. S. Barnes, E. Matisoo-Smith, and T. L. Hunt, "Ancient DNA in the Pacific Rat *(Rattus exulans)* from Rapa Nui," *Journal of Archeological Science* 33 (2006): 1536–1540.

10. Dumont d'Urville, French scientist and naval officer, sailed widely in the Pacific from 1822 to 1825 and returned in 1826 until 1829. The name "Polynesia" was first used by the French explorer Charles de Brosses in 1756, and the three-way division by D'Urville in 1831. See Lal and Fortune, *Pacific Islands*, 63–159.

11. A. Grimble, "Canoes of the Gilbert Islands," *Journal of the Royal Anthropological Institute* 54 (1924): 101–139.

12. Peter Bellwood, *The Polynesians: Prehistory of an Island People* (London: Thames and Hudson, 1987), 20.

13. John Young, "The Response of Lau to Foreign Contact," *Journal of Pacific History* 17 (1982): 29–50.

14. A. C. Haddon and James Hornell, *Canoes of Oceania*, 3 vols., Bernice P. Bishop Museum Special Publications 27–29 (Honolulu, 1936–1938).

15. M. Thomas, *Schooner from Windward*, 10–11.

16. John P. Twyning, *An Account of the Life and Adventures of John Payer Twyning: Comprising the Wreck of the Minerva and the Author's Years in Fiji and the Friendly Isles*, 2nd ed. (Bristol: for the benefit of the author, 1850), 161.

17. The painting is in the collection of the Fiji Museum, Suva.

18. G. S. Parsonson, "The Settlement of Oceania," in *Polynesian Navigation*, ed. Jack Golson (Wellington, New Zealand: Polynesian Society, 1965), 38.

19. Mifflin Thomas, in *Schooner from Windward*, describes Hawaiian vessels at the time of Cook, although not specifically the *wa'a kaulua*.

20. Robert Langdon, *The Lost Caravel* (Sydney: Pacific Publications, 1975), 108–110.

21. Grimble, "Canoes of the Gilbert Islands," 101–139.

22. Haddon and Hornell, *Canoes of Melanesia*, 2:8.

23. Clive Moore, "Hiri Trading Voyages," in Lal and Fortune, *Pacific Islands*, 131.

24. Philip Edwards, ed., *The Journals of Captain James Cook* (1769; reprint, London: Penguin Classics, 1999), 88. See also Anne Salmond *Two*

Worlds: First Meeting between Maori and Europeans 1642–1772 (Honolulu: University of Hawai'i Press, 1998).

25. Bellwood, *Polynesians*, 42.

26. Finney, *Voyages of Rediscovery*, 159–161. The *Hokule'a* in 2004 was still sailing to each of the islands of Hawai'i, traveling more than four thousand miles in support of coral reef conservation (*Honolulu Advertiser*, 3 May 2004).

27. Ernest Sabatier, *Sous l'equateur du Pacifique: Les iles Gilbert et la Mission Catholique* (Paris: Edition Dillen, 1939); and Grimble, "Gilbertese Astronomy," 200.

28. Hocart, *Lau Islands of Fiji*, 62.

29. Patrick D. Nunn, "Illuminating Sea-Level Fall around AD 1200–1510 in the Pacific Islands: Implications for Environmental Change and Cultural Transformation," *New Zealand Geographer* 56 (1993): 46–53.

30. Patrick D. Nunn, "Facts, Fallacies and the Future in the Island Pacific," in *A New Oceania: Rediscovering Our Sea of Islands*, ed. Eric Waddell, Vijay Naidu, and Epeli Hau'ofa (Suva: University of the South Pacific, 1993), 114. See also David Lewis, *We, the Navigators* (Canberra: Australian National University Press, 1972), 89–90.

31. Twyning, *Life and Adventures*, 96.

32. Paul Johnstone, *The Sea Craft of Prehistory* (London: Routledge, 1980), 210.

33. Rutter, *Journal of James Morrison*, 204.

34. G. H. Heyen, pers. comm., 1963.

35. Sabatier, *Sous l'equateur du Pacifique*, 94–95.

36. Grimble, "Gilbertese Astronomy," 197.

37. Francis X. Hezel, *The First Taint of Civilization* (Honolulu: University of Hawai'i Press, 1983), 53.

38. Thomas Gladwin, *East Is a Big Bird: Navigation and Logic in Puluwat Atoll* (Cambridge, MA: Harvard University Press, 1970), 128.

39. Lewis, *We, the Navigators*, 194–202.

40. A. D. Couper, "Seasat Images," in *Times Atlas and Encyclopedia of the Sea*, ed. A. D. Couper (London: Times Books, 1983), 205.

41. Gladwin, *East Is a Big Bird*, 150–151.

42. Raymond Firth, *We, the Tikopia* (Boston: Beacon Press, 1936), 27.

43. Gladwin, *East Is a Big Bird*, 182–183.

44. A. D. Couper, "Pacific Seafarers in Trade and Navigation," in *Localization and Orientation in Biology and Engineering*, ed. D. Varjú and H. U. Schnitzler (Berlin: Springer-Verlag, 1984), 227–243.

45. Dava Sobel, *Longitude* (London: Fourth Estate, 1995), 11–13.

46. J. C. Beaglehole, *The Life of Captain James Cook* (London: Adam and Charles Black, 1774), 192.

47. Francis X. Hezel and Maria Teresa del Valle, "Early European Contact

with the Western Carolines 1525–1750," *Journal of Pacific History* 7 (1972): 26–44.

48. Parsonson, "Settlement of Oceania," 15.

49. Sabatier, *Sous l'equateur du Pacifique*, 95.

50. Quoted by D'Arcy, *People of the Sea*, 215n125.

51. David Lewis, "Polynesian and Micronesian Navigation Techniques," *Journal of the Institute of Navigation* 23, no. 4 (1970): 432–447.

52. O. H. K. Spate, *The Spanish Lake* (Canberra: Australian National University Press, 1979), 47. See also William Bligh's journal, *The Mutiny on Board HMS Bounty* (reprint, New York: Airmont, 1965).

53. Glyn Williams, preface to *The Prize of All the Oceans* (London: Harper Collins, 1999), and 134.

54. Spate, *Spanish Lake*, 169.

55. Philbrick, *In the Heart of the Sea*, 14.

56. Kathy Marks, "Fishermen Rescued after Five Months Lost at Sea," *Independent*, (London), 13 November 2001.

57. Johannes, *Words of the Lagoon*, 14.

58. Dening, *Islands and Beaches*, 57.

59. Kate Fortune, "Traditional Healing Practices," in Lal and Fortune, *Pacific Islands*, 443.

60. Edwards, *Journals of Captain James Cook*, 281.

3. Settlements, Territories, and Trade

1. R. Gerard Ward and Muriel Brookfield, "The Dispersal of the Coconut: Did It Float or Was It Carried to Panama?" *Journal of Biogeography* 19 (1992): 467–479. See also P. S. Dale and P. A. Maddison, "Transport Services as an Aid to Insect Dispersal in the South Pacific," in *Commerce and the Spread of Pest and Disease Vectors*, ed. Laird Marshall (New York: Praeger Scientific, 1984), 225–256.

2. M. S. McGlone, A. J. Anderson, and R. N. Holdaway, "An Ecological Approach," in *The Origins of the First New Zealanders*, ed. Douglas G. Sutton (Auckland: Auckland University Press, 1994), 140.

3. Bonnemaison, "The Tree and the Canoe," 129–130.

4. Glen Petersen, "Indigenous Island Empires: Yap and Tonga Compared," *Journal of Pacific History* 35 (2000): 5–22.

5. J. C. Beaglehole, ed., *The Journals of Captain James Cook on His Voyages of Discovery* (Cambridge: Cambridge University Press, 1961), 385–386.

6. M. Thomas, *Schooner from Windward*, 12.

7. John Martin, ed., *An Account of the Natives of the Tongan Islands*, by William Mariner, 2 vols. (London: Hakluyt Society, 1817–1818).

8. Greg Dening, "The Geographical Knowledge of the Polynesians and the Nature of Inter-Island Contact," in Golson, *Polynesian Navigation*, 123.

9. Derrick, *History of Fiji*, 113.

10. John Young, "Lau: A Windward Perspective," *Journal of Pacific History* 28 (1993):165.

11. John Jackson, "Feejeean Islands," appendix to *Journal of a Cruise among the Islands of the Western Pacific*, ed. J. E. Erskine (Edinburgh: John Murray, 1853), 452–453.

12. Bellwood, *Polynesians*, 84.

13. Paul D'Arcy, "Connected by the Sea: Towards a Regional History of the Western Caroline Islands," *Journal of Pacific History* 36, no. 2 (2001): 163–182; and Petersen, "Indigenous Island Empires," 6–17.

14. Bellwood, *Polynesians*, 97.

15. Greg Dening, ed., *The Marquesan Journal of Edward Roberts, 1797–1824* (Honolulu: University of Hawai'i Press, 1974), 180–181.

16. Peter Corris, *Passage, Port and Plantation: A History of Solomon Island Labour Migration 1870–1914* (Melbourne: Melbourne University Press, 1973), 18. There is controversy over the extent in the past of cannibalism in the Pacific, many reports being considered exaggerated and ascribed to missionaries.

17. Fiji is a case in point. Marshall Sahlins provides a major contribution to the debate by reviewing the accounts of *bakola* in Fiji, leaving little doubt regarding the extent and veracity of most of the reports. See Sahlins, "Making Up Cannibalism?" *Anthropology Today* 19, no. 3 (2003): 44.

18. H. E. Maude, *The Evolution of the Gilbertese Boti*, Polynesian Society Memoir 35 (Wellington, New Zealand, 1963), 51.

19. Sabatier, *Sous l'equater du Pacifique*, 106–118.

20. M. Baraniko, T. Taam, and N. Tabokai, in *Kiribati Aspects of History* (Tarawa: Ministry of Education, Training and Culture, 1984), 44–64.

21. H. Carrington, ed., *The Discovery of Tahiti: A Journal of the Second Voyage of HMS Dolphin round the World, under the Command of Captain Wallis, RN in the Years 1766, 1767 and 1768*, by George Robertson (London: Hakluyt Society, 1948), 222.

22. Erskine, *Islands of the Western Pacific*, 269.

23. Hocart, *Lau Islands of Fiji*, 290.

24. Brookfield, *Melanesia*, 328–329.

25. Montague, "Kaduwaga," 60.

26. Charles Wilkes, *Narrative of the United States Exploring Expedition in the Years 1838–1842* (Ridgewood, NJ: Gregg Press, 1970), 362.

27. T. Williams, *Fiji and the Fijians* (London: Hodder and Singleton, 1870), 40.

28. Brookfield, *Melanesia*, 324–326.

29. D'Arcy, "Connected by the Sea," 169–170.

30. Bellwood, *Polynesians*, 51. See also Marshall I. Weisler, ed., *Prehistoric Long-Distance Interaction in Oceania: An Interdisciplinary Approach*, New Zealand Archaeological Association Monograph 21, Auckland, 1997.

31. Gladwin, *East Is a Big Bird*, 35.
32. Harold J. Weins, *Atoll Environment and Ecology* (New Haven, CT: Yale University Press, 1962), 182.
33. D'Arcy, "Connected by the Sea," 165–169. See also D'Arcy, *People of the Sea* (Honolulu: University of Hawai'i Press, 2006), 144–163.
34. Petersen, "Indigenous Island Empires," 5–18.
35. Hezel, *First Taint of Civilization*, 105.
36. Buell Quain, *Fijian Villages* (Chicago: University of Chicago Press, 1948), 173.
37. Hocart, *Lau Islands of Fiji*, 290.
38. Marshall D. Sahlins, *Moala: Culture and Nature on a Fijian Island* (Ann Arbor: University of Michigan Press, 1962), 422.
39. Erskine, *Islands of the Western Pacific*, 269.
40. Ben R. Finney, "Experimental Voyaging, Oral Traditions and Long-Distance Interaction in Polynesia," in *Prehistoric Long-Distance Interaction in Polynesia: An Interdisciplinary Approach*, ed. Marshall I. Weisler (Cambridge: Cambridge University Press, 1992), 72–73.
41. Edwards, *Journals of Captain James Cook*, 354.
42. Ibid., 473.
43. Ibid., 81.
44. Brookfield, *Melanesia*, 324–326.
45. Moore, "Hiri Trading Voyages," 139.
46. T. Williams, *Fiji and the Fijians*, 40.
47. Corris, *Passage, Port and Plantation*, 18.
48. Matthew Cooper, "Economic Context of Shell Money Production in Malaita," *Oceania* 41, no. 4 (1971): 270. The maintenance of peace may also have been the basis for the enormous scale of Arioi touring parties in Tahiti (D'Arcy, *People of the Sea*, 58–59).
49. Irwin, *Prehistoric Exploration*, 176–180.
50. Beaglehole, *Journals of Captain James Cook* (1961), 2:352, 357.
51. Jared Diamond, *Collapse* (London: Penguin Books, 2005), 80–135, provides a summary of archaeological results in Mangareva, adjacent islands, and Easter Island.
52. From my visit to Rapa Nui during February 2006, as lecturer with the *BBC History Magazine* team on MV *Discovery*.
53. Nunn, "Facts, Fallacies and the Future," 114.
54. Beaglehole, *Journals of Captain James Cook* (1955), 1:170.

4. The Arrival of Foreign Ships

1. Hezel, *First Taint of Civilization*, 2.
2. Ibid., 9–10.
3. Ibid., 28.

4. Spate, *Spanish Lake*, 128.
5. Ibid.
6. A. D. Couper, "Islanders at Sea: Change and the Maritime Economies of the Pacific," in *The Pacific in Transition*, ed. Harold Brookfield (London: Edward Arnold, 1973), 246.
7. A. D. Couper, "Historical Perspectives on Seafarers and the Law," in *Seafarers' Rights*, ed. D. Fitzpatrick and M. Anderson (Oxford: Oxford University Press, 2005), 3–39.
8. Edwards, *Journals of Captain James Cook*.
9. Ibid., 82.
10. J. C. Beaglehole, ed., *The Voyage of the Resolution and Adventure 1772–1775* (Cambridge: Cambridge University Press, 1955), 493.
11. Carrington, *Discovery of Tahiti*.
12. Ibid., 139, 154, 155.
13. Ibid., 123, 229.
14. Beaglehole, *Journals of Captain James Cook*, 1:114–116. See also Edwards, *Journals of Captain James Cook*, 61–64.
15. Edwards, *Journals of Captain James Cook*, 355–356.
16. Beaglehole, *Life of Captain James Cook*, 385.
17. Rutter, *Journal of James Morrison*.
18. Beaglehole, *Life of Captain James Cook*, 99.
19. Edwards, *Journals of Captain James Cook*, 532.
20. Rutter, *Journal of James Morrison*, 229.
21. J. C. Beaglehole, ed., *The Endeavour Journal of Joseph Banks, 1768–1771* (Sydney: Angus and Robertson, 1962), 2:130.
22. Beaglehole, *Life of Captain James Cook*, 192.
23. Johannes, *Words of The Lagoon*, 14.
24. Philip Edwards, *The Story of the Voyage: Sea-Narratives in Eighteenth-Century England* (Cambridge: Cambridge University Press, 1994), 115–117.
25. Ibid., 118. For a detailed appraisal of George Forster, see Nicholas Thomas, *Discoveries* (London: Penguin Books, 2003), 275–278.
26. Beaglehole, *Voyage of the Resolution and Adventure*, 277.
27. Rutter, *Journal of James Morrison*, 235.
28. Robert Langdon, *The Lost Caravel* (Sydney: Pacific Publications, 1975).
29. The Reverend Thomas Williams, quoted in Dorothy Shineberg, *They Came for Sandalwood: A Study of the Sandalwood Trade in the South West Pacific 1830–65* (Melbourne: Melbourne University Press, 1986), 14.
30. William Lockerby, *The Journal of William Lockerby, Sandalwood Trader in the Fijian Islands during the Years 1808–1809* (London: Hakluyt Society, 1925), 11:xiii.
31. Deryck Scarr, "European Visitors: First Contacts," in Lal and Fortune, *Pacific Islands*, 149.

32. I. C. Campbell, "Polynesian Perceptions of Europeans in the Eighteenth and Nineteenth Centuries," *Pacific Studies* 5, no. 2 (1982): 64–79.

33. A. D. Couper, songs collected in the Gilbert Islands and translated by Paul Laxton, from the author's field notes (Canberra, 1964).

34. John Martin, ed., *An Account of the Natives of the Tongan Islands*, by William Mariner (London: Hakluyt Society, 1817–1818), 1:256.

35. Erskine, *Islands of the Western Pacific*, 220.

36. A. H. Wood, *History and Geography of Tonga* (Nukualofa: Tupou College, 1952), 35–36.

37. John L. Nicholas, *Performed in the Years 1814 and 1815 in Company with the Rev. Samuel Marsden* (Auckland: Wilson and Horton, 1971), 2:19.

38. Beaglehole, *Life of Captain James Cook*, 176.

39. Ibid.

40. Rutter, *Journal of James Morrison*, 234.

41. Barrie MacDonald, *Cinderellas of the Empire: Toward a History of Kiribati and Tuvalu* (Canberra: Australian National University Press, 1982), 19.

42. J. Lamb, V. Smith, and N. Thomas, *A South Seas Anthology* (Chicago: University of Chicago Press, 2000), 65–66.

43. Campbell, "Polynesian Perceptions," 71.

44. Beaglehole, *Life of Captain James Cook*, 262.

45. Salmond, *Between Worlds*, 280.

46. John Turnbull, *A Voyage round the World in the Years 1801–1804* (Philadelphia: Benjamin and Thomas Kite, 1810), 1:133.

47. King's journal, entry for November 1778, in Beaglehole, *Journals of Captain Cook*.

48. Edwards, *Story of the Voyage*, 121.

5. Pacific Commercial Shipowners

1. H. E. Maude, "Post-Spanish Discoveries in the Central Pacific," *Journal of the Polynesian Society* 70, no. 1 (1961).

2. H. E. Maude and Ida Leeson, "The Coconut Oil Trade of the Gilbert Islands," *Journal of the Polynesian Society* 74 (1965): 399. The authors note that "Nanouti had a particularly sinister reputation."

3. Ibid., 405–406.

4. J. S. Cumpston, *Shipping Arrivals and Departures, Sydney, 1788–1825*, 2 vols. (Canberra: Campbell, 1964).

5. Ibid., 1788, *Lady Penrhyn*.

6. Hohepa, "My Musket," 196.

7. H. E. Maude, "The Tahitian Pork Trade 1800–1830," *Journal de la Société des Océanistes* (Paris) 15 (1959): 55.

8. Ibid., 74.

9. Rutter, *Journal of James Morrison*, 100–105.

10. Maude, "Tahitian Pork Trade," 58.

11. Turnbull, in *Voyage round the World*, 1:13, notes Otoo's addiction to liquor when he was king.

12. Turnbull appears to have been supercargo on this voyage of 1802–1803. He was part owner of the ship with Captain John Buyers and would also have invested in the cargo.

13. Maude, "Tahitian Pork Trade," appendix B, 84.

14. Turnbull, *Voyage round the World*, 1:153.

15. Ibid., 2:16–17.

16. Ibid., 2:94; Niel Gunson, "Pomare II of Tahiti and Polynesian Imperialism," *Journal of Pacific History*, 4 (1969): 78.

17. Turnbull, *Voyage round the World*, 2:118.

18. Turnbull described the ship as being absent for two months at the "Mottos," which were part of the Tuamotus. Ibid., 2:180.

19. A. T. Yarwood, *Samuel Marsden: The Great Survivor* (Melbourne: Melbourne University Press, 1977), 193.

20. *Sydney Gazette*, June 1819.

21. Maude, "Tahitian Pork Trade," 69.

22. Gunson, "Pomare II," 75–77. In some documents the name "Michael Fodger" is given as "Michael Folger"; for consistency, "Fodger" is used here.

23. Ibid., 69–70.

24. Cumpston, *Shipping Arrivals and Departures*, arrivals list for 1819–1825.

25. Sandalwood from Marquesas is recorded at Port Jackson from the *Queen Charlotte* in 1815, but the product was exhausted by about 1817.

26. Gunson, "Pomare II," 76–77.

27. Ibid.

28. The arrival of *Endeavour* with salt pork is mentioned in the *Sydney Gazette*, June 1825.

29. Gunson, "Pomare," 78.

30. Missionary insistence that people should wear decent clothing was prevalent on all islands, and this policy probably contributed to ailments, including tuberculosis, from dampness and sunshine deprivation.

31. Maude, in "Tahitian Pork Trade," records that there were twenty-one Australian-built, privately owned ships trading to the islands at this time.

32. James R. Gibson, *Otter Skins, Boston Ships, and China Goods* (Seattle: University of Washington Press, 1999), 23.

33. M. Thomas, *Schooner from Windward*, 11–12, 34, 35.

34. Ibid., 12.

35. O. H. K. Spate, *Paradise Found and Lost* (London: Routledge, 1988),

372. Records show that Metcalf was soon afterward killed by Indian tribes on the American northwest coast.

36. K. R. Howe, *Where the Waves Fall* (Melbourne: Allen and Unwin, 1984), 157.

37. M. Thomas, *Schooner from Windward*, 12.

38. Turnbull, *Voyage round the World*, 2:59–60.

39. Ibid., 2:60.

40. Howe, *Where the Waves Fall*, 161.

41. Stephen W. Reynolds, *Voyage of the New Hazard 1810–1813*, ed. F. W. Howay (Fairfield, WA: Ye Galleon Press, 1970), 111n314.

42. Thomas, *Schooner from Windward*, 13.

43. Ibid., 14.

44. J. R. Gibson, *Otter Skins*, 25, 34.

45. Ibid., appendix tables.

46. Reynolds, *Voyage of the New Hazard*, 3–158.

47. In ibid., Reynolds covers relationships between sailors and Hawaiian girls and the arrangements made to keep this activity on board.

48. Ibid., 5.

49. Ibid. Regarding slave trading on the coast, editor F. W. Howay points out that slavery was still an institution at that time in the southern states of the Union.

50. Ibid., 25n68.

51. The circumstances are somewhat obscure as conveyed by Reynolds, ibid. The manuscript "Log of the Hamilton" (25 July 1811; held in the Essex Institute, Salem, MA) does not apparently provide all the details either of this tragic event.

52. Reynolds, *Voyage of the New Hazard*, 143. The date of 1 July was taboo, and "no person allowed to go on the water."

53. The Fourth of July was celebrated on 5 July, according to Reynolds' journal, as the date had not been adjusted at 180°.

54. M. Thomas, *Schooner from Windward*, 18.

55. The *Prince Regent* is recorded in Sydney as sailing in the company of the *Mermaid* for the Sandwich Islands on 16 October 1821 *(Sydney Gazette)*.

56. Various aspects of the Erromango catastrophe are covered by Shineberg, *They Came for Sandalwood*. See also Gunson, "Pomare II," 18; and Spate, *Paradise Found and Lost*, 284.

57. Shineberg, *They Came for Sandalwood*.

58. Ibid.

59. Caroline Ralston, *Grass Huts and Warehouses: Pacific Beach Communities of the Nineteenth Century* (Honolulu: University of Hawai'i Press, 1978), 104.

60. Ibid., 108.

61. M. Thomas, *Schooner from Windward*, 27–29.

62. Howe, *Where the Waves Fall*, 96.

63. Raymond Firth, *Economics of the New Zealand Maori* (Wellington, New Zealand: R. E. Owen Government Printer, 1929), 284, 304, 351.

64. A. Murray Bathgate, "Maori River and Ocean Going Craft," *Journal of the Polynesian Society* 3, no. 78 (1969); Clifford W. Hawkins, "The Waka in Trade and Transport," *Marine News* 49, no. 1 (2000): 12–14.

65. Salmond, *Between Worlds*, 280.

66. Ibid., 368.

67. Nicholas, *Voyage to New Zealand*, 71–74. See also Richard A. Cruise, *Journal of a Ten Months' Residence in New Zealand* (London: Longman, 1832; facsimile, Christchurch, New Zealand: Capper Press, 1974), 74–77; and Peter Dillon, *Narrative and Successful Result of a Voyage in the South Seas* (London: Hurst Chance, 1829), 1:216–224.

68. Marsden in 1814 warned of the great cruelties toward the Europeans, particularly in the case of the *Boyd*. A young Tahitian who was married to the daughter of a Maori chief replied by asserting that the Europeans were the first aggressors and detailing other offenses. See "Rev. S. Marsden's Account of His First Visit to New Zealand," December 1814, in McNab, *Historical Records*, 350.

69. Government and General Order, 1 December 1813, in McNab, *Historical Records*, 316–317.

70. Quoted in H. D. Skinner, "Murdering, Beach Collecting and Excavating: 1850–1950," *Journal of the Polynesian Society* 68 (1959).

71. Ibid. An account of the archeological sites at which these incidents occurred is at the Otago Museum, Dunedin, New Zealand; and for information of the related fate of the *Mary & Elizabeth*, see Susan Chamberlain, "The Hobart Whaling Industry 1830 to 1900" (PhD thesis, La Trobe University, Victoria, 1982), 133.

72. Hohepa, "My Musket," 199.

73. Ibid.

74. Samuel Marsden, "Communication with Governor Darling 18 April 1831," in McNab, *Historical Records*, 716.

75. Samuel Marsden, response by Governor Darling, 25 April 1831, in ibid., 717.

76. Harry Morton, *The Whale's Wake* (Honolulu: University of Hawai'i Press, 1982), 84, 135.

77. Thomas Raine to Sir George Murray, Sydney, 3 January 1829, in McNab, *Historical Records*, 716.

78. Losses were high due to navigation on treacherous lee shores, as well as the poor state of these acquired vessels and rigging, but there are few details of their losses.

79. Similarly, N. Morarjee, in N. G. Jog, ed., *Narattam Morarjee: Architect of Modern Indian Shipping* (Bombay: Scindia Steam Navigation Co., 1977), notes that the introduction of Indian-owned shipping is seen as part of the independence movement in India.

80. Donald Denoon and Philippa Mein-Smith, with Marivic Wyndham, *A History of Australia, New Zealand and the Pacific* (Edinburgh: Blackwell, 2000), 108. See also Raewyn Dalziel, "Southern Islands: New Zealand and Polynesia," in *The Oxford History of the British Empire*, vol. 3, *The Nineteenth Century*, ed. Andrew Porter, 567–577 (Oxford: University Press, 1999), 577.

81. Records of Maori-owned vessels, circa 1850, Wellington Maritime Museum.

82. Hawkins, "Waka in Trade and Transport," 12–14.

83. Neil Atkinson, *Crew Culture: New Zealand Seafarers under Sail and Steam* (Wellington, New Zealand: Te Papa Press, 2001).

84. Clifford W. Hawkins, "The Passage of Sail: European Sailing Ship Building in the South West Pacific," *Great Circle* 5, no. 1 (1983): 90–97.

85. The lives of two women were spared: a black woman who was still in Tonga when Mariner was there, and a European named Elza Mosey (or Moray) became a wife of Teukava, a chief from Kolovai. She escaped to Australia on the ship *Union* in 1804 after that ship was nearly taken. Later she returned to her Tongan family on the ship *Favourite*. Wood, *History and Geography of Tonga*, 34; and H. E. Maude, "Beachcombers and Castaways," *Journal of the Polynesian Society* 73, no. 3 (1964): 260.

86. Martin, *Account of the Natives*.

87. Spate, *Paradise Found and Lost*, 159.

88. Ralston, *Grass Huts and Warehouses*, 107.

89. J. W. Davidson and Deryck Scarr, eds., *Pacific Island Portraits* (Canberra: Australian National University Press, 1970), 95.

90. Erskine, *Islands of the Western Pacific*, 269.

91. Hezel, *First Taint of Civilization*, 103–105.

92. Ibid., 224.

93. H. E. Maude and Edwin Doran, "The Precedence of Tarawa Atoll," *Annals of American Geographers* 56 (1966): 269–289.

94. R. L. Stevenson, *In the South Seas* (London: Chatto and Windus, 1920), 275.

95. Firth, *Economics*, 164, 304.

96. Peter R. Mills, "Neo in Oceania," *Journal of Pacific History* 135 (2003): 53–67.

97. Naval Intelligence Division, *Geographical Handbook*, vol. 1, *Pacific Islands*, edited by Raymond Firth and J. W. Davidson "for British Admiralty" (Royal Navy, 1942), 276.

6. Under Foreign Sail

1. Craig J. Forsyth, "The Creation and Maintenance of a Stigmatized Occupation: An Historical Analysis of the American Merchant Marine," *Maritime Policy and Management* 14, no. 2: 100–101.
2. Ibid., 101.
3. British Parliamentary Papers, *House of Commons Select Committee Appointed to Enquire into the Causes of Shipwrecks*, HC Paper, vol. 18 (London, 1836), 373.
4. Nicholas Rogers, "Liberty Road: Opposition to Impressment in Britain during the American War of Independence," in *Jack Tar in History*, ed. C. Howell and R. Twomey (Fredericton, NB: Acadiensis Press, 1991), 54.
5. P. Linebaugh and M. Rediker, "The Many-Headed Hydra: Sailors, Slaves and the Atlantic Working Class in the Eighteenth Century," in Howell and Twomey, *Jack Tar in History*, 15.
6. N. A. M. Rodger, *The Command of the Ocean: A Naval History of Britain 1649–1815* (London: Penguin Books, 2004), 62.
7. Linebaugh and Rediker, "Many-Headed Hydra," 16.
8. Andrew Gibson and Arthur Donovan, *The Abandoned Ocean: A History of United States Marine Policy* (Columbia: University of South Carolina Press, 2000), 33.
9. Ibid., 35.
10. Ibid., 43.
11. Craig Forsyth, "Stigmatized Occupation," 101.
12. Turnbull, *Voyage round the World*, 176.
13. Enclosure no. 3, letter to Colonel Nicolls from Enderby et al., NSW, 16 September 1823, in McNab, *Historical Records*, 608–609.
14. Colonel Torren's Proposal, 4 July 1826, in McNab, *Historical Records*, 664–665.
15. K. E. Larson, "Early Channels of Communication in the Pacific," *Ethnos* (1966): 117.
16. George I. Quimby, "Hawaiians in the Fur Trade of North-west America, 1785–1820," *Journal of Pacific History* 7 (1972): 93.
17. Reynolds, *Voyage of the New Hazard*, 33, 42. The *Tarquin* happens to have sunk when the captain, unable to free the ship of Indian boarders, set fire to the magazine. The explosion killed some one hundred Indians. Most of the crew were killed on board or when attempting to escape by boat. There are uncertainties regarding dates and the explosion. An account is given in the logbook of the *Hamilton* in the Essex Institute, Salem, MA.
18. Quimby, "Hawaiians in the Fur Trade," 97–98.
19. Richard Copping, "A Narrative of Pacific Seafaring 1826–1892," typescript (Crowther Archives, Hobart, Tasmania), 25.
20. Sailors were considered to be most dangerous people in the penal set-

tlements and elsewhere. So also were those from ships in port (see chapter 7). In 1796 sailors from the American fur trading ship *Otter* rescued the Scottish reformer Thomas Muir from Botany Bay, where he was serving a fourteen-year sentence for sedition in spreading the ideas of Tom Paine in Scotland. Many other convicts were smuggled on board ships and taken to the islands and America.

21. Rodger, *Command of the Ocean*, 397. Rodger comments that the only criminals the navy wanted were smugglers, "who had valuable skills."

22. Robert Hughes, *The Fatal Shore* (Sydney: Pan Books, 1988), 269–291. The *Trail* (not mentioned by Hughes) is listed in the *Sydney Gazette* as arriving on 10 August 1816 from the Marquesas and Tahiti with six tons of pork and twenty tons of sandalwood. She sailed on 28 September and was reported in the press as taken by "runaway convicts."

23. Jackson, appendix to "Feejeean Islands," 411.

24. Joseph Osborne on the whaler *Emerald* (1835), quoted in Howard, "Rotuman Seafaring," 129–130.

25. Examination of Andrew Henry (p. 45) and Captain H. Burns (p. 20), in *Inquiry by Royal Commission into Certain Alleged Cases of Kidnapping of Natives of the Loyalty Islands Held at Sydney, 9th August 1869*, under C. Rolleston. See also K. R. Howe, "Tourists, Sailors and Labourers," *Journal of Pacific History* 13 (1978): 22–24.

26. Hezel, *First Taint of Civilization*, 113.

27. Turnbull, *Voyage round the World*, 2:71, 3:125. Turnbull also observed the advantages of the trade to the NW coast for Hawaiian sailors who "acquire sufficient property to make themselves easy and comfortable, as well as respectable among their countrymen."

28. Yarwood, *Samuel Marsden*, 169. See also Chappell, *Double Ghosts*, 37–40.

29. Morton, *Whale's Wake*, 211.

30. Copping, "Narrative of Pacific Seafaring," 10.

31. Hugill, *Sailortown*, 157.

32. Frank T. Bullen, *The Cruise of the Cachalot* (London: Smith Elder and Co., 1879).

33. Turnbull, *Voyage round the World*, 2:72.

34. Copping, "Narrative of Pacific Seafaring," 35.

35. Ibid., 28.

36. Chamberlain, "Hobart Whaling Industry," 133.

37. F. Parbury, Evidence before the Select Committee of the House of Lords on the Navigation Laws, 23 March 1848, Ordered by the House of Commons and printed 19 May 1848, in Records of Parliament to Questions 1422–1426 of Committee.

38. *Sydney Shipping Gazette*, 24 January 1818.

39. Ibid., 12 April 1817.

40. Dillon, *Voyage in the South Seas,* 1:24, 25, 31, 96; 2:92, 98. See also Howe, *Where the Waves Fall,* 101.

41. C. R. Straubel, ed., *The Whaling Journal of Captain W. B. Rhodes of the Barque Australian of Sydney, 1836–1838* (Christchurch, New Zealand: Whitcombe and Tombs, 1954), xxxii.

42. H. E. Maude, *Slavers in Paradise: The Peruvian Slave Trade in Polynesia, 1862–1864* (Stanford, CA: Stanford University Press, 1981), 5–6.

43. Susan Chamberlain, *An Analysis of the Composition of the Tasmanian Whaling Crews Based on Their Crew Agreements 1860–1898* (Hobart, Tasmania: Crowther Whaling Archives, 1982).

44. Bullen, *Cruise of the Cachalot,* 2.

45. Morton, *Whale's Wake,* 170.

46. It was the debates over the British navigation laws in the 1840s that highlighted the fact that no examination was required for the position of an officer on board a British vessel. This situation was partially rectified by legislation in 1844, and by the 1870s, legislation also applied to foreign ships in the Pacific.

47. Reynolds, *Voyage of the New Hazard,* 387. Lang, who was promoted at the age of thirty-three as third mate and second mate, was the oldest man on the ship.

48. Copping, "Narrative of Pacific Seafaring," 10, 12.

49. Bullen, *Cruise of the Cachalot,* 2.

50. Turnbull, *Voyage round the World,* 2:11.

51. Margaret Creighton, "American Mariners and the Rites of Manhood, 1830–1870," in Howell and Twomey, *Jack Tar in History,* 142.

52. Ibid., 145.

53. Turnbull, *Voyage round the World,* 122.

54. Reynolds, *Voyage of the New Hazard,* 105.

55. Jackson, appendix to "Feejeean Islands," 327.

56. Creighton, "American Mariners," 143.

57. *Hobart Mercury,* 18 December 1858, Crowther Whaling Archives (Press Collection), Hobart, Tasmania.

58. See Sager, *Seafaring Labour.*

59. Ibid.

60. Reynolds, *Voyage of the New Hazard,* 155–156.

61. The mixture of whalers and missionaries at Lahaina from the 1820s was lethal. The clergy prevailed on the governor of Maui to stop the women from consorting on board with sailors. There were several riots, which are colorfully portrayed in *Rediscovering Hawaii* (National Geographic Society, Cartographic Division, 1995): "The conflict reached a crescendo in 1827 when incensed seamen whistled cannon balls at the mission house before sailing for less inhibited Honolulu."

62. Gavan Daws, "Honolulu in the Nineteenth Century," *Journal of Pacific History* 2 (1967): 89.

63. Deryck Scarr, ed., *A Cruise in a Queensland Labor Vessel to the South Seas*, by William A. Giles (Canberra: Australian National University Press, 1968), 34.

64. Bullen, *Cruise of the Cachalot*, 60.

7. Dangers, Mutinies, and the Law

1. British Parliamentary Papers, *Return of Deaths on British Ships, 1878*, vol. 60.

2. W. E. Home, "The Health of Merchant Seamen," *Lancet* (8 November 1924): 981.

3. M. Thomas, *Schooner from Windward*, 601.

4. Sarah Palmer and David Williams, "British Sailors 1775–1870," in *Those Emblems of Hell? European Sailors and the Maritime Labour Market 1570–1870*, ed. P. C. Van Royen, J. R. Bruijn, and J. Lucassen (St. John's: International Maritime Economic History Association, 1997), 99.

5. R. Gerard Ward, ed., *American Activities in the Central Pacific 1790–1870* (Ridgewood, NJ: Gregg Press, 1966), 4:596, 598, 600.

6. Ibid., 4:596, 598.

7. Morton, *Whale's Wake*, 167–168.

8. Ward, *American Activities*, 4:145.

9. Ibid., 3:360.

10. Chamberlain, "Hobart Whaling Industry," 130–133.

11. Memoirs of Duaterra as given by Mrs. Marsden, Parramatta, 28 October 1815, in Nicholas, *Voyage to New Zealand*, 380–381.

12. Morton, in *Whale's Wake*, notes that these reports and also the news brought by the ship *Vittoria* reported in 1832 that "two Europeans on sealing voyages were devoured by their Maori crew mates" (115).

13. Jim Gibbs, *A Maritime History of Hawaii: Shipwrecks in Paradise* (Seattle: Superior Publishing Co., 1922), 79–81.

14. Andrew Cheyne, *A Description of Some Islands of the Western Pacific* (London: J. D. Potter, 1852), 67.

15. Ward, *American Activities*, 3:550.

16. John Jackson, in Erskine, *Islands of the Western Pacific*, 486.

17. Ibid., 390–391.

18. Shineberg, *They Came for Sandalwood*, appendix 1, 219–245; appendix 2, 247–249.

19. Hezel, *First Taint of Civilization*, 119–120.

20. Morton, *Whale's Wake*, 168; Shineberg, *They Came for Sandalwood*, 191.

21. Cheyne, *Islands of the Western Pacific*, 89.
22. Chamberlain, "Hobart Whaling Industry," 126–129.
23. Reynolds, *Voyage of the New Hazard*, 59.
24. William Dalton, *Two Whaling Voyages to the South Seas 1823–1829*, ed. Niel Gunson (Canberra: National Library of Australia, 1990), 85.
25. Morton, *Whale's Wake*, 25.
26. Maude, "Tahitian Pork Trade," 66–67.
27. Copping, "Pacific Seafaring," 10.
28. Ward, *American Activities*, 4:570, 576–577. See also Edward A. Stackpole, *The Mutiny on the Whaleship Globe: A True Story of the Sea* (Nantucket, MA: published by the author, 1981).
29. Spate, *Paradise Found and Lost*, 284.
30. Yarwood, *Samuel Marsden*, 169.
31. Scarr, *Cruise in a Queensland Labour Vessel*, 38.
32. Reynolds, *Voyage of the New Hazard*, 39.
33. Ibid., 34.
34. Thomas Creighton, "Canadian Whalers in Micronesia (1840–1850)," *Journal of Pacific History* 24, no. 2 (1989): 228.
35. Reynolds, *Voyage of the New Hazard*, 119.
36. Barrie MacDonald, *Cinderellas of Empire: Toward a History of Kiribati and Tuvalu* (Canberra: Australian National University Press, 1982), 20.
37. Chamberlain, "Hobart Whaling Industry," 152.
38. Maude and Crocombe, "Rarotongan Sandalwood," 34–35.
39. Nicholas, *Voyage to New Zealand*, 380–390.
40. Chappell, *Double Ghosts*.
41. R. L. Stevenson, *In the South Seas*, 22. Tari's name could have been derived from the ship *Charles and Henry*, which was owned by Charles Coffin and his brother of Nantucket. Some Pacific sailors were stuck with the names of their last ship.
42. Rodger, *Command of the Ocean*, 490.
43. Ward, *American Activities*, 4:37.
44. Ibid., 3:39, 4:360–362, 5:36–37.
45. See *Mallacoota Memories 1841–1948* (Mallacoota, Victoria, Australia: Mallacoota District Historical Society, 1980), 12:87–88, for a detailed example of the combination of press reports and local oral history, which shows crew conditions and complaints leading to brutal punishment and mutiny on the *Junior*.
46. *Sydney Shipping Gazette*, 13 November 1813.
47. Ibid.
48. H. E. Maude and Marjorie Tuainekore Crocombe, "Rarotongan Sandalwood: An Ethnohistorical Reconstruction," *Journal of the Polynesian Society* 71 (1962): 34–35.

49. Ward, *American Activities*, 3:541, 4:583, 576–577. See also Stackpole, *Mutiny on the Whaleship Globe*.

50. Ward, *American Activities*, 6:141–151, 193. See also the account of the mutiny on the *William Little* in Gibbs, *Maritime History of Hawaii*, 52.

51. Couper, "Historical Perspectives," 3–35.

52. Maude, "Tahitian Pork Trade," 55.

53. Government and General Order, 9 November 1814, in ibid., 328–329.

54. Yarwood, *Samuel Marsden*, 192.

55. Forsyth, "Stigmatized Occupation."

56. The persistence of the views by authorities on seafarers is demonstrated by the quotation 119 years after Justice Story by the US Supreme Court in the case of *Garrett v. Moore-McCormack Co. Inc.* in 1942 (317 US 239, 247, AMC 1645). Similarly the views of Lord Stowell in 1825 regarding the case of the *Minerva* (contained in British Admiralty 1 Hagg Adm 347) persisted.

57. A. D. Couper, "Historical Perspectives," 19.

58. Ibid., 15–18.

59. Forsyth, "Stigmatized Occupation," 100–101.

60. Marion Diamond, "Queequeg's Crewmates: Pacific Islanders in European Shipping," *International Journal of Maritime History* 1, no. 2 (1989): 126.

61. Sarah Palmer, *Politics, Shipping and the Repeal of the Navigation Laws* (Manchester, UK: Manchester University Press, 1990), 174.

62. Diamond, "Queequeg's Crewmates," 132.

8. Companies, Colonies, and Crewing

1. T. Williams, *Fiji and the Fijians*, 465–466.

2. Consular Letter Books, *Western Pacific High Commission*, National Archives of Fiji, Suva (hereafter "CLB"), 26 December 1865, 469–486.

3. CLB (1863), 65, 338.

4. CLB (1874), 62–63.

5. See David Young, "Sailing to Levuka: The Cultural Significance of the Island Schooners in the Late 19th Century," *Journal of Pacific History* 28 (1993): 36–52. This paper provides a detailed account of the types of vessels used. See also Hawkins "Passage of Sail," 1.

6. F. M. Spoehr, *White Falcon: The House of Godeffroy and Its Commercial and Scientific Role in the Pacific* (Palo Alto, CA: Pacific Books, 1963), 46–47.

7. *Area, Population, Trade, etc., of the Principal Groups of Islands*, report by Mr. Steed (1874), in New Zealand Parliamentary Papers (Wellington; hereafter "NZPP"), A-3A.

8. R. W. Dalton, "Reports on the Trade of the Fiji Islands" and "Trade of Western Samoa and Tonga," typescript (Suva: Central Archives of the Western Pacific High Commission, 1918, 1919).

9. See also K. Buckley and K. Klugman, *The History of Burns Philp* (Sydney: Burns Philp and Co., 1981).

10. Gibbs, *Maritime History of Hawaii*, 72.

11. There are numerous accounts of colonization. Useful for this summary were W. P. Morrell, *Britain in the Pacific Islands* (Oxford: Oxford University Press, 1960); Lal and Fortune, *Pacific Islands;* and Denoon, Mein-Smith, and Wyndham, *History of Australia*.

12. A. Gibson and Donovan, *Abandoned Ocean*, 90.

13. Peter Hempenstall and Noel Rutherford, *Protest and Dissent in the Colonial Pacific* (Suva: University of the South Pacific, 1984), 49.

14. K. Buckley and K. Klugman, *South Pacific Focus* (Sydney: Allen and Unwin, 1986), report 1 of January 1910, 14.

15. See Frank Burnett, *Through Tropic Seas* (London, 1910), 98, for an account of Breckenfeldt on Nanouti, who had to padlock everything against the depredations of his many wives, in comparison with Captain Randall of Butaritari, whose wife was from a royal family and often acted as his supercargo. Described by J. J. Mahlmann, "Reminiscences of an Ancient Mariner," *Japan Gazette* (Yokohama, 1918), 22.

16. N. Chatfield, "Recollection of the Shipping Department of Burns Philp and Co. 1883–1914," typescript (Sydney: Mitchell Library, 1957).

17. Detailed information on subsidies is provided in "Memorandum re the Future of Australian Interests in the Pacific" (Sydney, 19 January 1915), in Burns Philp Papers, University of Sydney Library. See also Buckley and Klugman, *History of Burns Philp*.

18. Chatfield, "Shipping Department of Burns Philp," 104.

19. G. B. Smith-Rawse, *Ellice Islands Annual Report*, no. 9 of 1913 (London: Colonial Office).

20. Fiji, *Return of Customs Dues, Exports and Navigation 1881–1884* (Suva, 1885).

21. Dr. Stuebal to Prince Bismarck (1885), correspondence, NZPP, A-4D.

22. Henderson and MacFarlane, letter, 16 August 1893, Western Pacific High Commission, Central Archives, Suva.

23. Gibbs, *Maritime History of Hawaii*, 86, 90–91.

24. Chatfield, "Shipping Department of Burns Philp," 104.

25. Fiji, *Report of the Commission of Inquire into the Decrease of the Native Population* (Suva: Government Printer, 1896), 59.

26. Ibid., 60.

27. W. T. Campbell, *Gilbert and Ellice Islands: Report for the Years 1896–1900* (London: Colonial Office 225/61, 30340; Mitchell Library, Sydney).

28. A. W. Mahaffy, *Report on a Visit to the Gilbert and Ellice Islands in 1909*, Cd. 4992, CO225 (London, 1910).

29. M. Thomas, *Schooner from Windward*, 100.

30. Ibid., 99–100.

31. Burns Philp Papers, "Memorandum re the Future of Australian Interests," 3.

32. Conrad Bollinger, *Against the Wind* (Wellington: New Zealand Seamen's Union, 1968), 86.

33. Stephen Schwartz, *Brotherhood of the Sea: A History of the Sailors Union of the Pacific, 1885–1985* (San Francisco: Robert Matlock Printing Co., 1986). Also see National Maritime Union, *On a True Course: The Story of the National Maritime Union* (New York, 1967). Conrad Bollinger makes the point that militant New Zealand seamen were impressed by "the propaganda of the American Wobblies [IWW] on the Pacific coast"; Bollinger, *Against the Wind*, 90.

34. Charles Price, "White Restrictions on Colonial Immigration," *Race* 7, no. 3 (1966): 222.

35. Bollinger, *Against the Wind*, 84.

36. Myra Willard, *History of the White Australia Policy to 1920* (Melbourne: Melbourne University Press, 1974), 51.

37. Buckley and Klugman, *History of Burns Philp*, 83.

38. Atkinson, *Crew Culture*, 124.

39. A. Gibson and Donovan, *Abandoned Ocean*, 116–117, 182.

40. Bollinger, *Against the Wind*, 86.

9. Island Protests and Enterprises

1. Derived from the personal records of Captain G. Heyen in the 1960s and the logbooks of the SS *Macquarie*. These were subsequently deposited at the Research School of Pacific Studies, Australian National University, Canberra.

2. Other, less commercial protests included the many actions against land alienation and bids for independence, such as the 1826 Mamaia movement in Tahiti; the Maori wars of the 1860s; the Tuka movement in Fiji during the 1870s; the 1878 rebellions in New Caledonia; the recurring fighting against European forces in Samoa, 1887–1899; the attempts to reinstate the power of the king in Hawai'i during 1889; the 1904–1912 rebellions in New Guinea; the rise of Mau a Pule in Samoa, 1908; and the "Vailala Madness" in Papua New Guinea, 1919. See entries in Lal and Fortune, *Pacific Island*.

3. CLB (1864), 324, 338.

4. Greenwood to Rabone (21 August 1872), in Methodist Overseas Mission Letters, Mitchell Library, Sydney, item 170.

5. G. Ruthven Le Hunte, *Six Letters from the Western Pacific, by a Judicial Commissioner,* NZPP, letter 2 (1883), 13.

6. *Pendergast Report to the New Zealand Government* (1898), NZPP, A3.

7. H. E. Maude, "The Sword of Gabriel: Account of the Disturbances on Onotoa Island," seminar paper (Canberra: Australian National University, 1964).

8. E. Osborne, *The Copra Trader* (Sydney: NSW Bookstall, 1924), 60, 105.

9. Doug Munro, "The Lives and Times of Resident Traders in Tuvalu: An Exercise in History from Below," *Pacific Studies* 10, no. 2 (1987): 82.

10. F. Wallen, *Report No. 1, 30 Jan 1910, to Managing Director, Messrs Burns Philp Ltd.,* in Buckley and Klugman, *South Pacific Focus,* 18.

11. Ibid., *Report No. 2,* 31. Price fixing on copra buying is recognized in Buckley and Klugman, *History of Burns Philp,* 265–267.

12. Moshe Rappaport, "Oysterlust: Islanders, Entrepreneurs and Colonial Policy over Tuamotu Lagoons," *Journal of Pacific History* 30, no. 1 (1995): 43.

13. Doug Munro and Teloma Munro, "The Rise and Fall of the Vaitupu Company," *Journal of Pacific History* 20, no. 4 (1985): 184. The Munros record that, as part of the process of repaying the debts, a returned seaman named Ahatagi handed over his entire savings to the island fund. See also Doug Munro and Teloma Munro, "Vaitupu's Debt: An Exercise in Combined Use of Documentary Records and Oral History," *Oral History Association of Australia Journal* 5 (1982–1983): 58–64.

14. H. E. Maude, "The Co-operative Movement in the Gilbert and Ellice Islands," *South Pacific* (May 1950).

15. J. W. Davidson, *Samoa mo Samoa: The Emergence of the Independent State of Western Samoa* (Melbourne: Oxford University Press, 1967), 80–87.

16. *Tonga Government Gazette* 25 (1910).

17. In T. C. T. Potts to Secretary of State for the Colonies, appendix A of "Communication on the Kautaha."

18. For details of Tonga Ma'a Tonga Kautaha, see A. D. Couper, "Protest Movements and Protocooperatives in the Pacific Islands," *Journal of the Polynesian Society* 77, no. 3 (1968): 268–271; and Hempenstall and Rutherford, *Protest and Dissent,* 44–49.

19. Viti Company Papers, Western Pacific High Commission, Suva.

20. A. Alexander, *From the Middle Temple to the South Seas* (London, 1927). For details and references to the Viti Company, see A. D. Couper, "The Viti Company and the Apolosi Movement," in Couper, "Protest Movements," 268–271. See also *Fiji Law Reports 1875–1946,* 88–97, and "Situ-

ation in Fiji," report, 10 February 1916, CO83-130, both at Public Records Office, London.

21. Couper, "Protest Movements," 271–272. Memos relating to the resident commissioner and Schutz for 1938 onward were consulted in the Kiribati government archives in Tarawa (2001).

22. M. E. Jull, "My Trip to New Zealand and a Group of Islands in the South Seas 1883–1884," 2 vols., unpublished MS (1575), National Library of Australia, Canberra.

23. R. L. Stevenson, *In the South Seas*, 282.

24. Hezel, *First Taint of Civilization*, 224.

25. Quoted by Philip C. Coombe, *Transport and Development: Shipping in the Cook Islands* (MA thesis, University of Auckland, 1982), 33.

26. Hawkins, "Passage of Sail," 95.

27. Complaint of Messrs. Donald and Edenborough of Seizure of the Schooner Norval, Western Pacific High Commission, Fiji, Relating to the Cook Islands, Minutes on Civil Proceedings (1893). See also Deputy Commission Office, Apia, re *Litigations of Abandoned Vessels*, 103/99, Central Archives of Fiji, 4 December 1899.

28. Jull, "My Trip to New Zealand," 65.

29. Hawkins, "Passage of Sail," 95.

30. Fiji, *Report of the Commission Appointed to Inquire into the Decrease of the Native Population* (Suva: Government Printer, 1896), 49.

31. *Fiji Provincial Council Reports, Western District*, Vatulele (Central Archives of Fiji, 1910).

32. *Kadavu Provincial Council Report* (Central Archives of Fiji, 1902), 144. See also Howard, "Rotuman Seafaring," 138.

33. C. Percy Smith, "Six Months in the Pacific," unpublished MS (1919), Auckland Museum Library.

34. Anne C. Dunbar, "Transport and Development: Inter-island Shipping in Vanuatu" (PhD thesis, Australian National University, 1981), 83.

35. Fiji, *Legislative Council Debates, Steamship Subsidies* (Central Archives of Fiji, 21 November 1917), 249–283.

36. Fiji, *Shipping Commission 1915* (CP 19), pars. 30–33.

37. Fiji, *Legislative Council Debates* (1917), 251.

38. Colonial Office Reports, *Fiji, 1906–1918,* Cmd. 508–530 (1919); *Pacific Islands Yearbook, 1932* (Sydney: Pacific Publications, 1932), 55.

39. See Clive Moore, Jacqueline Leckie, and Doug Munro, eds., *Labour in the South Pacific* (Queensland: James Cook University Press, 1990); and B. V. Lal, *Broken Waves: A History of the Fiji Islands in the Twentieth Century* (Honolulu: University of Hawai'i Press, 1992).

40. Bill Gammage, "The Rabaul Strike, 1929," *Journal of Pacific History* 10 (1975): 3–29.

41. Edward Johannessen, *The Hawaiian Labor Movement: A Brief History* (Boston: Bruce Humphries, 1956).

10. Contemporary Local and Regional Shipping

1. Epeli Hau'ofa, "A Beginning," in Waddell et al., *New Oceania*, 136.
2. Couper, "Islanders at Sea," 236.
3. Mrs. R. L. Stevenson, *The Cruise of the Janet Nichol* (London: Chatto and Windus, 1915), 163.
4. Lal, *Broken Waves*, 168–169; Pramod K. Rae, "Ethnic Factors in Trade Unionism in Fiji 1942–1975," *Pacific Perspective* 8, no. 1 (1979): 32–37; Jacqueline Leckie, "Colonial Inheritance and Labor: Structure, Conditions and Identities in Fiji," in *Lines across the Sea*, eds. Brij V. Lal and Hank Nelson (Brisbane: Pacific History Association, 1995), 185–197.
5. Basil Thomson, *The Fijians: A Study of the Decay of Customs* (1908; London: Dawsons of Pall Mall, 1968), 286.
6. Derived from interviews with participants, notes by John Taka and sailors on Nairai, and information from Fiji Police Headquarters reports (May 1964).
7. Howard, "Rotuman Seafaring," 138.
8. A. D. Couper, *Report to the Government of Fiji on Inter-insular Shipping and Trade* (Suva, 1965).
9. "Samoa's MV *Queen Salamasina* Sold to Fiji Company," *Pacific Islands Monthly*, January 2000, 45.
10. *South Pacific Maritime Code* (Suva: South Pacific Bureau for Economic Co-operation, 1986). The code was adapted to include small vessels in the region not covered by international conventions.
11. Lloyd's Register Casualty Returns (1980–1988) and Maritime Industry Authority (MARINA), Philippines.
12. Avnita Goundar of the Pacific Regional Maritime Programme also wrote "Captain Carol Dunlop: Fiji's First Female Sea-going Captain," in *Regional Maritime Programme Newsletter* (2006). This publication carries the news of the formation of the Pacific Women in Maritime Association (PacWIMA) in 2005 (http://www.spc.int/maritime).
13. UNCTAD, *Establishment or Expansion of Merchant Marines in Developing Countries*, TD/26/Rev 1 (1968); United Nations, *Convention on a Code of Conduct for Liner Conferences*, NYTD/Code/13/1974.
14. Captains of every ship must deposit a crew list on entering and leaving a port. Sometimes these can be accessed, as in this example and others referred to in chapter 11. I am grateful also to John MacLennan, chief executive of the Pacific Forum Line, for access to PFL crew lists and other information.
15. Tony Nightingale, *The Pacific Forum Line* (Christchurch, New Zealand: Glestory Press, 1998), 111.

11. The Global Pacific Seafarer

1. UNCTAD, *Review of Maritime Transport 2003* (Geneva, 2003), 135–139; Lloyd's Register of Shipping (1 January 2004).

2. A. D. Couper, *Voyages of Abuse* (London: Pluto Press, 1999).

3. Lloyd's Register of Shipping (1 January 2004); *ITF Seafarers' Bulletin* (2005): 28. It was also clear that operating under a FOC is not always easy money for small Pacific states. The *Karine A*, flying the flag of Tonga, was arrested for illegal arms trading. Tonga had no idea who the owners were, except that the ship was managed by a Greek person. This cost the Kingdom of Tonga in both money and reputation. In 2005 the Solomon Islands was considering introducing an FOC register.

4. Second registers (or international registers) have been established by Norway (NIS), UK (Isle of Man), Denmark (DIS), France (Antarctic Territory), Germany (GIS), and the Netherlands (Antilles).

5. Many positions ashore require people with seafaring skills and qualifications, and such jobs pay well to attract them. For officers, these positions are found in the fields of education, maritime law, brokering, surveying, marine management, marine equipment, safety, and government, in addition to numerous port positions. For ratings, the demand is in stevedoring, rigging, towage, rescue, and salvage. The most cost-effective way, and often the only way, to fill these posts is to recruit from the sea. Few such positions are called for in small islands.

6. The Tuvalu Maritime Training Institute is for ratings, most of whom are supplied to German companies.

7. See Couper, *Voyages of Abuse*.

8. The sample information on mortality of Kiribati seafarers was derived from the data papers of the *Study of Occupational Mortality among Merchant Seafarers on the British, Singapore and Hong Kong Fleets*, conducted by Dr. Steven Roberts, Seafarers International Research Centre (SIRC), Cardiff, November 1998. The totals of Pacific fatalities on board these flag ships over twelve years: Kiribati, 4; Fijian, 2; Papua New Guinea, 2; Tuvalu, 1.

9. SIRC, *The Sailing Chaplain and Outreach Welfare Schemes* (Cardiff, 2003), 1–64. See also Minghua Zhao, X. Shi, and T. Feng, *The Political Commissar and His Shipmates aboard Chinese Merchant Ships* (Beijing: Chinese Social Sciences Documentation Publishing House, 2004).

10. *Pacific Islands Monthly*, December 1964, 25. See also Hemantha D. Wickramatillake, *Infectious Diseases among Seafarers* (Cardiff: SIRC, 1998). The writer notes, "An inquiry in New York revealed that 80 seamen had called at a total of 1,124 ports in 45 countries and had intercourse with 615 women." See P. Vuksanovic, W. H. Goethe, H. V. Burchard, et al., "Seamen and AIDS," *Travel Medicine International* 6 (1988): 18–19.

11. Tangaru Central Hospital lab, Kiribati records (2001); World Health

Organization, *Second Generation Surveillance Surveys of HIV, Other STIs and Risk Behaviours in Six Pacific Island Countries* (Geneva, 2006), 46–62.

12. Leckie, "Colonial Inheritance and Labor," 188.

13. GEIOSU meeting, 13 April 1972, from union minutes, Tarawa.

14. According to ITF policy, all FOC ships must be covered by an ITF collective bargaining agreement signed by the union in the country of beneficial ownership and control and, often, the unions in the country of labor supply. FOC ships that fall significantly below minimum standards for seafarers are likely to be penalized at ports by affiliated unions. The ITF-affiliated unions have a membership of 4.6 million in 120 countries.

15. For comparative levels of crew wages internationally, see Drewry Shipping Consultants, *Ship Operating Costs Annual Review and Forecast 2004/05* (London, 2005).

16. Toatu, "Seamen and Cultural Change," 264.

17. Bernd Lambert, "Makin and the Outside World," in *Pacific Atoll Populations,* Association for Social Anthropology in Oceania monograph 3, ed. Vern Carroll (Honolulu: University of Hawai'i Press, 1975), 264.

18. For detailed data on remittances provided by SPMS, see Maria Borovnik, "Seafarers in Kiribati—Consequences of International Labor Circulation" (PhD thesis, University of Canterbury, 2003).

19. BIMCO/ISF, *Manpower 2005 Update: The World Demand for and Supply of Seafarers,* (Coventry: Warwick Institute for Employment Research, 2005).

20. See Te'o Ian Fairbairn, *The Kiribati Economy* (Canberra: AIDAB, 1992), 37. See also Te'o Ian Fairbairn, *Island Entrepreneurs* (Honolulu: University of Hawai'i Press, 1989).

Epilogue: Some Contemporary Resonances

1. Giff Johnson, "Mau's Keen Eye Keeps Hawaiian Canoe on Track," *Pacific Islands Monthly,* April 1999, 50–51.

2. Some basic principles are described in A. D. Couper, "The Economics of Sail," *Journal of Navigation* 30 (1977): 164–171.

BIBLIOGRAPHY

Alexander, A. *From the Middle Temple to the South Seas.* London, 1927.
Atkinson, Neil. *Crew Culture: New Zealand Seafarers under Sail and Steam.* Wellington, New Zealand: Te Papa Press, 2001.
Baraniko, M., T. Taam, and T. Tabokai. In *Kiribati Aspects of History,* 44–66. Tarawa: Ministry of Education, Training and Culture, 1984.
Barnes, S. S., E. Matisoo-Smith, and T. L. Hunt. "Ancient DNA in the Pacific Rat *(Rattus exulans)* from Rapa Nui." *Journal of Archeological Science* 33 (2006): 1536–1540.
Bathgate, Murray. "Maori River and Ocean Going Craft." *Journal of the Polynesian Society* 3, no. 78 (1969): 344–377.
Beaglehole, J. C. *The Endeavor Journal of Joseph Banks, 1768–1771.* 2 vols. Sydney: Angus and Robertson, 1962.
———, ed. *The Journals of Captain James Cook on His Voyages of Discovery.* 4 vols. Cambridge: Cambridge University Press, 1955, 1961, 1967.
———. *The Life of Captain James Cook.* London: Adam and Charles Black, 1974.
———, ed. *The Voyage of the Resolution and Adventure 1772–1775.* Cambridge: Cambridge University Press, 1955.
Becke, Louise. *Notes from My South Sea Log.* London: Faber and Unwin, 1905.
Bellwood, Peter. "Footsteps from Asia: The Peopling of the Pacific." In Lal and Fortune, *Pacific Islands,* 53–58.
———. *The Polynesians: Prehistory of an Island People.* London: Thames and Hudson, 1987.
BIMCO/ISF. *Manpower 2005 Update—The World Demand for and Supply of Seafarers.* Coventry: Warwick Institute for Employment Research, 2005.
Bligh, William. *The Mutiny on Board HMS Bounty.* Reprint. New York: Airmont, 1965.
Bollinger, Conrad. *Against the Wind.* Wellington: New Zealand Seamen's Union, 1968.

Bònnemaison, Joel. "The Tree and the Canoe: Roots and Mobility in Vanuatu Societies." *Pacific Viewpoint* 25, no. 2 (1984): 117–151.
Borovnik, Maria. "Seafarers in Kiribati—Consequences of International Labor Circulation." PhD thesis, University of Canterbury, 2003.
British Parliamentary Papers. "Evidence of Samuel Browning, March 1847." *Select Committee on Navigation Laws.*
———. *First Report of the Royal Commission on Loss of Life at Sea (1885).*
———. *Return of Deaths on British Ships, 1878.* Vol. 60.
———. *House of Commons Select Committee Appointed to Enquire into Causes of Shipwrecks.* HC Paper, vol. 18. London, 1936.
Brookfield, H. C. *Melanesia.* London: Metheuen and Co., 1971.
Buckley, K., and K. Klugman. *The History of Burns Philp.* Sydney: Burns Philp and Co., 1981.
———. *South Pacific Focus.* Sydney: Allen and Unwin, 1986.
Bullen, Frank T. *The Cruise of the Cachalot.* London: Smith Elder and Co., 1879.
Burnett, Frank. *Through Tropic Seas.* London, 1910.
Burns Philp Papers. University of Sydney Library.
Campbell, I. C. "Polynesian Perceptions of Europeans in the Eighteenth and Nineteenth Centuries." *Pacific Studies* 5, no. 2 (1982): 64–79.
Campbell, W. T. *Gilbert and Ellice Islands: Report for the Years 1896–1900.* London: Colonial Office 225/61, 30340; Mitchell Library, Sydney.
Carrington, H., ed. *The Discovery of Tahiti: A Journal of the Second Voyage of HMS Dolphin round the World, under the Command of Captain Wallis, RN in the Years 1766, 1767 and 1768,* by George Robertson. London: Hakluyt Society, 1948.
Carroll, Vern, ed. *Pacific Atoll Populations.* Honolulu: University of Hawai'i Press, 1975.
Carucci, Lawrence Marshall. "Symbolic Imagery of Enewetak Sailing Canoes." In *Polynesian Seafaring and Navigation: Ocean Travel in Anutan Culture and Society,* ed. Richard Feinberg, 16–37. Kent, OH: Kent University Press, 1995.
Chamberlain, Susan. *An Analysis of the Composition of the Tasmanian Whaling Crews Based on Their Crew Agreements 1860–1898.* Hobart, Tasmania: Crowther Whaling Archives, 1982.
———. "The Hobart Whaling Industry 1830 to 1900." PhD thesis, La Trobe University, Victoria, 1982.
Chappell, David A. *Double Ghosts: Oceanian Voyagers on Euroamerican Ships.* Armonk, NY: M. E. Sharpe, 1997.
Chatfield, N. "Recollection of the Shipping Department of Burns Philp and Co. 1883–1914." Typescript. Sydney: Mitchell Library, 1957.
Cheyne, Andrew. *A Description of Some Islands of the Western Pacific.* London: J. D. Potter, 1852.

Colonial Office Reports. *Fiji, 1906–1918.* Cmd. 508–530 (1919).
Consular Letter Books (CLB). *Western Pacific High Commission.* Suva: Central Archives of Fiji, 1863–1876.
Coombe, Philip C. "Transport and Development: Shipping in the Cook Islands." MA thesis, University of Auckland, 1982.
Cooper, Matthew. "Economic Context of Shell Money Production in Malaita." *Oceania* 41, no. 4 (1971): 266–275.
Copping, Richard. "A Narrative of Pacific Seafaring 1826–1892." Typescript. Crowther Archives, Hobart, Tasmania.
Corris, Peter. *Passage, Port and Plantation: A History of Solomon Island Labour Migration 1870–1914.* Melbourne: Melbourne University Press, 1973.
Couper, A. D. "The Economics of Sail." *Journal of Navigation* 30 (1977): 164–171.
———. "Historical Perspectives on Seafarers and the Law." In *Seafarers' Rights,* ed. D. Fitzpatrick and M. Anderson, 3–35. Oxford: Oxford University Press, 2005.
———. "Islanders at Sea: Change and the Maritime Economies of the Pacific." In *The Pacific in Transition,* ed. Harold Brookfield, 229–247. London: Edward Arnold, 1973.
———. "Pacific Seafarers in Trade and Navigation." In *Localization and Orientation in Biology and Engineering,* ed. D. Varjú and H. U. Schnitzler, 227–243. Berlin: Springer-Verlag, 1984.
———. "Protest Movements and Protocooperatives in the Pacific Islands." *Journal of the Polynesian Society* 77, no. 3 (1968): 263–274.
———. *Report to the Government of Fiji on Inter-insular Shipping and Trade.* Suva, 1965.
———. "Seasat Images." In *Times Atlas and Encyclopedia of the Sea,* ed. A. D. Couper, 205. London: Times Books, 1983.
———. *Voyages of Abuse.* London: Pluto Press, 1999.
Creighton, Margaret S. "American Mariners and the Rites of Manhood, 1830–1870." In Howell and Twomey, *Jack Tar in History,* 143–163.
Creighton, Thomas. "Canadian Whalers in Micronesia (1840–1850)." *Journal of Pacific History* 24, no. 2 (1989): 225–238.
Cruise, Richard A. *Journal of a Ten Months' Residence in New Zealand.* London: Longman, 1832; facsimile, Christchurch, New Zealand: Capper Press, 1974.
Cumpston, J. S. *Shipping Arrivals and Departures, Sydney, 1788–1825.* 2 vols. Canberra: Campbell.
Dale, P. S., and P. A. Maddison. "Transport Services as an Aid to Insect Dispersal in the South Pacific." In *Commerce and the Spread of Pest and Disease Vectors,* ed. Laird Marshall, 225–256. New York: Praeger Scientific, 1984.

Dalton, R. W. "Reports on the Trade of the Fiji Islands; Also Trade of Western Samoa and Tonga." Typescript. Suva: Central Archives of the Western Pacific High Commission, 1918, 1919.

Dalton, William. *Two Whaling Voyages to the South Seas 1823–1829*. Edited by Niel Gunson. Canberra: National Library of Australia, 1990.

Dalziel, Raewyn. "Southern Islands: New Zealand and Polynesia." In *The Oxford History of the British Empire*, vol. 3, *The Nineteenth Century*, ed. Andrew Porter, 567–577. Oxford: University Press, 1999.

Danielsson, Bengt, and Marie-Thérèse Danielsson. "Polynesia's Third Sex: The Gay Life Starts in the Kitchen." *Pacific Islands Monthly*, August 1978, 10–13.

D'Arcy, Paul. "Connected by the Sea: Towards a Regional History of the Western Caroline Islands." *Journal of Pacific History* 36, no. 2 (2001): 163–182.

———. *The People of the Sea: Environment, Identity and History in Oceania*. Honolulu: University of Hawai'i Press, 2006.

Davidson, J. W. *Samoa mo Samoa: The Emergence of the Independent State of Western Samoa*. Melbourne: Oxford University Press, 1967.

Davidson, J. W., and Deryck Scarr, eds. *Pacific Island Portraits*. Canberra: Australian National University Press, 1970.

Daws, Gavan. "Honolulu in the Nineteenth Century." *Journal of Pacific History* 2 (1967): 77–96.

Dening, Greg. "The Geographical Knowledge of the Polynesians and the Nature of Inter-Island Contact." In Golson, *Polynesian Navigation*, 102–131.

———. *Islands and Beaches: Discourse on a Silent Land; Marquesas, 1774–1880*. Honolulu: University of Hawai'i Press, 1980.

———, ed. *The Marquesan Journal of Edward Roberts, 1797–1824*. Honolulu: University of Hawai'i Press, 1980.

Denoon, Donald, and Philippa Mein-Smith, with Marivic Wyndham. *A History of Australia, New Zealand and the Pacific*. Edinburgh: Blackwell, 2000.

Derrick, R. A. *A History of Fiji*. Suva: Government Press, 1963.

Diamond, Jared. *Collapse*. London: Penguin Books, 2005.

Diamond, Marian. "Queequeg's Crewmates: Pacific Islanders in European Shipping." *International Journal of Maritime History* 1, no. 2 (1989) 123–142.

Dillon, Peter. *Narrative and Successful Result of a Voyage in the South Seas*. 2 vols. London: Hurst Chance, 1829.

Drewry Shipping Consultants. *Ship Operating Costs Annual Review and Forecast 2004/05*. London, 2005.

Dunbar, Anne C. "Transport and Development: Inter-island Shipping in Vanuatu." PhD thesis, Australian National University, 1981.

Edwards, Philip, ed. *The Journals of Captain James Cook*. London: Penguin Classics, 1999.
———. *The Story of the Voyage: Sea-Narratives in Eighteenth-Century England*. Cambridge: Cambridge University Press, 1994.
Erskine, J. E. *Journal of a Cruise among the Islands of the Western Pacific*. Edinburgh: John Murray, 1853.
Fairbairn, Teʻo Ian. *Island Entrepreneurs*. Honolulu: University of Hawaiʻi Press, 1989.
———. *The Kiribati Economy*. Canberra: AIDAB, 1992.
Feinberg, Richard. "The Island and Its People." In *Polynesian Seafaring and Navigation: Ocean Travel in Anutan Culture and Society*, ed. Richard Feinberg, 5–21. Kent, OH: Kent State University Press, 1988.
———, ed. *Seafaring in the Contemporary Pacific Islands*. DeKalb: Northern Illinois University Press, 1995.
Fiji. *Legislative Council Debates, Steamship Subsidies*. November 1917.
———. *Report of the Commission Appointed to Inquire into the Decrease of the Native Population*. Suva: Government Printer, 1896.
———. *Report of the Shipping Commission 1915*. Council Paper 19.
———. *Return of Customs, Dues, Exports and Navigation 1881–1884*. Suva, 1885.
Fiji Marine Board. Records of the Fiji Marine Board, Office of the Harbour Master, Suva.
Finney, Ben R. "Experimental Voyaging, Oral Traditions and Long-Distance Interaction in Polynesia." In Weisler, *Prehistoric Long-Distance Interaction*, 38–52.
———. *Voyages of Rediscovery*. Berkeley: University of California Press, 1994.
Firth, Raymond. *Economics of the New Zealand Maori*. Wellington, New Zealand: R. E. Owen Government Printer, 1929.
———. *We, the Tikopia*. Boston: Beacon Press, 1936.
Forsyth, Craig J. "The Creation and Maintenance of a Stigmatized Occupation: An Historical Analysis of the American Merchant Marine." *Maritime Policy and Management* 14, no. 2 (1987): 99–108.
Fortune, Kate. "Traditional Healing Practices." In Lal and Fortune, *Pacific Islands*, 443.
Gammage, Bill. "The Rabaul Strike, 1929." *Journal of Pacific History* 10 (1975): 3–29.
Gibbs, Jim. *A Maritime History of Hawaii: Shipwrecks in Paradise*. Seattle: Superior Publishing Co., 1922.
Gibson, Andrew, and Arthur Donovan. *The Abandoned Ocean: A History of United States Marine Policy*. Columbia: University of South Carolina Press, 2000.

Gibson, James R. *Otter Skins, Boston Ships, and China Goods*. Seattle: University of Washington Press, 1999.

Gladwin, Thomas. *East Is a Big Bird: Navigation and Logic on Puluwat Atoll*. Cambridge, MA: Harvard University Press, 1970.

Golson, Jack, ed. *Polynesian Navigation*. Wellington, New Zealand: Polynesian Society, 1965.

Grimble, Arthur. "Canoes of the Gilbert Islands." *Journal of the Royal Anthropological Institute* 54 (1924): 101–139.

———. "Gilbertese Astronomy and Astronomical Observations." *Journal of the Polynesian Society* 40 (1931): 197–224.

Goodenough, W. H. *Native Astronomy in the Central Carolines*. Philadelphia: University of Pennsylvania, 1953.

Goundar, Avnita. "Captain Carol Dunlop: Fiji's First Female Sea-going Captain." *Regional Maritime Programme Newsletter*, 2006.

Gunson, Niel. "Pomare II of Tahiti and Polynesian Imperialism." *Journal of Pacific History* 4 (1969): 67–82.

———. "The Tongan-Samoa Connection 1777–1845." *Journal of Pacific History* 32 (1990): 139–152.

Haddon, A. C., and James Hornell. *Canoes of Oceania*. 3 vols. Bernice P. Bishop Museum Special Publications 27–29 Honolulu, 1936–1938.

Hauʻofa, Epeli. "A Beginning." In Waddell et al., *New Oceania*, 126–193.

———. "Our Sea of Islands." *Contemporary Pacific* 6 (1994): 148–161.

Hawkins, Clifford W. "The Passage of Sail: European Sailing Ship Building in the South West Pacific." *Great Circle* 5, no. 1 (1983): 90–97.

———. "The Waka in Trade and Transport." *Marine News* 49, no. 1 (2000): 12–14.

Helu, I. Futa. "South Pacific Mythology." In *Voyages and Beaches: Pacific Encounters, 1769–1840*, ed. Alex Calder, Jonathan Lamb, and Bridget Orr, 45–54. Honolulu: University of Hawaiʻi Press, 1999.

Hempenstall, Peter, and Noel Rutherford. *Protest and Dissent in the Colonial Pacific Suva*. University of the South Pacific, 1984.

Henry, Teuira. "Tahitian Astronomy." *Journal of the Polynesian Society* 16 (1907): 101–104.

Heyen, G. H. *Sailing Direction on Navigating in and between the Islands of the Gilbert Group*. Suva: Government Printer, 1937.

Heyerdahl, Thor. *The Kon-Tiki Expedition*. London: George Allen and Unwin, 1951.

Hezel, Francis X. *The First Taint of Civilization*. Honolulu: University of Hawaiʻi Press, 1983.

Hezel, Francis X., and Maria Teresa del Valle. "Early European Contact with the Western Carolines 1525–1750." *Journal of Pacific History* 7 (1972): 26–44.

Hill, J. M. M. *The Seafaring Career.* London: Tavistock Institute of Human Affairs, 1972.
Hoare, M. E., ed. *The Resolution Journal of Johann Reinhold Forster 1772–1775.* 4 vols. London: Hakluyt Society, 1982.
Hocart, A. M. *The Lau Islands of Fiji.* Bernice Bishop Museum Bulletin 69. Honolulu, 1929.
Hohepa, Pat. "My Musket, My Missionary, and My Mana." In *Voyages and Beaches: Pacific Encounters, 1769–1840,* ed. A. Calder, J. Lamb, and B. Orr, 180–201. Honolulu: University of Hawai'i Press, 1999.
Home, W. E. "The Health of Merchant Seamen." *Lancet* (8 November 1924): 981–982.
Hope, Ronald. *A New History of British Shipping.* Edinburgh: John Murray, 1990.
———. *Poor Jack.* London: Chatham Publishing, 2001.
Howard, Alan. "Rotuman Seafaring in Historical Perspective." In Feinberg, *Seafaring in the Contemporary Pacific Islands,* 114–143.
Howe, K. R. *The Loyalty Islands.* Canberra: Australian National University Press, 1977.
———. "Tourists, Sailors and Labourers." *Journal of Pacific History* 13 (1978): 22–36.
———. *Where the Waves Fall.* Sydney: Allen and Unwin, 1984.
Howell, C., and Richard Twomey, eds. *Jack Tar in History.* Fredericton, NB: Acadiensis Press, 1991.
Hughes, Robert. *The Fatal Shore.* Sydney: Pan Books, 1988.
Hugill, Stan. *Sailortown.* London: Routledge and Kegan Paul, 1967.
Inquiry by Royal Commission into Certain Alleged Cases of Kidnapping of Natives of the Loyalty Islands Held at Sydney, 9th August 1869 under C. Rolleston. Canberra: National Library of Australia.
Irwin, Geoffrey. *The Prehistoric Exploration and Colonisation of the Pacific.* Cambridge: Cambridge University Press, 1992.
Jackson, John. "Feejeean Islands." Appendix to *Journal of a Cruise among the Islands of the Western Pacific,* ed. J. E. Erskine, 411–477. Edinburgh: John Murray, 1853.
Jog, N. G., ed. *Narottam Morarjee: Architect of Modern Indian Shipping.* Bombay: Scindia Steam Navigation Co., 1977.
Johannes, R. E. *Words of the Lagoon: Fishing and Marine Lore in the Palau District of Micronesia.* Berkeley: University of California Press, 1981.
Johannessen, Edward. *The Hawaiian Labor Movement: A Brief History.* Boston: Bruce Humphries, 1956.
Johnson, Giff. "Mau's Keen Eye Keeps Hawaiian Canoe on Track." *Pacific Islands Monthly,* April 1999, 50–51.
Johnson, Samuel. *Journal of a Tour of the Hebrides.* 3rd ed. London, 1773.

Johnstone, Paul. *The Sea Craft of Prehistory*. London: Routledge, 1980.

Jonge, Nico de, and Toos Van Dijk. *Forgotten Islands of Indonesia*. Leiden: Periplus Editions 1995.

Jull, M. E. "My Trip to New Zealand and a Group of Islands in the South Seas 1883–1884." 2 vols. Unpublished MS (1575). National Library of Australia, Canberra.

Kennedy, D. G. *Field Notes on the Culture of Vaitupu, Ellice Islands*. New Plymouth, New Zealand: Polynesian Society, 1931.

Kirch, Patrick Vinton. *On the Road of the Winds*. Berkeley: University of California Press, 2002.

Knipe, Ed. *Gamrie: An Exploration in Cultural Ecology*. New York: University Press of America, 1984.

Lal, Brij V. *Broken Waves: A History of the Fiji Islands in the Twentieth Century*. Honolulu: University of Hawai'i Press, 1992.

Lal, Brij V., and Kate Fortune, eds. *The Pacific Islands: An Encyclopedia*. Honolulu: University of Hawai'i Press, 2000.

Lal, Brij V., and Hank Nelson, eds. *Lines across the Sea*. Brisbane: Pacific History Association, 1995.

Lamb, J., V. Smith, and N. Thomas. *A South Seas Anthology*. Chicago: University of Chicago Press, 2000.

Lambert, Bernd. "Makin and the Outside World." In *Pacific Atoll Populations*, ed. Vern Carroll, 212–216. Honolulu: University of Hawai'i Press, 1975.

Langdon, Robert. "The Bamboo Raft as Key to the Introduction of the Sweet Potato in Prehistoric Polynesia." *Journal of Pacific History* 36 (2001): 32–58.

———. *The Lost Caravel*. Sydney: Pacific Publications, 1975.

Larson, K. E. "Early Channels of Communication in the Pacific." *Ethnos* (1966): 112–119.

Lawson, R. M., and E. Kwei. *African Enterprise and Economic Growth: A Case Study of the Fishing Industry of Ghana*. Accra: Ghana University Press, 1974.

Leckie, J. "Colonial Inheritance and Labour: Structure, Conditions and Identities in Fiji." In *Lines across the Sea*, ed. Brij V. Lal and Hank Nelson, 185–197. Brisbane: Pacific History Association, 1995.

———. "Trade Union Rights and Politics in Post-Coup Fiji." *Pacific Studies* 16, 3 September 1993), 112–119.

———. "Workers in Colonial Fiji." In *Labour in the South Pacific*, ed. G. Moore, J. Leckie, and D. Munro, 47–66. Queensland: James Cook University, 1990.

Le Hunte, G. Ruthven. *Six Letters from the Western Pacific, by a Judicial Commissioner*. New Zealand Parliamentary Papers. Wellington.

Lepowsky, Maria. "Voyaging and Cultural Identity in the Louisiade Archi-

pelago of Papua New Guinea." In Feinberg, *Seafaring in the Contemporary Pacific Islands*, 34–54.
Lewis, David. "Polynesian and Micronesian Navigation Techniques." *Journal of the Institute of Navigation* 23, no. 4 (1970): 432–447.
———. *We, the Navigators*. Canberra: Australian National University Press, 1972.
Linebaugh, P., and M. Rediker. "The Many-Headed Hydra: Sailors, Slaves and the Atlantic Working Class in the Eighteenth Century." In Howell and Twomey, *Jack Tar in History*, 11–35.
Linnekin, Jocelyn. "New Political Orders." In *The Cambridge History of the Pacific Islanders*, ed. Donald Denoon, 185–216. Cambridge: Cambridge University Press, 2004.
Lockerby, William. *The Journal of William Lockerby, Sandalwood Trader in the Fijian Islands during the Years 1808–1809*. London: Hakluyt Society, 1925.
MacDonald, Barrie. *Cinderellas of the Empire: Toward a History of Kiribati and Tuvalu*. Canberra: Australian National University Press, 1982.
MacFarlane, Deborah. "Transsexual Prostitution in Polynesia: A Tradition Defiled?" *Pacific Islands Monthly*, February 1983, 11–12.
Mahaffy, A. W. *Report on a Visit to the Gilbert and Ellice Islands in 1909*. Cd. 4992, CO225. London, 1910.
Mahlmann, J. J. "Reminiscences of an Ancient Mariner." *Japan Gazette* (Yokohama), 1918.
Mallacoota Memories 1841–1948. Vol. 12. Mallacoota, Victoria, Australia: Mallacoota District Historical Society, 1980.
Marks, Kathy. "Fishermen Rescued after Five Months Lost at Sea." *Independent* (London), 13 November 2001.
Martin, John, ed. *An Account of the Natives of the Tongan Islands*. By William Mariner. 2 vols. London: Hakluyt Society, 1817–1818.
Mason, Michael, Basil Greenhill, and Robin Craig. *The British Seafarer*. London: Hutchinson/BBC in association with the National Maritime Museum, 1980.
Maude, H. E. "Beachcombers and Castaways." *Journal of the Polynesian Society* 73, no. 3 (1964): 254–293.
———. "The Co-operative Movement in the Gilbert and Ellice Islands." *South Pacific* (May 1950).
———. *The Evolution of the Gilbertese Boti*. Polynesian Society Memoir 35. 1963. Wellington, New Zealand.
———. "Post-Spanish Discoveries in the Central Pacific." *Journal of the Polynesian Society* 70, no. 1 (1961): 67–111.
———. *Slavers in Paradise: The Peruvian Slave Trade in Polynesia, 1862–1864*. Stanford, CA: Stanford University Press, 1981.
———. "The Sword of Gabriel: Account of the Disturbances on Onotoa

Island." Seminar paper. Canberra: Australian National University, 1964.

———. "The Tahitian Pork Trade 1800–1830." *Journal de la Société des Océanistes* (Paris) 15 (1959): 55–95.

Maude, H. E., and Marjorie Tuainekore Crocombe. "Rarotongan Sandalwood: An Ethnohistorical Reconstruction." *Journal of the Polynesian Society* 71 (1962): 32–56.

Maude, H. E., and Edwin Doran. "The Precedence of Tarawa Atoll." *Annals of American Geographers* 56 (1966): 269–289.

Maude, H. E., and J. Leeson. "The Coconut Oil Trade of the Gilbert Islands." *Journal of the Polynesian Society* 74 (1965): 397–437.

McGlone, M. S., A. J. Anderson, and R. N. Holdaway. "An Ecological Approach." In *The Origins of the First New Zealanders*, ed. Douglas G. Sutton, 136–163. Auckland: Auckland University Press, 1994.

McNab, Robert, ed. *Historical Records of New Zealand*. Government and general orders from 1805 and letters. 2 vols. Wellington.

Melville, Herman. *Moby Dick*. London: Penguin Books, 1994.

Mills, Peter R. "Neo in Oceania." *Journal of Pacific History* 135 (2003): 53–67.

Montague, Susan P. "Kaduwaga: A Trobriand Boat Harbour." In Feinberg, *Seafaring in the Contemporary Pacific Islands*, 55–67.

Moore, Clive. "Hiri Trading Voyages." In Lal and Fortune, *Pacific Islands*, 139.

Moore, Clive, Jacqueline Leckie, and Doug Munro, eds. *Labour in the South Pacific*. Queensland: James Cook University, 1990.

Morrell, W. P. *Britain in the Pacific Islands*. Oxford: Oxford University Press, 1960.

Morton, Harry. *The Whale's Wake*. Honolulu: University of Hawai'i Press, 1982.

Munro, Doug. "The Lives and Times of Resident Traders in Tuvalu: An Exercise in History from Below." *Pacific Studies* 10, no. 2 (1987): 73–106.

Munro, Doug, and Teloma Munro. "The Rise and Fall of the Vaitupu Company." *Journal of Pacific History* 20, no. 4 (1985): 174–190.

———. "Vaitupu's Debt: An Exercise in Combined Use of Documentary Records and Oral History." *Oral History Association of Australia Journal* 5 (1982–1983): 58–64.

National Maritime Union. *On a True Course: The Story of the National Maritime Union*. New York, 1967.

Naval Intelligence Division. *Geographical Handbook*. Vol. 1, *Pacific Islands*, edited by Raymond Firth and J. W. Davidson. British Admiralty, 1942.

New Zealand Parliamentary Papers (NZPP). Wellington. Nicholas, John L. *Narrative of a Voyage to New Zealand Performed in the Years 1814*

and 1815 in Company with the Rev. Samuel Marsden. 2 vols. Auckland: Wilson and Horton, 1971.
Nightingale, Tony. *The Pacific Forum Line.* Christchurch, New Zealand: Glestory Press, 1998.
Nunn, Patrick. "Facts, Fallacies and the Future in the Island Pacific." In Waddell et al., *New Oceania,* 112–115.
———. "Illuminating Sea Level Fall around AD 1200–1510 in the Pacific Islands: Implications for Environmental Change and Cultural Transformation." *New Zealand Geographer* 56 (1993): 46–53.
Osborne, E. *The Copra Trader.* Sydney: NSW Bookstall, 1924.
Pacific Islands Yearbook, 1932. Sydney: Pacific Publications, 1932.
Palmer, Sarah. *Politics, Shipping and the Repeal of the Navigation Laws.* Manchester, UK: Manchester University Press, 1990.
Palmer, Sarah, and David Williams. "British Sailors 1775–1870." In *Those Emblems of Hell? European Sailors and the Maritime Labour Market 1570–1870,* ed. P. C. Van Royen, J. R. Bruijn, and J. Lucassen 93-118. St. John's: International Maritime Economic History Association, 1997.
Parsonson, G. S. "The Settlement of Oceania." In Golson, *Polynesian Navigation,* 11–63.
Pérez-Mallaína, Pablo E. *Spain's Men of the Sea: Daily Life on the Indies Fleet in the 16th Century.* London: Johns Hopkins University Press, 1998.
Péron, Francoise. "Seamen of the Island and the Faith: The Example of Quessant." *INSULA: International Journal of Island Affairs* (Paris) 1, no. 1 (1992): 36–41.
Petersen, Glen. "Indigenous Island Empires: Yap and Tonga Compared." *Journal of Pacific History* 35 (2000): 5–22.
Petit-Skinner, Solange. "Traditional Ownership of the Sea in Oceania." In *Ocean Yearbook,* vol. 4, ed. Elizabeth Mann Borgese and Norton Ginsberg, 308–318. Chicago: University of Chicago Press, 1983.
Philbrick, Nathaniel. *In the Heart of the Sea.* London: Harper Collins, 2001.
Price, Charles. "White Restrictions on Colonial Immigration." *Race* 7, no. 3 (1996).
Quain, Buell. *Fijian Villages.* Chicago: University of Chicago Press, 1948.
Quimby, George. "Hawaiians in the Fur Trade of North-west America, 1785–1820." *Journal of Pacific History* 7 (1972): 92–104.
Rae, Pramod K. "Ethnic Factors in Trade Unionism in Fiji 1942–1975." *Pacific Perspectives* 8, no. 1 (1979): 32–37.
Ralston, Caroline. *Grass Huts and Warehouses: Pacific Beach Communities of the Nineteenth Century.* Honolulu: University of Hawai'i Press, 1978.
Rappaport, Moshe. "Oysterlust: Islanders, Entrepreneurs and Colonial Policy

over Tuamotu Lagoons." *Journal of Pacific History* 30, no. 1 (1995): 39–52.

Reynolds, Stephen W. *The Voyage of the New Hazard 1810–1813*, ed. F. W. Howay. Fairfield, WA: Ye Galleon Press, 1970.

Roberts, Steven. *Study of Occupational Mortality among Merchant Seafarers on the British, Singapore and Hong Kong Fleets*. Cardiff: Seafarers International Research Centre. 1998.

Rodger, N. A. M. *The Command of the Ocean: A Naval History of Britain 1649–1815*. London: Penguin Books, 2004.

Rogers, Nicholas. "Liberty Road: Opposition to Impressment in Britain during the American War of Independence." In Howell and Twomey, *Jack Tar in History*, 55–75.

Rutter, Owen, ed. *The Journal of James Morrison, Boatswain's Mate of the Bounty*. London: Golden Cockerel Press, 1935.

Sabatier, Ernest. *Sous l'equateur du Pacifique: Les iles Gilbert et la Mission Catholique*. Paris: Edition Dillen, 1939.

Sager, Eric. *Seafaring Labour: The Merchant Marine of Atlantic Canada 1820–1914*. Montreal: McGill-Queens University Press, 1989.

Sahlins, Marshall. "Making up Cannibalism?" *Anthropology Today* 19, no. 3 (2003): 3–6.

———. *Moala: Culture and Nature on a Fijian Island*. Ann Arbor: University of Michigan Press, 1962.

Salmond, Anne. *Between Worlds: Early Exchanges between Maori and Europeans, 1773–1815*. Auckland: Viking Press, 1997.

———. *Two Worlds: First Meetings between Maori and Europeans 1642–1772*. Honolulu: University of Hawai'i Press, 1998.

"Samoa's MV *Queen Salamasina* Sold to Fiji Company." *Pacific Islands Monthly*, January 2000, 45.

Scarr, Deryck, ed. *A Cruise in a Queensland Labour Vessel to the South Seas*. By William A. Giles. Canberra: Australian National University Press, 1968.

———. "European Visitors: First Contacts." In Lal and Fortune, *Pacific Islands*, 147–150.

Schwartz, Stephen. *Brotherhood of the Sea: A History of the Sailors' Union of the Pacific, 1885–1985*. San Francisco: Robert Matlock Printing Co., 1986.

Seafarers International Research Center (SIRC). *The Sailing Chaplain and Outreach Welfare Schemes*. Cardiff, 2003.

Shineberg, Dorothy. *They Came for Sandalwood: A Study of the Sandalwood Trade in the South West Pacific 1830–65*. Melbourne: University of Melbourne Press, 1986.

———, ed. *The Trading Voyage of Andrew Cheyne 1841–44*. Canberra: Australian National University Press, 1971.

Skinner, H. D. "Murdering, Beach Collecting and Excavating: 1850–1950." *Journal of the Polynesian Society* 68 (1959): 219–239.
Smith, Percy C. "Six Months in the Pacific." Unpublished MS. Auckland Museum Library, 1919.
Smith-Rawse, G. B. *Ellice Islands Annual Report*, no. 9 of 1913. London: Colonial Office.
Sobel, Dava. *Longitude*. London: Fourth Estate, 1995.
South Pacific Maritime Code. Suva: South Pacific Bureau for Economic Co-operation, 1986.
Spate, O. H. K. *Paradise Found and Lost*. London: Routledge, 1988.
———. *The Spanish Lake*. Canberra: Australian National University Press, 1979.
Spoehr, F. M. *White Falcon: The House of Godeffroy and Its Commercial and Scientific Role in the Pacific*. Palo Alto, CA: Pacific Books, 1963.
Stackpole, Edouard A. *The Mutiny on the Whaleship Globe: A True Story of the Sea*. Nantucket, MA: published by the author, 1981.
Stevenson, Mrs. R. L. *The Cruise of the Janet Nichol*. London: Chatto and Windus, 1915.
Stevenson, R. L. *In the South Seas*. London: Chatto and Windus, 1920.
———. *Treasure Island*. 1881; London: Penguin Classics, 1999.
Straubel, C. R., ed. *The Whaling Journal of Captain W. B. Rhodes of the Barque Australian of Sydney, 1836–1838*. Christchurch, New Zealand: Whitcombe and Tombs, 1954.
Sutton, D. G. *The Origins of the First New Zealander*. Auckland: Auckland University Press, 1994.
Thomas, Mifflin. *Schooner from Windward*. Honolulu: University of Hawai'i Press, 1983.
Thomas, Nicholas. *Discoveries*. London: Penguin Books, 2003.
———. *Entangled Objects*. Cambridge, MA: Harvard University Press, 1991.
———. *Oceanic Art*. London: Thames and Hudson, 1995.
Thomas, Stephen D. *The Last Navigator*. New York: Ballantine Books, 1987.
Thomson, Basil. *The Fijians: A Study of the Decay of Customs*. London: Dawsons of Pall Mall: 1968. Originally published in 1908.
Toatu, Teuea. "Seamen and Cultural Change in Kiribati." *Pacific Perspective* 8, no. 2 (1975): 31–32.
Tui, Novosa. "Foretellers of Ships." *Pacific Islands Monthly* 42 (1946).
Turnbull, John. *A Voyage round the World in the Years 1801–1804*. 3 vols. Philadelphia: Benjamin and Thomas Kite, 1810.
Twyning, John P. *An Account of the Life and Adventures of John Payer Twyning; Comprising the Wreck of the Minerva and the Author's Years in Fiji and the Friendly Isles*. 2nd ed. Bristol: for the benefit of the author, 1850.

UNCTAD. *Establishment or Expansion of Merchant Marines in Developing Countries.* TD/26/Rev 1. 1968.

———. *Review of Maritime Transport 2003.* Geneva, 2003.

United Nations. *Convention on a Code of Conduct for Liner Conferences.* NYTD/Code/13/1974.

Vuksanovic, P., W. H. Goethe, H. V. Burchard, et al. "Seamen and AIDS." *Travel Medicine International* 6 (1988): 18–19.

Waddell, Eric, Vijay Naidu, and Epeli Hauʻofa, eds. *A New Oceania: Rediscovering Our Sea of Islands.* Suva: University of the South Pacific, 1993.

Wallen, F. Reports 1 and 2 to managing directors of Burns Philp. In Buckley and Klugman, *South Pacific Focus.*

Ward, R. Gerard, ed. *American Activities in the Central Pacific 1790–1870.* 8 vols. Ridgewood, NJ: Gregg Press, 1966.

———. *Widening Worlds, Shrinking Worlds? The Reshaping of Oceania.* Canberra: Australian National University, 1999.

Ward, R. Gerard, and Muriel Brookfield. "The Dispersal of the Coconut: Did It Float or Was It Carried to Panama?" *Journal of Biogeography* 19 (1992): 467–479.

Weins, Harold J. *Atoll Environment and Ecology.* New Haven, CT: Yale University Press, 1962.

Weisler, Marshall I. "Hard Evidence for Prehistoric Interaction in Polynesia." *Current Anthropology* 39, no. 4 (1998): 521–532.

———, ed. *Prehistoric Long-Distance Interaction in Oceania: An Interdisciplinary Approach.* New Zealand Archaeological Association, Monograph 21. Auckland, 1997.

Western Pacific High Commission, Central Archives of Fiji, Suva.

Wickramatillake, Hemantha D. *Infectious Diseases among Seafarers.* Cardiff: Seafarers International Research Centre, 1998.

Wigen, Kären. "Oceans of History." *American Historical Review* 3 (2006): 717–721.

Wilkes, Charles. *Narrative of the United States Exploring Expedition in the Years 1838–1842.* Ridgewood, NJ: Gregg Press, 1970.

Willard, Myra. *A History of the White Australia Policy to 1920.* Melbourne: Melbourne University Press, 1974.

Williams, Glyn. *The Prize of All the Oceans.* London: Harper Collins, 1999.

Williams, Thomas. *Fiji and the Fijians.* London: Hodder and Singleton, 1870.

Wood, A. H. *History and Geography of Tonga.* Nukualofa: Tupou College, 1952.

World Health Organization. *Second Generation Surveillance Surveys of HIV, Other STIs and Risk Behaviours in the Six Pacific Island Countries.* Geneva, 2006.

Yarwood, A. T. *Samuel Marsden: The Great Survivor.* Melbourne: Melbourne University Press, 1977.

Young, David. "Sailing to Levuka: The Cultural Significance of the Island Schooners in the Late 19th Century." *Journal of Pacific History* 28 (1993): 36–53.

Young, John. "Lau: A Windward Perspective." *Journal of Pacific History* 28 (1993): 159–180.

———. "The Response of Lau to Foreign Contact." *Journal of Pacific History* 17 (1982): 29–50.

Zhao, Minghua, X. Shi, and T. Feng, *The Political Commissar and His Shipmates aboard Chinese Merchant Ships.* Beijing: Chinese Social Sciences Documentation Publishing House, 2004.

INDEX

abandonment of sailors: by Captain Fodger, 127; case of Ruatara, 127–128; the law, 127; occurrences, 76, 114, 126, 193; Stevenson's account, 129

abuses: floggings, 86, 101, 126; forced to desert, 125–126; illegal hanging, 122, 131; reprisal concerns of governments, 133; theft of identities, 125; wage discrimination, 125–126

accidents at sea: categories, 118; induced to take risks, 120; modern hazards, 195; in whaling, 120–121

alcohol, 112, 194–196

allotments to dependents from sailors, 201

Anson, George, 38

Anuta (Polynesian outlier), sailors social behavior, 18

Aotearoa (New Zealand): exploration by Kupe, 8–9; Polynesian arrivals, 9, 23; return voyages and climate, 32; settlement names, 44; traditional vessels, 30; vessels of Europeans, 59; violence and armaments trade, 90–93. *See also* Maori

arms race: attacks on ships for guns, 71, 96; guns by trade, 78, 80, 83, 96

art at sea, 112

astronomy (indigenous): Carolines, 34; Kiribati, 9; Tahiti, 9

Austral Islands, source of sandalwood, 81–82

Australian Maritime College (AMC), 177, 179

Australian Waterside Workers' Federation, 200

Baintabu (navigator), 37
bakola (human flesh), 48
Banks, Joseph, 67, 68
beachcombers: as commercial agents, 91; as crimps, 105; as mercenaries, 78; their origins, 76; as traders 139
bêche de mer trade, 122
Binoka, Tem, 96, 157
birds: arrivals and island sustenance, 43; indicators of fish, 39; of land, 36; shipbuilding timber, 28; totemic species, 13
blackbirders: Pacific crewing, 107–108; people stealing ships, 107
Bligh, William, 38, 39, 62
Boki (Governor), 88, 89
Bougainville, Louis de, 60, 61, 66
bubuti (Kiribati), obligations to share, 7
Bullen, Frank, 105, 111
Buyers, John, 80

253

Cakobau (King), 46, 47, 96
Cameron, Alister D., 154
Campbell, Telford, 146, 155
Campbell, William, 125
cannibalism at sea, 39; attitudes of Europeans, 67–68; on bakola raids, 48; on lifeboats, 39; in sealing, 121
canoes (oceanic): baurua, 30; drua, 28; kalia, 28; lakatoi, 30; pahi, 29; puka, 30; wa (generic name), 25; wa kaulua, 29; waka tana, 30; waka taua, 30
Cape Horn, 102, 116
capitalism into Pacific: different ethics, 97; environmental and social impacts, 98
captains: of foreign ships, 125, 129; functions, 33–34; of indigenous craft, 9, 44; as part owners, 77
Caroline Islands (Micronesia), navigators' skills and status, 34, 44
Carteret, Philip, 60, 61, 66
castaways: driven away in conflicts, 48; expelled from ships, 38; by famine, 47; reception on islands, 47, 48
ceremonies at sea: bonding of crew, 18; ducking chair, 18; King Neptune, 18, 112–113; old horse, 18
Chatfield, N., 144
China trade: Outer Eastern Passage from Australia, 76; tea cargoes, 76; cross Pacific from northwest America and Hawai'i calls, 85; voyages of *New Hazard* in fur trade, 85–88
Chinese traders, in islands, 144, 166, 205
climate change: deterioration of climate curtailing voyaging, 32; environmental impacts, 57; favorable sailing periods, 32

coal, 141, 150–151
coastal hazards: lee shores, 41; reefs, 41–42
coconut oil trade, 76, 82
Collingwood, Cuthbert, 130
colonial shipping: curtailment of traditional trading, 146; reduced employment of island sailors, 146; trade unions against cheap labor, 148–149; White Australia Policy, 149
colonization: annexation by imperial powers, 140–141; early steamships, 141; flag preferences, 143; ports of entry and subsidies, 143; redistributing German territories, 150; small and remote islands suffer, 144
company shipping: establishing spheres of trade, 138–140; national lines cover Pacific, 141; technical improvements, 141–143
Comstock, Samuel, 132
conflicts: attacks by island people, 71, 91, 96, 121, 122; attacks on Pacific people, 60–61, 83, 91–93; wars between islands, 37, 45–48, 71, 81, 90, 96
convicts: employed as sailors, 103–104, 224n20; escape to islands, 76; stealing ships, 104; women convicts and crews, 102
Cook, James: attitudes to social complexities, 72; to deserters, 65–66; and the Maori, 59; to Pacific navigators, 37, 73; to taking possession of territories, 63–64; on trading values, 54; to venereal disease, 66, 74; voyages of, 62–63; on wars, 45–50; on women's conditions, 69
Cook Islands (eastern Polynesia) own ships, 157–158, 181

cooperatives and protocooperatives, 153–154
Copping, Edward, 121
crews (historic): bonding, 18; multi-ethnic, 117; multinational, 107; officer appointments, 109. *See also* seafarers recruitment (historical)
Crowther, Dr. W. L., 123
currents (ocean), 12, 30; becalmed, 34; drifting, 39; hazardous, 146

Davis, Isaac, 84
death at sea (historical): ancient voyages, 12; British figures, 12, 118, 210n17; Hawaiian, 119; Nantucket, 12; opinion of medical officer, 118–119; sailors souls to Davy Jones' locker or Fiddler's Green, 13; underreporting of deaths, 119
deaths (contemporary): autopsy examples, 196; common causes, 195; delays in medical attention at sea, 195; suicide, 196–197
desertion: attraction of islands, 102; driven to desert, 76, 126; from time of Cook, 65–66, 76, 79, 91, 102, 105
destroying canoes as punishment, 15, 64
Dillon, Peter, 107
diseases: exposure in ports, 123; in foc'sles, 110; nutritional defects, 123; sexual infections, 123–124, 195; tuberculosis, 123
diving: for cable and hull repairs, 106; deep for pearls, 106, 130; mutiny by pearl divers, 130; protests at exploitation of lagoons, 152; skills of Pacific sailors, 106
DNA, dating in archaeology, 24
droughts, 6, 47

Dunlop, Carol, 180
dynasties: founding in Hawai'i, Kamehameha, 83; Tahiti, Pomare, 78; Tonga, chiefs Ha'apai, Tongatapu, Vava'u, 46; victorious Tupou dynasty, 46

East India Company, 76
Easter Island. *See* Rapa Nui
El Niño: droughts and migrations, 9; generation of westerly winds, 23
engine rooms, change in ship social structure, 147
English language, advantages in global seafaring, 189, 206
explorers (Western): American, 50; British, 62; Dutch, 61; French, 61, 62; Portuguese, 61; Spanish, 60–61

fei (Yapese stone money), 51
Fiji (Melanesia/Polynesia): arrival, 23; Bua sea power, 46–47; cargoes, 49, 53; cession to Britain, 140; foreign companies and subsidies, 166, 168; inter-island fleet (contemporary), 166–167; *Kandavulevu* lost, 174, 175; passengers and cargo, 167–168; safety regulations, 174–176; seafarers' profiles, 177–179; ship losses, 168–169; social changes, 178–180; solevu, 171–175; technical changes in shipping and ports, 175; tourist craft, 175; trade unions, 170, 180; trading, informal by passengers and sailors, 170–171; training, 176–177
Finney, Ben, 30, 207
first fleet, convict arrivals, 76
first migrant arrivals, primacy accorded, 44
flag of convenience, 186–187, 193, 200, 235n3

Fodger, Michael, 81, 127, 130
food at sea: on migratory voyages, 40–41; in modern interisland vessels, 170; on sailing ships, 123; serving modern mixed crews, 7, 194
food from the sea: Anson, Bligh, and Magellan, 38–39; indigenous techniques successful, 39–40
Forster, George, 68, 69, 74
Forster, Johann Reinhold, 68
French Polynesia: shortage of ships' officers, 192; trade unions, 199

geographical knowledge (indigenous): evidence of early trading networks, 49; Micronesia map conveyed to Cantova, 36; Tupaia's map of Polynesia, 1, 36
Gilbert, Thomas, 76
Gilbert and Ellice International Overseas Seamen's Union, 200
Glen, John, 91
gods and sea spirits: Batiauea, Baretoka (Kiribati), 7; Dakuwaga, Degei, Rokola (Fiji), 14, 16; Maui, Tangaroa, Oro (Polynesia), 7, 8, 54; Motikitiki (Solomons), 8; ship as god, 11
golden rivet, 11
Gordon, Sir Arthur (Governor, Fiji), 145, 146; policies, 145
Grimble, Arthur, 9, 34
Guam (Marianas): arrival of Magellan, 38; galleon staging post, 61

Hamburg Süd line, 188–189
Hanson, Thomas, 81
Hart, Charles, 122
Hawai'i (Polynesia): Cook on *Resolution,* 66; first arrival Polynesians, 23; fur traders, 83; Kamehameha dynasty established, 83; killings by Metcalf, 83–84; obtained *Fair American,* 84; royal commercial fleet initiated, 84; sailors from Hawai'i, 86; sea power and conquests, 83; ship purchases with sandalwood, 84; shipbuilding, 84; shipping regulations from America, 146; trade to China, 87; trade to northwest Pacific, 77; unprofitable businesses, 88; voyage disaster, Erromango sandalwood, 88–89
Hawaiki (Polynesia), legendary homeland of Maori, 9, 30
Henry, Samuel, 81
Heyen, G. H., 34, 138
Hicks, Zachary, 67
Hipour (navigator), 207
HIV/AIDS in Pacific, 21, 197–199
Hokule'a, 30, 207
homosexual: death sentence, 19; *Largs Bay* marriage, 19; Polynesian attitudes, 114, 212n41
hotel and cruise ships, 175

Indo Fijian traders, 166
Indonesia: ships as symbolic family, 10; swell in navigation, 13
International Labour Organization (ILO), 200
International Maritime Organization (IMO), conventions, 176, 178
International Overseas Seamen's Union (Kiribati), 200
International Shipping Federation (ISF), 200
International Transport Workers' Federation (ITF): contracts, 200; Kiribati negotiations, 200–201, 236n14; rates, 182
iron, economic impacts: George Forster claims moral corruption, 74

Japanese, as crews: Hawai'i, 147
Jones, John Coffin, 89
junior officers, literacy, 109

Kameeiamoku, 83
Kamehameha I, 46, 83–84, 86, 88
Kamehameha II (Liholiho), 88
Kamehameha III, 88
kanaka, crews, 103, 130
Kau, Moala (navigator), 46, 71
kava (yaqona): carried to islands, 40, 43; feasts, 53; traded, 172
Kelly, James, 93
Kete, Tomasi Cama, 177–178
King, Philip Gidley (Governor, NSW), 77–79
Kiribati (contemporary): allotments, 201; analysis of crew lists, 190; community attitudes to seafarers, 201–202; Hamburg Süd line, 188; health, 195; life at sea, 193; maneaba discussions, 193; Marine Training Centre, 189; national income, 205; recruitment by quota, 189; retirement, 205; sailors' profiles, 193; sexual behavior of seafarers, 198–199; sexually transmitted infections, 197–198; stresses on marriage, 203; Tarawa alternative residence, 203–204; value added prospects in seafaring, 206; wages of seafarers, 200; wives' responsibilities, 203; women and equality, 204; women in maneaba, 202; women's maritime organizations, 204
Kiribati (historical): colonial prohibition of indigenous voyaging, 146; conflicts, 37, 48; diversity of origins, 24; driven away by wars, 37, 48; navigational training, 34; protest organizations, 156; shipping services, 188; trade unions, 199–201
Kupe, 8–9

Lapita, Neolithic migrants: pottery routes, 23

Lau Islands (Fiji/Polynesia): sea power, 47; shipbuilding, 47; vesi timber, 46
law of the sea (historical): ancient rules, 132; coastal states rights, 63; customs of the sea, 75, 132–133; freedom of the sea, 63; indigenous laws, 71; naval officer views, 63; regulations New South Wales, 77, 78, 92, 94, 134; safety legislation, 134–135; seafarers adversely affected by new laws, 134–135, 229n56; seafarers' legal isolation, 133
law of the sea (modern): conventions IMO, 176; ILO, 200
lays payments: induced risk taking, 120; unfair on sealers, 126; on whalers dangerous, 120
Le Maire, Isaac, 61
Legazpi, Miguel Lopez de, 61
Lewis, David, 36
longitude problems, 36
loss of ships in Pacific (historical): Hawai'i, 121; most prone whalers, 119; on reefs, 120; survival prospects, 120; wages cease on loss, 119
Loyalty Islands (Melanesia) seafarers, 104

Ma'afu (Chief), 96
Macquarie, Lachlan (Governor, NSW), 92, 133
Magellan, Ferdinand, 38, 60
Mahaffy, Arthur, 146, 152, 155
Mahan, Alfred, 141
mana, of chiefs, 77
maneaba (Kiribati): indigenous navigation school, 34; meetings, 20; place of refuge, 48; rights to speak, 202
Manui'a (Chief), 88
Maori: arms in demand, 90; beachcombers in commerce, 91; flax,

food, kauri trades, 77, 91; intertribal conflicts, 94; ship shore conflicts, 91–93; technically advanced Maori craft developed, 91; temporarily controlled all shipping, 94–95; Treaty of Waitangi, 95
Margaret, voyages of, 79–81
Mariana Islands (Micronesia), links with Carolines, 52
Marine Training Centre (MTC), 16, 189–190
Mariner, William, 3, 71, 96
maritime education and training, IMO regulations, 178
maritime heritage: ancestor voyages, 207; regional links revived, 208
Marquesas (eastern Polynesia): arrivals, 23; drought, 47; kidnapping for crews, 104; raiding, 47
Marsden, Samuel, 92, 94, 133
Marshall, John, 76
Marshall Islands (Micronesia): flag of convenience, 186; schooners, 157; stick charts, 35
Meares, John, 103
medical care: on ancient voyages, 40; contemporary examples, 195–196; on merchant ships, 124; surgeons, 124; on whalers, 124
Mendana, Alvera de, 61
mental health at sea: isolation and stress, 197; priests, political commissars, and unions on merchant ships, 197; suicides, 196
merchant shipping companies, 139–140
mess rooms, 194–195
Metcalf, Simon, 83
missionaries on islands: in arms trading, 81; in shipowning, 81
Missions to Seafarers: facilities in ports, 197; modern problems reaching crews, 197
Morrison, James, 14, 66, 69, 72

multinational crews, 118, 133, 145, 188, 193
mutiny: defined, 129–130; incidents, 130–132; killing of captains and officers, 130–131; piracy a factor in mutinies, 131–132; on ships with divers, 131; yardarm hangings as penalty, 132

navigation training (indigenous) in Carolines, 34; Kiribati, 34; Marshalls, 35; techniques, 35
Nawai, Apolosi, 155–156
near Oceania, 23
New Caledonia (Melanesia): attacks on sandalwood ships, 122; people's protests, 231n2
New Guinea: arrivals, 22; trading, 30, 49, 54–55
New Hazard, voyages of, 86–88
New Hebrides (Vanuatu) condominium, 141
Nicholson, John, 81
Norfolk Islands, arrival of Polynesians, 23
nutrition, 123
Nye, David, 123

Ocean Island (Banaba), 160
Outer Eastern passage to China, 76
Overseas Seafarers Wives Association (Kiribati), 199

Pacific Forum: agreements on shipping, 166; membership, 181
Pacific Forum Line (PFL): agreements, 165; crew and officers, 185; developing the fleet, 182–183; services, 182–183; shareholders, 181; subsidies, 183
Pacific national shipping lines: Cook Islands, Nauru, Papua New Guinea, Tonga, 181
Pacific women in maritime (Pac Wima), 21

Palau (Micronesia): sharks, 40; trade with Yap, 51–52
Panama Canal, 150
passengers (interisland), 168; trading, 171
Pattison, Simeon, 92
pearls, 106
Piailug, Mau (navigator), 207
Pitcairn Island (eastern Polynesia): depopulated, 56; mutineers arrived, 57
Pleistocene voyages, 22; obsidian trading, 23
poems and songs, 1, 13, 18, 51, 69–71, 73, 105, 116
Polynesian outliers, 23
Polynesian perceptions of foreign sailors, 70, 73–74
Polynesian Voyaging Society, 207
Pomare (King), 78, 81–82
Pomare (Queen), 82
Pomare (V), 152
pork trade, New South Wales: Tahiti, 79
press gangs, 101
price fixing, trading companies, 152
prostitution: disease, 117; sailor town establishments, 19, 116; sailors' misconceptions, 72–73; views by Cook, 69; views by Forster, 68; views by Morrison, 69
protests against foreign companies: boycotts, 151; copra production strikes, 152; defense of lagoon rights, 152–153; government interventions, 152, 157; island trading enterprises in Cook Islands, 158; island trading enterprises in Fiji, 155–156; island trading enterprises in Kiribati, 156–157; island trading enterprises in Samoa, 154; island trading enterprises in Tonga, 154–155; island trading enterprises in Vaitapu, 153–154

Quiros, Pedro Fernandez, 61

race relations at sea: discrimination in Pacific employment, 149; foc'sle unity eroded, 145; maritime union actions, 148; race exclusiveness in Fiji trade unions, 170, 179; White Australia Policy, 149
Rapa Nui (eastern Polynesia): arrivals, 24; boat forms (hare paenga), 57–58; climatic factors and environmental destruction, 57; isolation, 57; people stolen, 107; warfare, 57; Western ships, 57
Raratonga (eastern Polynesia), prayer for Cook's arrival, 69–70
rats *(rattus exulans)*: destruction ashore, 43; sources of protein on voyages, 38, 41; use of rat DNA in archaeology, 24
Ratu Mara, 185
reefs, 11–12, 41; *Minerva* reef losses, 119–120; passes, 41–42
Reynolds, Stephen, 3, 86–87, 116
Robertson, George, 3, 49, 64–65
Roggeveen, Jacob, 57
Rotuma (western Polynesia): seafarers, 19, 104; ship losses, 159, 175; ships, 159
Royal Society, on humane behavior, 63–64
Ruatara (Chief), 121, 127–128

sailing ships (Western): accommodation, 111–112; free time, 112; hazards of work, 112; social organization, 110–112; reduced manning, 137; technical advance topsail schooners, 137
sailor towns: brothels and crimps, 19, 212n42; diseases, 117; going home, 117; independence of sailors, 117; riots, 117, 226n61; tattoo parlors, 20
Samoa: first arrivals, 23; political

260   Index

divisions American and Western, 141
Schouten, William, 61
Schutz, Willy, 156–157
scientists (exploring ships): collecting specimens, 67; human classification, 68
Scott, William, 79
seafarer rights, 134–135
seafarers recruitment (contemporary): international shipping, 186–188; multinational, 193, 208; Pacific, 187; ratings surplus, 206; world officer shortages, 188
seafarers recruitment (historical): kidnapping, 104, 105, 107, 134; law, 134; numbers, 106–109; Pacific crews preferred, 102–103, 106; press gang, 101; shanghaiing, 105; shortages of seafarers, 101
sealers, deaths ashore in remote places, 121
seamanship, prehistoric, "intuitive perception," 2
seapower (indigenous): Bau, 46–47; Hawai'i, 46; Lau, 47; Tahiti, 45, 47; Tonga, 46
second registry, 187
Secretariat of the Pacific Community, 176
settlements, high and low islands: site values, 44
sexual behavior of sailors: sexually transmitted infections, 197–199; survey, 198–199; treatment, 199
sexual customs, Pacific, 72–73, 212n41
sharks, respect for, 40
Shetlands Islands, mother wave, 14
ship stability, 168–169
ship symbolism: a family, 10; of female gender, 10; figureheads, 15; mother, 11; sacred names, 16

shipbuilding (indigenous): builder status (Matia), 28; ceremonies, 14; launching, 15
shipbuilding (Western): birth of a ship, 15, 211n28; launching ceremony, 15; new types to Pacific, 99
shipowning (colonial policies): attitudes to island enterprises, 158–159; flag preferences, 143; ports of entry, 144; profitable routes, 160; subsidies, 143–145, 159
shipwrecks: dedication of sailors, 119; Hawaiian coast, 121; loss of wages, 119
slop chest, 105, 112
small vessel revival (indigenous): Abemama, 157; Cook Islands, 157; Fiji, 158–159; Kiribati, 160; Rotuma, 159; Samoa, 159; Tahiti, 158; Tanna, 159
Society Islands (French Polynesia), Spanish influence, 29
Solander, Daniel, 67
solevu, 172–175
Solf, William (Governor, Samoa), 154–155
Solomon Islands: arrival of Pleistocene era, 22; launching ceremonies, 14; raiding, 48; trade, 55–56
South America, contacts and sweet potato, 24
South Pacific Marine Services (SPMS), 189, 193
South Pacific Regional Maritime Programme, 188
steam versus sail, 141–143, 150
Storey, Justice (US), 134
Stowell, Lord, 134
stress at sea: fast turnaround, 197; loneliness, 196
strike breaking, 135, 162
strikes: America, 148–149; Austral-

asia, 149; Fiji, 161; Hawai'i, 162; naval strikes, 130; Papua New Guinea, 149, 161–162
Sumsuma, campaigner for seafarer rights, 161–162
superstitions (taboos): females, 16–17; priests, 17; sailing days, 16; words, 17
swells, 13–14, 35

tabua (Fiji), whales' teeth, 53, 55
Tahiti (eastern Polynesia): arrival of Polynesians, 23; European ships, 78; internecine wars, 79, 81; mercenaries recruited, 78; New South Wales salt pork for arms, 79, 81; Pomare ascendancy, 78; royal fleet, 81–83; shipbuilding, 81; Tahitian crews, 79–80
tapa (bark cloth), 28
Tasman, Abel, 61
tattoo: Pacific, 10, 20; sailors, 66; trade in human heads, 94
te Pahi (Chief), 92
te Puki (Chief), 92
te Taniwha Horeta, 11
Tevaki (navigator), 207
thieving on board, 18, 19; punishments, 19
Thompson, Nainoa (navigator), 207
Thurston, John Bates (Governor, Fiji), 140
Tikopea (Polynesian outlier), navigational methods, 35
tobacco, addiction and currency, 70–71
Tonga (eastern Polynesia): alliances with Fiji, 46; destroyed vessels, 71, 96; European ships, 54; foreigners ashore, 96, 223n85; navigators and raiders, 46; seafarers, 117; Tupoa dynasty, 46; warfare, 71, 96. See also Pacific national shipping lines

Tonga Ma'a Tonga Kautaha, 154–155
trade dependence, isolated islands, 56–57
trade, informal, passengers and sailors, 171
trade rooms, 143
trade unions, 164, 193, 199; America (mainland), 148; Australia, 148; Fiji, 161; French Polynesia, 200; Hawai'i, 162; Kiribati, 199–200; New Guinea, 200; New Zealand, 148
trading systems (indigenous), 50–57; fei (Palau-Yap), 51; Hiri (Papua New Guinea), 54–55; Kula ring (Trobriand Islands), 54; nodal islands, 49; sawei (Carolines), 51–52; Siassi (nodal), 50; solevu (Fiji), 53, 172–175; specialists in sea trade, 50
tribute requirements: Carolines to Yap, 47; Lau Islands to Lakeba, 47; Rotuma to Tonga, 46; Tuamotus to Tahiti, 47, 80
Tuamoto (eastern Polynesia): Godefroy depot, 138; pearls, 80; vessel building, 158
Tui, Lakeba (Chief), 47
Tupaia (navigator), 1, 36, 42, 67
Tupoa (King), 155
Turnball, John, 3, 79–80, 84, 98, 102, 106, 113
Tuvalu (eastern Polynesia), Marine Training Centre, 190

United Nations Conference on Trade and Development (UNCTAD), 181

Vaitupu Company, 153–154
Vanuatu (Melanesia): first arrivals, 23; flags of convenience, 186, 192
Viti Company, 155–156

wages of sailors: cheap labor issues Pacific, 106, 182; ILO minimum levels, 201; informal agreements, 169
Walker, Theodore, 131
Wallis, Samuel, 60, 62, 64, 66, 78
Western Pacific High Commission, 155
whalers (historical): conditions, 111; crews, 108–109; dangers, 119–120; insane people, 124; Pacific officers, 109; surgeons, 124
Whippy, David, 71
Wilkes, Charles, 50
Williams, John, 82
Williams, Thomas William, 153

winds: calms, 33, 141; hurricanes (typhoons), 32, 51; local, 11; planetary, 30; planning passages improved, 141; sailing seasons, 32
women at sea: captains' wives, 113; global numbers, 17; Pacific, 178–180, 187; prejudices, 16–17, 113–114, 180. *See also* Fiji; Kiribati
women traders, 17, 37, 55–56
women's organizations, 179, 199, 204
World Health Organization, 198
World Maritime University, 178

Yap Islands (Micronesia), relations with Carolines, 50–51, 55

ABOUT THE AUTHOR

Alastair D. Couper was born in Aberdeen, Scotland. He attended nautical school and spent ten years at sea, qualifying as a master mariner. He earned an MA degree in geography at the University of Aberdeen and a PhD in human geography at the Research School of Pacific Studies, Australian National University, and was awarded an honorary DSc from the University of Plymouth, England. He was a lecturer in international transport at Durham University and professor of maritime studies, dean of applied sciences, and director of the Seafarers International Research Centre (SIRC) at Cardiff University (1970–1998). He spent two years as a professor at the World Maritime University, Malmö, Sweden, and is a visiting professor at Greenwich Maritime Institute, London. He has professional and research experience over many years in the Pacific, including sailing with island crews. His activities have also included performing United Nations surveys and serving as a trustee of the National Maritime Museum, Greenwich; a member of the Executive Board, Law of the Sea Institute, Honolulu; and editor and founder of the international journal *Maritime Policy and Management*. He has published extensively in the field of maritime studies, including *Voyages of Abuse* (1999) and Part 1 of *Seafarers' Rights* (2005).